COMBATING TERRORISM
Counterterrorism and Related Activities

COMBATING TERRORISM
Counterterrorism and Related Activities

Dr. Vijay Kumar Verma

MD PUBLICATIONS PVT LTD
NEW DELHI
www.mdppl.com

Published by :

MD Publications Pvt Ltd
'MD House', 11, Darya Ganj
New Delhi - 110 002
Phone : +91-11-41563325 (Customer Service)
+91-11-41562846 (Editorial)
E-mail (orders): contact@mdppl.com
Website: www.mdppl.com

ISBN: 978-81-7533-189-1

Published and Printed by Mrs. Rajni Gupta on behalf of **MD Publications Pvt Ltd** at Times Press, New Delhi.

Contents

Preface

Counterterrorism (also spelled counter-terrorism) refers to the practices, tactics, techniques, and strategies that governments, militaries, police departments and corporations adopt in response to terrorist threats and/or acts, both real and imputed.

Counterterrorism refers to offensive strategies intended to prevent a belligerent, in a broader conflict, from successfully using the tactic of terrorism. Counterterrorism is a set of techniques for denying an opponent the use of terrorism-based tactics, just as counter-air is a set of techniques for denying the opponent the use of attack aircraft. Counterterrorism includes both the detection of potential acts and the response to related events.

If the terrorism is part of a broader insurgency, counterterrorism may also form a part of a counter-insurgency doctrine, but political, economic, and other measures may focus more on the insurgency than the specific acts of terror. Foreign internal defense (FID) is a term used by several countries for programs either to suppress insurgency, or reduce the conditions under which insurgency could develop.

Building a counterterrorism plan involves all segments of a society or many government agencies. In dealing with foreign terrorists, the lead responsibility is usually at the national level. Because propaganda and indoctrination lie at the core of terrorism, understanding their profile and functions increases the ability to counterterrorism more effectively.

Most counterterrorism strategies involve an increase in standard police and domestic intelligence. The central activities are traditional, interception of communications, and the tracing of persons. New technology has, however, expanded the range of military and law enforcement operations.

Today, many countries have special units designated to handle terrorist threats. Besides various security agencies, there are elite tactical units, also known as special mission units, whose role is to directly engage terrorists and prevent terrorist attacks. Such units perform both in preventive actions, hostage rescue and responding to on-going attacks. Countries of all sizes can have highly trained counterterrorist teams. Tactics, techniques and procedures for man hunting are under constant development.

Most of these measures deal with terrorist attacks that affect an area, or threaten to do so. It is far harder to deal with assassination, or even reprisals on individuals, due to the short (if any) warning time and the quick infiltration of the assassins. Of course, if the assassination is done by a suicide bomber, infiltration becomes moot. These units are specially trained in tactics and are very well equipped for CQB with emphasis on stealth and performing the mission with minimal casualties. The units include take-over force (assault teams), snipers, EOD experts, dog handlers and intelligence officers.

There are many ways to combat terrorism. First, would be an international team that is always on call to respond to terrorist threats, and retrieve hostages with minimal loss of life. The second is gun control, which would limit the weapons accessed by potential terrorists. The last thing is to recognize terrorist organizations before they have a chance to attack.

One way to combat terrorism is with a team that is specially designed to go into buildings, planes, or any other place hostages are taken, and rescue the hostages, and neutralize all of the terrorists. This would help not only to prevent terrorism, but save the lives of the hostages. On the morning of September 5, 1972, eight Arab commandos broke into the Olympic compound in Munich, West Germany. They shot and killed two Israelis outright, one a wrestling coach, the other a weight-lifting coach. The commandos then took nine others of the eighteen-member Israeli Olympic team hostage and settled into the compound for a siege.

I am very grateful to Mr. Pranav Gupta, Director, MD Publications Pvt Ltd, New Delhi who has readily expressed his acceptance and supported me fully for completing this book.

Dr. Vijay Kumar Verma

1

Introduction

Introduction

The terrorist attacks in November 2008 on Mumbai did more than raise Indian hackles against Pakistan for failing to rein in terrorist groups operating on its soil. The scale and coordination of the attacks, a senior Indian government official said, suggest that at least one terrorist cell, made up of fewer than a dozen local people and probably directed and financed by militants, carried out the attacks, which killed many people. In the past, Indian operatives have aided foreign militants in what he called a benign fashion, sometimes providing little more than shelter or food. "The change is that some of them really know what they are up to," the official said, speaking on condition of anonymity because the investigation was in progress. None of the four counterterrorism goals identified by the U.S. government—defeating terrorist organizations with global reach; denying sponsorship, support, and sanctuary to terrorists; diminishing the underlying conditions that terrorists seek to exploit; and defending U.S. citizens and interests—can be achieved through unilateral action alone.

Although in February 2003 U.S. National Strategy for Combating Terrorism explicitly recognizes that an effective campaign against terrorism will require extensive multilateral cooperation, it says little about how to bring about such cooperation and next to nothing about the role of the United Nations. U.S. observers have paid scant attention to the UN's role in the international campaign against terrorism, yet the UN Security Council has made, and can continue to make, critical contributions to this effort. UN- imposed sanctions regimes have changed the attitudes of state sponsors of terrorism and helped stigmatize terrorism. After the attacks of September 11, the Security Council made the fight against terrorism a global one by ordering every UN member state to implement a wide array of measures to prevent and stop terrorist activities. The council also militarized the response to terrorism by legitimizing unilateral military action in response to terrorist threats.

The UN can continue to be an effective force against terrorism by enhancing the legitimacy of military actions and increasing the effectiveness of economic and political sanctions; strengthening and sustaining multilateral collaboration in the fight against terrorism; and establishing and maintaining international standards of accountability. Moreover, through its efforts to resolve regional conflicts, foster economic and social development, and develop the rule of law and standards of good governance, the UN can improve the political, economic, and social conditions that terrorists seek to exploit. Only with U.S. leadership, however, can the UN remain strong on terrorism and become an even stronger force. The diplomatic standoff in the UN over the war in Iraq is not the rule but the exception.

Indeed, the UN's track record since the end of the Cold War shows that, when the United States demonstrates leadership and determination, it frequently convinces other Security Council members to follow its lead and take effective multilateral action. In the future, this will require the United States to exercise political restraint and a willingness to listen to the concerns of other states.

Enlightened leadership will generate substantial payoffs in the form of multilateral cooperation and action.

Terrorism in a Changing World

The last decade has seen extraordinary changes in the international security environment. Decades of Cold War assumptions and strategies have been overthrown, and new debates have emerged on how to explain and address today's more diverse and ambiguous risks. Yet much of the discussion on terrorism remains tied to images drawn from previous epochs. Recent experience, from the bombings of the embassies in Kenya and Tanzania, the World Trade Center, the federal building in Oklahoma City, and Khobar Towers to the use of chemical weapons in the Tokyo subway and Hamas suicide attacks in Israel, has galvanized public and expert attention, and reminds us that terrorism is capable of starkly affecting U.S. citizens and U.S. interests. It also suggests troubling new dimensions, including the potential for terrorist action on U.S. territory and terrorist use of weapons of mass destruction—nuclear, chemical, biological, and radiological.

The old image of a professional terrorist motivated by ideology or the desire for "national liberation," operating according to a specific political agenda, armed with guns and bombs, and backed by overt state sponsors, has not quite disappeared. It has been augmented— some would say overtaken—by other forms of terrorism. This new terrorism has different motives, different actors, different sponsors, and, as Bruce Hoffman discusses, demonstrably greater lethality. Terrorists are organizing themselves in new, less hierarchical structures and using "amateurs" to a far greater extent than in the past. All of this renders much previous analysis of terrorism based on established groups obsolete, and complicates the task of intelligence-gathering and counterterrorism. Three points are worth noting as background.

First, this study was undertaken for the U.S. Air Force at a time when the attack on the Khobar Towers military housing complex in Dhahran, Saudi Arabia, was fresh in the minds of policymakers, the military, and the public. The Air Force was concerned about understanding the current and future terrorist threat to deployed forces and vigorously addressing the problem of "force protection." Although some aspects of our study treated the problem of close-in defense against terrorist risks to the Air Force, the bulk of our effort was broader, tracing the recent evolution of international terrorism against civilian and U.S. military targets, looking ahead to where terrorism is going, and assessing how it might be contained. We use the term "contained" because, unlike some other security challenges such as nuclear deterrence or the defense of borders, absolute prevention of terrorism is not a realistic objective.

Second, our research was conducted against the background of a wider national debate on aspects of international terrorism, especially the threat of weapons of mass destruction as a prominent "transnational risk." The Defense Science Board and others have examined these risks in detail over the past few years, and recent congressional and National Security Council initiatives have also made this their focus. In addition, it has become fashionable—with some reason—to consider the risk of information-based terrorism. Our study touches on each of these issues, but with less emphasis on the proliferation of technologies and techniques *per se,* and more emphasis on how changes in the sources and nature of terrorism may encourage—or discourage—the use of unconventional terror.

Third, we have been struck by the limited scope of most analyses of contemporary terrorism. Perhaps because the study of the behaviour of specific groups was the hallmark of most terrorism research in the recent past, expert analyses of terrorism tend to be just that— analyses of terrorist phenomena with little attempt to characterize the overall nature of the terrorist threat to national security or national objectives. We have therefore tried to place terrorism and counterterrorism in strategic perspective (for example, how the terrorist instrument may relate to other forms of conflict, or its application as an "asymmetric strategy" by less-capable adversaries). In conceptualizing counterterrorism strategy, we have applied a strategic planning framework used successfully in other RAND studies outside the terrorism field. Unlike many countries around the world, and unlike some of our allies, the United States has not faced an "existential" threat from terrorism, that is, a threat to our survival and basic way of life.

The viability of the United States as a society and as a political system has not been, and very likely will not be, threatened by terrorist acts, however lethal. That said, terrorism affects our national interests directly and indirectly, and can constrain our international freedom of action. The potential for enormous increases in lethality and disruption as the result of unconventional terrorism reinforces the importance of counterterrorism as a part of our national security strategy. The stakes go beyond the protection of American lives and property and our capacity for global engagement, and involve the reasonable expectation that the government will keep its citizens from being terrorized. The bulk of the research for this study was completed prior to the August 1998 bombings of the American embassies in Tanzania and Kenya, and the consequent U.S. strikes against terrorist-related targets in Afghanistan and Sudan, but reference has been made to them in the analysis where it seemed useful to do so.

Approach and Structure

We build on a large body of previous RAND research on terrorism and political violence, and make extensive use of the RAND St. Andrews Chronology of International

Terrorism, documenting incidents from 1968 to the present. The three papers in this volume were chosen because they give a good sense of the project and its key findings. Although the papers are broadly complementary, the reader will note some useful differences of perspective. We have not attempted to eliminate these differences, which, in any case, serve as further contributions to informed debate. Bruce Hoffman, charts trends and future patterns in international terrorism against civilian and military targets, and their implications. It also offers some broader observations on terrorist risks to the United States and the utility of military responses.

The chapter describes the rise of new types of terrorists, changing motivations, and the traditionally incremental character of terrorists' tactical innovations (and suggests that most—but not all—terrorism will continue to follow this pattern). The author identifies the key factors behind the increasing lethality of international terrorist acts, despite a steady decrease in the overall number of incidents worldwide. John Arquilla, David Ronfeldt, and Michele Zanini take up the controversial question of terrorism in the information age. They go beyond the discussion of "information warfare" by terrorists to assess the significance and organization of information-age terrorism and possible responses. Adopting a "netwar" perspective, they argue that future terrorism will often feature disruption rather than destruction, especially in a "war paradigm" where unconventional terrorism may be an attractive alternative to direct confrontation with the United States.

Their chapter includes a revealing analysis of the information competence of terrorist organizations in the Middle East, and suggests that the more active and lethal of these make extensive use of information techniques and are increasingly organized as networks rather than hierarchies. The authors go on to propose ways in which the United States and the U.S. Air Force can equip themselves to address this modern form of terrorism, including opportunities for new information-intensive approaches to counterterrorism. In the concluding, I seek to place terrorism and counterterrorism in strategic context, with special emphasis on the new dimensions of terrorism. I offer a typology of terrorist risks to U.S. interests, and discuss the changing geopolitics of terrorism. New regional and functional sources will compel us to look beyond the traditional centers of terrorism in Europe and the Middle East, and come to grips with terrorism as a transnational phenomenon, occupying an expanded place on the conflict spectrum.

The discussion draws on the comparative experience of Israel, France, and Britain in addressing their own terrorism challenges. Finally, the chapter offers a framework for conceptualizing national counterterrorism strategy, with "core," "environment shaping," and "hedging" dimensions, and with special attention to the role of air and space power in relation to each. Conclusions point to a strategy—and national capabilities— tailored to dealing with the very challenging problems of individuals, small nonstate actors, and networks in addition to the identifiable state sponsors that have been the traditional objects of air power in the service of counterterrorism. Counterterrorism strategy will be global, of necessity, but will also have to address the growing problem of homeland defense—a neglected dimension of American strategy.

UN Counterterrorism Sanctions in the 1990s

In January 1992, at the Security Council's first ever meeting of heads of state and government to define a new post–Cold War agenda for the council, the heads of state and government "expressed their deep concern over acts of international terrorism and emphasized the need for the international community to deal effectively with all such acts." In March 1992, for the first time the Security Council backed up its rhetorical commitment with action, imposing mandatory economic sanctions on Libya, which had been accused of involvement in the 1988 and 1989 bombings of UTA flight 772 and Pan Am flight 103.

The Security Council imposed mandatory—as defined in Chapter VII of the UN Charter—sanctions to fight terrorism on two other occasions: against Sudan in 1996 and against the Taliban regime in Afghanistan in 1999. The changing nature of the terrorist threat throughout the decade made it imperative to tackle this problem in concert with other nations. Five trends in international terrorist activity continued to attract U.S. and Security Council attention to the issue:

- An increasing proportion of terrorist attacks targeted U.S. facilities or citizens. According to some calculations, attacks on U.S. targets increased from about 20 percent of total attacks in 1993–1995 to almost 50 percent of the total in 2000.
- The average number of casualties per incident was increasing. U.S. Department of State statistics revealed a fourfold increase in the number of casualties per attack in the latter half of the 1990s.
- More and more terrorist groups seemed to be operating worldwide as part of global networks. The attacks on U.S. embassies in East Africa in 1998 underscored the global reach of the Al Qaeda network, which was estimated to have 4,000–5,000 well-trained fighters scattered around the world. Compared to the 500 members of the Abu Nidal organization, the 200–400 activists of the Irish Republican Army or the Basque Fatherland and Liberty (ETA), or the 50–75 hard- core members of the Red Brigades, Al Qaeda was significantly larger and a qualitatively different type of terrorist organization.
- Fears that terrorists might one day use chemical, biological, or nuclear weapons were increasing. The

1995 sarin nerve gas attack in the Tokyo subway by Aum Shinrikyo made such fears less theoretical. The possibility that terrorists could obtain biological, chemical, or nuclear weapons, either by buying, stealing, or colluding with states that were developing weapons of mass destruction (WMD), was a growing concern.

- The United States became particularly concerned about certain nations' role in supporting and sponsoring terrorism.

State support enhances the reach and power of terrorist groups and might provide them with WMD; states could also use terrorist groups as proxies for their own fights. Throughout the 1990s, economic sanctions were the main policy instrument employed in the campaign against terrorism. By imposing sanctions on Libya, Sudan, and the Taliban in Afghanistan, the Security Council not only sought the extradition of certain individuals but also hoped to send a more general message and to change the behaviour of state sponsors of terrorism. Washington in particular viewed "this type of concerted multilateral response to terrorism as an important deterrent to states considering support for terrorist acts or groups." Sanctions were fairly effective against Libya, getting it to meet both the specific and the more general demands. Even before the 1992 sanctions took effect, Libya offered to surrender the suspects in the UTA bombing to a French court and those responsible for the Pan Am explosion to an international court.

Washington, however, insisted that the suspects of the Pan Am bombing be turned over to either a U.S. or a British court. The imposition of sanctions also helped to achieve the broader security objective of weakening Libya's support of terrorist groups. This broader objective was largely achieved by the late 1990s. In 1996 the State Department noted that Libya's support of terrorism had been sharply reduced. Consequently, it became difficult to justify continuing imposition of UN sanctions against the country.

In addition, international support for the sanctions regime was crumbling. In response, the United States and United Kingdom developed a compromise proposal whereby the two Libyan suspects would be tried under Scottish law in a court in the Netherlands. The Security Council made this plans its own in August 1998.

After several months of negotiations, spearheaded by UN secretary general Kofi Annan, the Libyan government accepted the plan and handed over the two Libyan suspects in April 1999. Sanctions were suspended that same day. UN sanctions limiting the travel of Sudanese officials were imposed in April 1996 after Sudan refused to extradite three suspects in the assassination attempt of Egypt's President Husni Mubarak. Although Sudan subsequently expelled some members of terrorist groups, notably a number of Egyptians, Palestinians, and "Arab Afghans," including Osama bin Laden, sanctions were left in place and then strengthened by the adoption of an air embargo in August 1996. Indeed, the United States argued—and other Security Council members concurred—that Sudan continued to be used as a safe haven by other terrorist groups such as Al Qaeda. The more stringent sanctions, however, were never implemented because Security Council members feared the humanitarian consequences of an air embargo, particularly on a country already ravaged by a humanitarian crisis and civil war.

In this case, sanctions were used less to punish a particular state and more to transmit a general message that supporting terrorist activities was not acceptable and would provoke a substantial response by the international community. UN sanctions were lifted in September 2001, once Sudan pledged its full support for the global campaign against terrorism. At Washington's urging, the Security Council imposed financial and air travel sanctions on Afghanistan's Taliban regime in October 1999 because of its support for international terrorists and because it refused to extradite bin Laden, who was accused of involvement in the 1998 bombings of the U.S. embassies in Kenya and Tanzania. Unfortunately, the UN sanctions had no noticeable effect on the Taliban's behaviour because of the country's economic isolation: the extent of Taliban-controlled air traffic was negligible, the Taliban had limited funds abroad, and it was not active in the aboveboard global economy, deriving much of its money from illegal opium and heroin trade. A strengthened UN sanctions package, which had been adopted in December 2000, could not change these economic fundamentals.

Although the UN sanctions regimes of the 1990s failed to stop worldwide terrorist activities, they made supporting terrorist activities more costly for states and helped to change at least the declared attitudes—what they say if not what they do—of states toward terrorist groups, particularly the attitudes of state sponsors of terrorism. The State Department recognized this transformation in the late 1990s and again in 2001 when it noted the continuation of a slow trend away from state sponsorship of terrorism. At the same time, terrorist groups such as Al Qaeda adapted by becoming less dependent on state support, diversifying their organizational structures as well as their funding sources to make themselves more autonomous.

Most importantly, the UN sanctions regimes of the 1990s stigmatized terrorist activities and secured the growing international consensus that terrorism is an illegitimate activity that must be countered through collective international action. By designating terrorist activities as "threats to international peace and security," UN sanctions paved the way for more forceful international responses to terrorism after September 11, 2001.

International Response after September 11

Within hours of the attacks in New York and Washington, D.C., the Security Council president, French ambassador Jean-David Levitte, circulated a draft resolution strongly condemning the attacks and paving the way for military action. On September 12, 2001, Resolution 1368 was adopted unanimously. Two weeks later, the council adopted Resolution 1373, obligating all 191 UN member states to take far-reaching domestic legislative and executive actions designed to prevent and suppress future terrorist activities. At that time, the U.S. permanent representative to the Security Council, Ambassador John Negroponte, called the UN "a unique partner in troubled times" and described Resolution 1373 as the UN's "single most powerful response" in the war on terrorism.

The two UN resolutions took the unprecedented steps of legitimizing military action against terrorism and globalizing the ban on terrorism. Before Resolution 1368, the use of force in response to terrorist attacks often provoked condemnations in the UN General Assembly as well as among legal scholars. Prior to the September 11 attacks, the United States was well aware of the weak legal basis for the use of force in such situations and had used military force in response to terrorist acts on only three occasions: against Libya in 1986 in retaliation for its involvement in the bombing of a nightclub in Berlin that was frequented by U.S. service members; against Iraq in 1993 in retaliation for its attempt to assassinate former U.S. president George H. W. Bush and the emir of Kuwait; and against Afghanistan and Sudan in 1998 in retaliation for the bombings of the U.S. embassies in Kenya and Tanzania.

By invoking a state's right to self-defense and thus legitimizing the unilateral use of force against terrorist attacks, the Security Council set an important precedent that poses risks to the general prohibition on the use of force, as embodied in the UN Charter. Indeed, the United States seemed to consider Resolution 1368 a blank check. In its letter informing the Security Council of U.S. action against Al Qaeda and the Taliban, the United States hinted that military action would be taken against other targets when it stated that "our inquiry is in its early stages. We may find that our self-defense requires further actions with respect to other organizations and other states."

This declaration concerned Annan, UN diplomats, and legal scholars because, in the absence of international agreement on the definition of terrorism, they saw a legion of possibilities for abuse. China and Russia, on the other hand, were quick to endorse the U.S. position: Beijing believed that it helped to legitimize China's suppression of opposition groups in Xinjiang, while Russia saw it as a useful precedent in its fight against Chechen rebels. In fact, in September 2002, Moscow invoked Resolution 1368 to justify possible military attacks against Chechen rebels operating in Georgia—with or without the authorization of the Georgian government.

The UN Charter recognizes the right to self-defense as an inalienable right of states, but it is generally accepted that this right is not open-ended. Specifically, it ceases to operate when the Security Council takes action. In addition, the use of force in self-defense is subject to four critical conditions to judge the lawfulness of unilateral actions: whether there was an armed, or an imminent, attack and whether the military response was necessary, proportionate, and timely. To date, the broader implications of Resolution 1368 on the legality of the use of force have received little attention. Yet, the UN did not wait to debate these far-reaching implications on September 12, 2001; the UN acted by passing the resolution unanimously the day after the unforeseen attacks.

The Ban on Terrorism

Just two weeks later, on September 28, the Security Council adopted U.S. - sponsored Resolution 1373 that obligated all 191 UN member states to change and/or adopt domestic legislation that would criminalize terrorist acts, including the support and financing of such acts; deny safe haven to terrorists and prohibit any other support for terrorists, such as the provision of arms; and prompt cooperation with other states in the implementation of these measures.

Many of the measures mentioned in the resolution were present in two important conventions negotiated in the late 1990s: the 1997 Convention for the Suppression of Terrorist Bombings, which entered into force in May 2001, and the 1999 Convention on the Suppression of Financing of Terrorism, which at that time had not yet entered into force (but did in April 2002). Prior to September 2001, only two states had ratified both conventions: Cuba and the United Kingdom. Resolution 1373 made many of the provisions of these conventions binding on all states. To monitor implementation of Resolution 1373, the Security Council established the Counter-Terrorism Committee (CTC) and elected Jeremy Greenstock, the United Kingdom's permanent representative on the council, as the CTC's first chair.

During his tenure, Greenstock emphasized the technical nature of the CTC, describing its functions as "to monitor, to be analytical and to report facts to the Security Council for consideration." The goal, he said, was "to help the world system to upgrade its capability, to deny space, money, support, haven to terrorism, and to establish a network of information-sharing and co-operative executive action." The CTC initiated a multistage program. In the first stage, the committee reviewed member states' existing legislative and executive measures to combat terrorism, which Resolution 1373 had ordered states to provide to the CTC within 90 days.

The second stage focused on strengthening institutional mechanisms and providing assistance to improve states' capacity to combat terrorism. By January 2002, the CTC had received 117 of 191 reports—a remarkable response by historical standards—and by December 2002, 175 reports had been delivered. By April 2003, only three states—Sao Tome and Principe, Swaziland, and Vanuatu—had not yet filed reports with the CTC. An initial review of these reports pointed to several problems. States often had different understandings of Resolution 1373's key terms and provisions. For example, states equated the "financing of terrorist acts" with money laundering and dealt with it only in that context. Money used to finance terrorism, however, is not necessarily generated by illegal business transactions; on the contrary, much of this money is legal and is acquired legitimately. Similarly, member states were confused about freezing, seizing, confiscating, and suspending accounts.

Many states reported dealing with terrorist activities in their own territories but were silent with respect to terrorist acts carried out by their nationals elsewhere. Moreover, the information provided on international cooperation was sketchy, focusing mainly on formal judicial issues, particularly extradition. Finally, although many states lacked the legislative and administrative capacity to implement Resolution 1373, few requested CTC assistance toward this end. Many states preferred to adopt a wait-and-see attitude. Would the CTC be a serious body or not? Similar problems had surfaced in UN sanctions regimes in the 1990s. For example, two noted scholars who reviewed UN sanctions regimes in the 1990s estimated that only 12 countries had enacted laws enabling them to enforce financial sanctions.

In September 2002, the UN group monitoring sanctions on the Taliban and Al Qaeda reported that the latter continued to have access to considerable financial and other economic resources. The report noted that, even though $112 million had been frozen in the first three months after the September 11 attacks, in the following eight months only $10 million of that amount had actually been blocked. The report concluded that "al-Qaeda is by all accounts 'fit and well' and poised to strike again at its leisure." Implementation problems also hamper the safe haven provisions of Resolution 1373. In many countries, border controls are weak. Indeed, many countries do not have the capacity to police the territories under their jurisdiction effectively; they need additional resources to deal with these problems.

The CTC, with a staff of a dozen and no independent budget, is waging a heroic battle but a losing one. If properly empowered, the CTC could help states put into place machinery to implement and enforce counterterrorism legislation crucial for the global battle against terrorism. For this purpose, the CTC should become "a fulltime, professional and global body of experts" that can work with the Security Council and follow up on all avenues opened by Resolution 1373. Such a body would also be well suited to monitor and review implementation of Resolution 1373. Unfortunately, the United States is resisting this approach and prefers to handle these problems bilaterally. The United States also rejected a proposal to set up an Assistance Trust Fund because Washington preferred that funds for assistance be provided through bilateral channels. Washington's reluctance to provide sufficient resources to the UN—and to the CTC—is severely undercutting the international campaign against terrorism.

Policy Challenges and Responses

By ordering all UN member states to take legislative and executive measures to combat terrorism at home and abroad, the Security Council has made the fight against terrorism a global one. Although this approach should be applauded and is the only approach that has the potential to deal with a global threat effectively, five important problems persist. First, although a declaratory consensus exists on the importance of outlawing terrorist activities, states continue to have widely divergent views on the exact nature of these threats. The United States has designated seven nations as "state sponsors of terrorism"—Cuba, Iran, Iraq, Libya, North Korea, Syria, and Sudan —but not all UN members agree with this assessment.

The United States should take the lead in forging a consensus on the nature of the terrorist threat. Sustained attention to the concerns of other states, consultation with other governments, and genuine efforts to come to a multilateral understanding of the magnitude of the threat terrorism poses to international stability will help convince other states that the United States is concerned not only about its own national interests but also about the international community as a whole. The second problem deals with identifying who will have the authority to determine whether Resolution 1373 is being violated and who will have the authority to decide on policy responses to noncompliance. The United States and Russia have been the most outspoken in stating that the Security Council does not have an exclusive right to determine policy on this issue.

Washington and Moscow have argued that they can unilaterally decide whether other states are complying with Resolution 1373, and the two powers have argued that a unilateral determination of noncompliance would allow them to exercise their right to self-defense. Unilateral responses to noncompliance with Security Council resolutions, however, can set dangerous precedents: they can lead to abuse and can provoke serious rifts among Security Council members. In that sense, the contentious Security Council debate over Iraq in early 2003 could be a forerunner of other debates as the campaign against terrorism unfolds. The Security Council's leading powers should not dodge discussion of this issue but rather recognize that, when noncompliance with Resolution 1373 leads to imminent and direct security threats, individual states always retain the right to self-defense.

If not faced with imminent and direct threats, however, states have an obligation to develop collective responses. The Security Council should define minimum standards for all states to comply with Resolution 1373 and develop guidelines on how to respond when states do not comply. A state's behaviour below the minimum standard should trigger punitive measures such as political, economic, and even military sanctions, whereas performance above and beyond minimum international standards should reap rewards. For example, states that demonstrate a willingness to build up their counterterrorism capacities and cooperate with international authorities could get preferential treatment when applying for international loans. To avoid suspicion that punitive measures and rewards would be controlled by the political agenda of any one state—the United States, for example—the Security Council should decide on these matters collectively.

The long-term implications of recent Security Council actions with respect to the use of force constitute a third problem area. By legitimizing the unilateral use of military force in response to terrorist attacks, the Security Council has broadened the conditions under which states can use military force for self-defense. Because there is no commonly accepted definition of terrorism, the possibilities for abuse are obvious and dangerous. U.S. officials have argued that terrorist threats, including state sponsors, need to be countered by preemptive and possibly covert military actions, and this position further complicates the issue of using military force for self-defense. Rather than continue to emphasize its unilateral right to use force against noncompliant states, the United States should take the lead in defining criteria for the use of force in self-defense against terrorists and state sponsors of terrorism and engage the members of the Security Council in collectively addressing this issue.

Defining such criteria will require resolving when

terrorist acts are the equivalent of armed attacks, what defines an imminent attack, and whether threats of imminent attack always justify a military response. The United States must tread carefully in handling this issue. Weakening the existing norm on the prohibition of the use of force could yield widespread regional and international instabilities and thus prove contrary to Washington's long-term interests.

The UN can help to isolate state sponsors of terrorism politically and economically. Implementing the UN's counterterrorism measures promises to provide the fourth challenge. The financial and safe haven provisions of Resolution 1373 require monitoring and enforcement capabilities that most countries do not possess and that may be too expensive to acquire. The Security Council's response to this problem thus far has been inadequate. Although the CTC's political credibility has been established, its minimal resources allow it to provide only minimal technical assistance. Thus, those countries needing assistance will have to rely on it coming through bilateral channels, making the aid ad hoc and selective.

Ultimately, if the United States and the other Security Council members are serious about their determination to fight terrorism, they must provide states with the resources needed for them to implement the counterterrorism measures expected of them. Beyond providing technical assistance, the Security Council should also push to establish a UN mechanism that can help finance counterterrorism programs in states that have problems monitoring and enforcing the provisions of Resolution 1373. Members should therefore consider transforming the Counter-Terrorism Committee into a Counter-Terrorism Organization—an independent UN agency designed to address these technical and implementation issues and with the responsibility to review and monitor the effectiveness of these measures.

Finally, as recognized in the U.S. National Strategy for Combating Terrorism, the fight against international terrorism is a long-term battle against the "underlying conditions that promote the despair and the destructive visions of political change that lead people to embrace, rather than shun, terrorism." This campaign thus involves tackling broader societal problems: poverty, social disorder, lack of democracy, and poor governance. Although limited, the UN's track record in dealing with such problems is promising and should be enhanced. Its capacity to help states set up good governance structures that can provide law and order, economic development, and respect for human rights is notable. The technical and political expertise it gained in the 1990s should be utilized. Investing in social and development programs ultimately will pay off significantly in the campaign against terrorism. Terrorism is not just a military problem; defeating it will require a wide range of policy responses in nonmilitary areas, toward which the UN can make important contributions.

U.S. Leadership

As the largest and most powerful state in the world and as the Security Council member most directly targeted by Al Qaeda, the United States has a special responsibility—and a special interest—in making the Security Council an effective instrument in the fight against terrorism. Having demonstrated its ability to respond to U.S. concerns since the end of the Cold War, the UN has great political and operational value in the war on terror. The UN can do more, but how much more depends largely on leadership and support from the United States. The UN can make four critical contributions to the campaign against terrorism. First, it can enhance the legitimacy of state actions, including military actions against state sponsors of terrorism. Multilateral actions through the UN can also help to isolate state sponsors politically and economically and hence diminish their influence and reach. Second, the UN can help to create and develop international norms and international standards of accountability.

The UN sanctions regimes of the 1990s played an important role in associating terrorist activities with criminal acts. In the next decade, the United States and other states will want to make sure that terrorist acts are prosecuted and punished around the world. Only then can Al Qaeda and other terrorist organizations be contained. Third, the UN can help share the economic burden of the fight against terrorism. Building up state capacities to combat terrorism will require material resources. The United States has an interest in sharing these costs with others. Fourth, the UN can also help share the burden politically. The fight against terrorism is a long-term fight that will see both successes and failures.

The UN has been and will continue to be a useful political bulwark in this ongoing struggle. Although the United States profoundly disagreed with some UN member states over the war in Iraq, Washington has continued to recognize the usefulness of the UN and the CTC in "fostering a global counter-terrorism net- work."

Significantly, the harsh political dispute over the war on Iraq has not affected cooperation between the United States and France in the war against terrorism. As the terrorist threat mutates into a more complex and increasingly transnational and global threat, countering it through multilateral efforts that use the full spectrum of policy responses—not just military ones—becomes all the more important. Washington must therefore continue to work with, build on, and enhance the capacities of the UN to en- force counterterrorism strategies effectively.

2

Risk Management and Establishing Priorities

Assessing Threats

When pressure builds up under the earth, lava erupts; when there is oppression in the nation, rebellion releases; when an employer abuses his employees, revolt occurs; and when there is oppression in a family, either the spouse or children will do what needs to be done to bring the balance. The United States government has moved rapidly to address the dangers posed by new trends in terrorism that emerged in the last decade. With local responder training ongoing in many cities around the nations, the establishment of the Joint Task Force, and a number of important R&D program underway, now is an appropriate time to review national efforts and make improvements where necessary.

While I believe the United States has made great strides in recent years to enhance federal, state and local capabilities to combat terrorism, particularly terrorist use of weapons of mass destruction (WMD), I am concerned that many of the efforts launched in the mid-1990s need to be reconsidered. I particularly fear that our national anxiousness to address the so-called "New Terrorism" may be inadvertently adding to the danger. As a result, we are spending big, but not spending smart. There clearly are new trends in terrorist behaviour. But we must make sure that we are drawing accurate lessons from the past and guarding against future developments that are credibly in the realm of possibility and not merely reflections of our wildest nightmares.

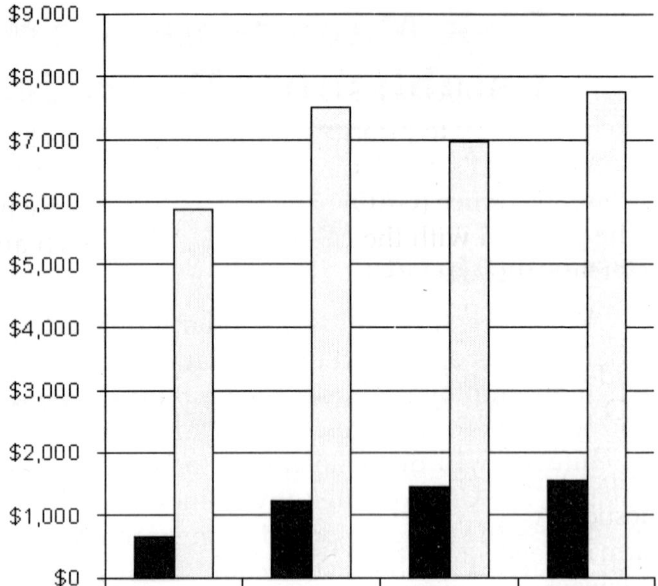

	FY 1998	FY 1999	FY 2000	FY 2001 - Req
■ WMD Terrorism	$645.3	$1,238.4	$1,453.7	$1,555.0
□ Non-WMD Terrorism	$5,870.8	$7,518.9	$6,966.0	$7,756.3

Figure: Federal Funding to Combat Terrorism ($ in Millions)

In addition to the committee's important oversight function, I strongly urge the committee and its staff to engage in a regular dialogue with the executive branch on this issue. As a nation, we are more likely to be most effective in combating the threat of terrorism if a variety of government and private institutions are working on this problem. There are no silver bullets, no special individuals and no single institution for defeating terrorism. To check the threat posed by domestic and international terrorism will require sustained effort by many different entities.

Terrorism Threat Assessments and Risk Management Strategies

The United States currently lacks a comprehensive and integrated intelligence assessment to inform policymaker thinking on how to prioritize spending decisions to support the government's programs to combat terrorism. The General Accounting Office (GAO) has indicated repeatedly that part of the problem with the current executive branch approach to terrorism is the lack of "threat and risk assessments that would suggest priorities and appropriate countermeasures." The GAO's observation is extremely important and should be addressed in a serious manner. The importance of the GAO view is that we lack a reasoned basis for making a case that we are spending too little, too much or just enough to combat terrorism. How much is enough remains an open question. As one renowned scholar succinctly noted, "without a firm understanding of the threat based on rigorous, ongoing reviews of evolving or changing terrorist behaviour and capabilities, continued efforts to address this problem may prove as ineffective as they are misplaced."

The last formal National Intelligence Estimate (NIE) on terrorist threats occurred three years ago. While this estimate was broad in scope, it was not intended to serve as a national assessment to assist policymakers in calibrating government efforts and spending decisions. Currently there is no single person who serves as a National Intelligence Officer (NIO) for terrorism. In a de facto fashion, the Director of Center Intelligence's (DCI) Counterterrorist Center generally serves this role. Given the jurisdictional restraints on the Central Intelligence Agency, the Counterterrorist Center cannot assemble an assessment that combines information on both domestic and international terrorism.

With a security threat as fluid and elusive as terrorism, the challenge of crafting effective short and long term measures is very difficult. Intelligence on terrorist threats is significantly different than intelligence on military threats from nation-states. Intelligence on the military programs of nation-states is comparatively more static and large enough to be covered by a variety of intelligence means. Numerous intelligence assessments on the threat posed by ballistic missiles have been conducted in recent years. Similarly, a number of special commissions have also sought to provide the Congress, the President and the American people with their view of the threat. These assessments have contributed to the national debate on the threat posed by ballistic missiles and the measures that may be required to address the threat. The short and long-term measures addressing the proliferation of ballistic missiles bear significant financial implications for the country.

While the threat posed by terrorism is much more difficult to gauge, analysis of the threat certainly deserves as thorough a review. Several special commissions have contributed to our collective understanding of the threat posed by emerging trends in terrorism, but their mandates have not specifically focused on assessing the threat. What is missing from our national discussion on how to best combat terrorism is a regular, comprehensive threat assessment that integrates assessment of both domestic and international terrorist threats?

Without a regular, comprehensive and integrated threat assessment of the security challenge posed by terrorism, policymakers draw conclusions on raw and finished intelligence information that comes across their desks. Policymakers prioritize spending and programming emphasis via a variety of tools, but intelligence is an essential one. The view of the intelligence community should serve as a critical baseline for the decisions of policymakers.

Policymakers should not assemble the intelligence assessment in a piecemeal and episodic fashion. Rather, policymakers should have the benefit of a regular, comprehensive and integrated terrorism threat assessment that informs both short-term and long-term policy decisions. Moreover, given the transnational and increasingly loose networks of individuals conducting terrorist acts, policymakers must have a picture of both domestic and international terrorist threats. Examining one set of threats in isolation from the other may hinder early identification of key warning signs.

A regular, comprehensive, and integrated threat assessment will help ensure that intelligence information that withstands the scrutiny of the entire intelligence community informs program and spending decisions. While policymakers can call upon portions of the intelligence community at any given time for information, a regular, comprehensive and integrated community-wide assessment would provide a process and a document that they take into account when making program and spending decisions.

The Congress should consult with the President about modalities for generating a comprehensive and integrated terrorism threat assessment on a regular basis. One option, and the best in my opinion, is to have the Interagency Intelligence Committee on Terrorism conduct a comprehensive and integrated assessment every year or two. Another option is to establish a National Intelligence Officer for terrorism. In order to ensure that the assessment integrated information on foreign terrorism with domestic terrorism, it is worth considering an equivalent officer in the Federal Bureau of Investigation.

Given the constitutional restrictions, the FBI's Counterterrorism Threat Assessment and Warning Unit may be the proper office to charge with stitching together the assessments of foreign and domestic terrorist threats. And finally, a third option and in my opinion the least desirable option, is for the National Security Council to generate an assessment based on the information it reviews from existing intelligence assessments. In a de facto fashion, this is what currently occurs. The only difference is that a formal NSC assessment might accompany the Office of Management and Budget's Annual Report to Congress on Combating Terrorism.

A regular terrorism threat assessment will lessen the possibility that long-term investment and program decisions are made according to vicissitudes of raw intelligence and ensure that at least on a regular basis there is a community benchmark calibrating the threat. Finally, and importantly, assembling this report on a periodic basis requires appropriate resources to meet the increased tasking on the intelligence community. Too often the intelligence and law enforcement communities are given new responsibilities without the resources to carry them out and they end up pulling resources from other existing duties and stretching personnel beyond desirable limits.

Creating a national strategy to address a threat for which there is not a clear consensus on the magnitude of the threat leaves the task of crafting a strategy without context. In recent years, United States policy to combat the threat of terrorist use of weapons of mass destruction has been driven by perceptions of vulnerability to such attacks rather than the likelihood. A comprehensive threat assessment would presumably factor in capabilities and motivations in addition to vulnerabilities. The inordinate focus of our antiterrorism policy on vulnerabilities and worst-case planning may skew precious federal resources to less critical aspects of the terrorism problem.

The recent scare over the vulnerability of the national monuments is just the most recent example of how the lack of a comprehensive assessment of threat that takes into account the likelihood of an attack can be exploited by government bodies seeking to call attention to their budgetary needs. News reporting on a study conducted by a private contractor for the National Park Services just prior to the our national Independence Day, as hundreds of thousands of Americans planned to visit our national monuments, was a case of threat manipulation for budgetary benefit in the extreme.

The release of information from this report just prior to this national holiday and prior to the conclusion of the congressional budget process seems hardly a coincidence. As two private experts pointed out in the news reporting, the National Park Police are not alone in our nation's Capitol when it comes to protecting the city from terrorist attacks, nor is it possible to completely eliminate all vulnerability. Addressing the communications or overtime needs of the National Park Service should be possible without scaring citizens away from visiting national monuments on Independence Day or unnecessarily drawing attention to vulnerabilities that might be exploited by individuals or groups with malicious designs.

Basing threat perception on vulnerabilities and gearing much of our terrorism response capabilities according to worst-case scenarios is skewing our approach to terrorism. A number of problems stem from a focus on vulnerabilities and worst-case response planning. First, the historical record on terrorism and the intelligence community both suggest that conventional explosives continue to be the weapon of choice for terrorists. Low consequence attacks with multiple-use chemicals and non-contagious biological agents' trails behind conventional explosives as the likely weapon of choice. There is a low probability of high consequence attacks that may involve the full range of unconventional weapons materials.

Second, by focusing on the low probability, high consequence events we may tend to categorize too many of them involving unconventional weapons materials as federal events when state and/or local resources may be more appropriate. Given the potential for demands on federal assets to meet American interest abroad as well as at home, they should be saved for when they are appropriately required. Third, frequent discussion about our vulnerabilities draws attention to them. Most of the WMD cases the FBI investigated in recent years were anthrax hoaxes. Our public communication about the terrorist threat is inadvertently eliciting threats that distract our resources from real attacks by determined terrorists.

Fourth, we must guard against inflating the potential of this threat to such a large degree that we create conflicts between funding for antiterrorism measures at home and important missions for our military abroad. Inordinate concern about catastrophic domestic terrorism may lead policymakers to call upon the military to perform missions at home that should be the domain of non-military service government organizations. Mission dilution of our military is something that constantly warrants the attention of the President and the Congress. We should keep the military's missions few and well defined such that it can perform at the highest level of effectiveness.

An open society such as ours cannot eliminate completely danger from all aspects of life. Prudent risk assessments will help us reduce the danger and improve our ability to respond in the unlikely event of an attack. We accept risk in many other areas of American society that result in the tragic loss of life. We want to guard against any terrorist attack that not only threatens the lives of our citizens, but also calls into question the authority of our government. This balance can be achieved at acceptable cost bearing in mind some risk.

Both executive and legislative branches of government seek to address the threat posed by catastrophic terrorist attacks. Senior officials say that they will accept criticism for being over-prepared and over-compensating for the threat. Some congressional staff suggest that the political danger of being parsimonious with spending to combat terrorism is too great to do anything but prepare for the worse-case scenario. While some hedge against the unpredictability of the future is commendable, we must not confuse prudent measures with efforts to avoid political blame for failure to take necessary precautions. Government has a responsibility to prepare for unlikely events that could produce catastrophic consequences. However, a balance must be struck between responsible preparedness and mere political hedging.

A comprehensive terrorism threat assessment will presumably be informed by a thorough analysis of past terrorist incidents with unconventional weapons. Far too many policymakers and researchers rendering assessments about terrorist use of unconventional weapons focus on what they *imagine* terrorists could do, not on what they have done in the past, which leads them to substitute their thinking for that of the terrorists. Acknowledging that history is not a perfect guide to the future and that government has a responsibility to take precautions against even unlikely eventualities, there must be some baseline, some historical context in order to consider potential eventualities.

Comprehensive Terrorism Threat Assessment

A comprehensive terrorism threat assessment is an essential component for crafting a national strategy for combating terrorism. A national strategy should guide the creation of programs and allocations of resources to implement the strategy. The report submitted by the Director of the Office of Management and Budget (OMB) pursuant to section 1051 of the Fiscal Year 1998 National Defense Authorization Act (Public Law 105-85) entitled "Director of the Office of Management and Budget's Annual Report to Congress on Combating Terrorism" (hereafter "the OMB Annual Report") provides a useful basis for congressional and public review of the executive branch's policies and programs. The year 2000 version of this report does describe a sound budget review process. The document as a whole is a considerable improvement over previous versions of the report.

The OMB Annual Report notes that the Clinton administration's terrorism policy is outlined in Presidential Decision Directives (PDD) 39, 62 and 63 and specific agency guidance such as the Attorney General's "Five-Year Interagency Counter-Terrorism Plan." These documents, issued over the course of the last several years, form a basis for a national strategy. The current budget review process described in the OMB annual report is not a substitute for a comprehensive threat assessment. Both a comprehensive threat assessment and a sound budget review process are needed. However, they do not amount to a national strategy. PDD-39 was issued in 1995 shortly after the sarin attack on the Tokyo subway and the bombing of the Murrah Federal Building in Oklahoma City. PDD-62 and PDD-63 were issued in 1999. Each document was prepared at a different time, in reaction to terrorist events or developing circumstances, or designed to address specific policy gaps and meet new circumstances confronting the United States. A collection of policy documents is simply not equivalent to a national strategy like that recommended by the Gilmore commission. If this national security threat is as important as the President and many of his advisors suggest, then a comprehensive strategy is an important roadmap to guide programmatic and budgetary aspects of governmental activities.

US Funding to Combat Terrorism

The OMB Annual Report provides a useful basis for congressional and public review of the executive branch's spending on antiterrorism and counterterrorism. Funding to combat terrorism is difficult to segment into sub-categories, separating funding that specifically addresses WMD from other non-WMD related programs.

Undoubtedly there is overlap that requires a judgment call as to which federal dollar spent contributes to a particular activity. The OMB is to be commended for generating this useful document.

Each annual version of the Report prepared by the OMB and submitted to the Congress provides more budgetary detail on US antiterrorism and counterterrorism activities than the previous year's version. Not only does this high degree of budgetary transparency serve as a modest testament to the strength of the American political system, it creates the basis for congressional and public review that is vital to sustaining a consensus on government policy in this important area of national security.

The 2000 OMB Annual Report states that "information gleaned since the submission of the FY 2001 budget" and the submission of the Report indicates the nature of the terrorism threat has increased. Further explanation of the increased threat in the period — February 2000 to May 2000 — is not provided. The OMB Annual Report argues that this augmented threat is the justification for an amendment to the budget amounting to $235.5 million submitted in conjunction with the report.

How financial resources are allocated serves as a critical indicator of actual, as opposed to declared, policy implementation. The OMB Annual Report is a valuable tool for understanding the direction, scope and dimensions of USG efforts to combat terrorism. However, in order to ensure that these reports serve their full potential in the future, the OMB should strive to be consistent from year to year. An imperfection in the OMB Annual Reports over the course of the past three years is that the dollar figures described as enacted in past years are not consistent from year to year.

Presumably the OMB can account for the discrepancies, by grouping items under the spending category in one report from that of the following year. For example, in the

Report's general mission category of Law Enforcement and Investigative Activities, the 1999 version of the OMB Annual Report indicates that $2.587 billion was enacted in 1999, there was a supplemental appropriation of $350 million, and that the FY 2000 requested amounted to $2.757. Yet, the OMB Annual Report for 2000 indicates that $2.687 was enacted in 1999 and $2.797 was requested. Thus, the 1999 dollar amount for this category plus the supplemental does not equal the amount the 2000 OMB Annual Report indicates as "enacted" in 1999, nor are the "requested" figures equivalent between the two annual reports. The confusions these apparent discrepancies sow must be rectified in future annual reports to Congress.

Clearly defining the spending items under each spending category may be one way to improve the value of these annual reports. Some analysts argue that the only way to truly understand what has been spent from year to year is to examine the Treasury accounts per department and agency. By tracking the spending according to the Treasury accounts the Congress could determine not only how it agreed with the executive branch on how funds would be spent, but also would actually see how the executive branch implemented the spending as directed by annual budget acts.

Important Budget Issues

A constructive dialogue between the President and the Congress on funding to combat terrorism is critical. At present the dialogue seems satisfactory, but there is room for improvement. On the part of the executive branch, the President's representatives should consult more regularly and transparently with the Congress. On the part of the Congress, the process should be streamlined and rationalized. The plethora of committees with jurisdiction over portions of the budget supporting the government's programs to address the terrorist threat makes the consultation process cumbersome. The National Commission's recommendation that the appropriation committees in each house of Congress assign an individual staff member to track funding for combating terrorism is a useful suggestion.

Shifting Funding Emphasis to Prevention and Preemption

Tremendous improvements have been made in our national preparedness to respond to mass casualty terrorism incidents, particularly those involving weapons of mass destruction. More progress is required and training of the next generation of local responders and officials at all levels of government will remain an ongoing task. The focused emphasis on improving capabilities to respond to a WMD attack on American soil followed the Tokyo subway attack. At the time, there was tremendous fear that Aum Supreme Truth's attack marked the start of a new pattern of sub-national terrorist activity involving unconventional weapons. Since the Tokyo subway incident much has been learned about the attack and the cult, which should help recalibrate the magnitude of the danger of sub-national groups and WMD terrorism.

Putting aside the question of whether the US is allocating too little or too much funding to combat terrorism, and considering the figure of $9.3 billion requested by the Clinton administration for Fiscal Year 2001, a shift in programmatic emphasis and funding seems warranted at this stage in the evolution of American terrorism policy. Increasing emphasis should be place on the front end of the problem, by preemption and prevention of attacks, with less emphasis placed on the back end in post-attack consequence management. The OMB Annual Report notes that from 1998 to 2001 spending for preparing for and responding to terrorist acts increased from $126 million to $627 million, an increase of 398%.

This shift is particularly relevant for funding relating to WMD terrorism and incident response. The increase in funding for preparing for and responding to WMD terrorist acts increased from $89 million in 1998 to $566 million three years later, an increase of 536%. In contrast, funding for law enforcement and investigative activities has increased only $6% over the same period. While the President has asked for significant increases in this area of funding over the last two years, the end result has been only a modest increase.

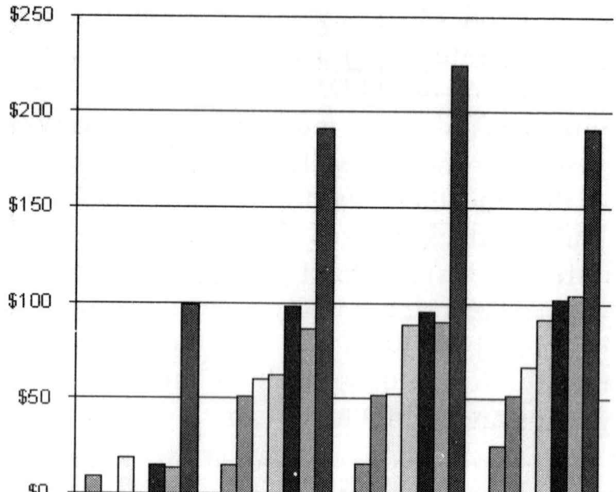

	FY 1998	FY 1999	FY 2000	FY 2001 - Req
Other	$8.9	$15.0	$15.7	$25.8
Stockpile of Vaccines and Therapeutics	$0.0	$51.0	$52.0	$52.0
Other Planning and Assistance to State/Local	$18.8	$60.0	$52.4	$66.7
Public Health Infrastructure/Surveillance	$0.0	$62.0	$88.6	$91.4
Equipment for First Responders	$15.1	$98.4	$95.2	$102.2
First Responder Training and Exercises	$13.3	$86.1	$90.4	$104.0
Special Response Units	$99.2	$191.5	$224.5	$191.4

Figure: Funding to Combat WMD Terrorism - By Mission Area ($ in Millions)

Comparatively modest increases in law enforcement, intelligence and diplomatic tools may dollar per dollar

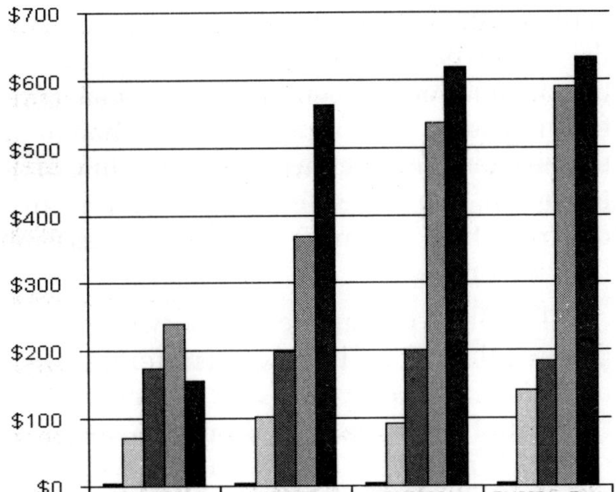

	FY1998	FY1999	FY2000	FY2001 - Req
■Physical protection of national population/infrastructure	$3.4	$3.8	$3.6	$3.6
□Law enforcement & investigative activities	$71.8	$102.3	$93.8	$142.5
■Physical security of govt facilities/employees	$175.1	$199.4	$200.6	$185.4
■Research and Development	$239.8	$368.8	$537.0	$589.9
■Preparing for & responding to terrorist acts	$155.3	$564.2	$618.7	$633.5

Figure: Preparing for and Responding to WMD Terrorism ($ in Millions)

contribute more to diminishing the threat. Using the OMB Annual Report's language, this means shifting emphasis from downstream investments to upstream investments. Currently, 82% of the funding goes to these downstream investments and 18% to upstream investments. Some downstream investment, such as R&D into pharmaceuticals and improvements in facilities security, may entail huge costs, while more FBI agents and CIA case officers might be comparatively less. Thus, the percentage balance in favor of antiterrorism measures as opposed to counterterrorism measures is understandable. Yet, a comparatively modest shift in funding emphasis would greatly enhance our effort to preempt and prevent attacks, while not neglecting defensive measures.

The law enforcement and intelligence communities perform critical "front end" missions to combat terrorism.

While both communities have received extra tasking with the increased concern about the dangers of new terrorist trends, neither has benefited from a sustained increase in funding support to fundamentally change their impact on the problem. Intelligence is the front line of defense against terrorism. The more we know about a security threat from the front line, the more tools we can assemble to address the challenge.

The State Department deserves special mention as a potential tool in the government's effort to combat terrorism. For comparatively modest amounts of funding the State Department could play a larger role to prevent terrorist attacks. Collaboration with allies to thwart attacks and pressure states that aid terrorism could hem in the problem in important ways. The intelligence community and the Department of Defense can also play an important role by collaborating with their counterparts in foreign countries to thwart attacks before they occur and sap the resources that terrorist group need to wage their attacks. Finally, it may be helpful to establish a separate line item in the State Department for combating terrorism. Currently, funding for terrorism is lumped in with the Department's Nonproliferation, Anti-terrorism, Demining and Related Programs Account (NADR). As a result of the other programs in this account, sustained support for the Department's activities is precarious.

By suggesting a shift in the emphasis of spending, I am not proposing that domestic preparation to respond to terrorist incidents be diminished significantly or discontinued. It is my view that a more systematic approach to assessing the threat and devising programmatic guidelines with the benefit of a comprehensive and integrated threat assessment will lead to a recalibration of the threat we face in the short and medium term. It is important to establish a balance of spending that can be sustained over time and this balance will, in my opinion, require a shift in funding emphasis.

In regard to domestic preparation and response mission, the balance should shift from programs unique to terrorism to be broadened in a way to that will meet the challenges of a wider range of public disasters. Wise spending on defensive measures will have a dual-use capability that benefits American society today and serves as an asset to deter, detect or respond to a terrorist incident. Funding to improve the health and agricultural surveillance systems to guard against disease outbreaks is an example of dual-use benefit spending. Capabilities that benefit society at the moment of a catastrophic attack may be warranted, but they should be considered with a clear sense of spending trade-offs.

Sustainability of US Terrorism Policy

It is vitally important to forge a consensus on those essential programs and provide adequate support for them. Sustained support is particularly important in the areas of law enforcement and intelligence. Critical to the effectiveness of these mission areas is the development and retention of good personnel. The law enforcement and intelligence communities must be directed to make combating terrorism an organizational priority that is reflected in the value of such work for career advancement. Furthermore, it is important to enable personnel working terrorism issues to develop the needed expertise. Frequent rotation or multi-tasking prevent personnel from building valuable expertise.

Funding for improving the protection of our embassies abroad is one area where our inability to provide adequate funding over a sustained period of time is particularly disturbing. Funding for embassy security always seems to go up the year after American embassy has been bombed and then the funding tapers off each year thereafter until another bombing occurs. The OMB Report notes that since military installations abroad have become tough targets for terrorists, there is some evidence that American embassies are preferred targets. Both the Congress and the President should strive to sustain funding in this area.

Funding in the Medical Response Area

The Department of Health and Human Services (HHS) has received the most significant increases in funding in the shortest period of time. The research agenda for many HHS programs is especially challenging. It is a Department that critically needs the grounding of a comprehensive threat assessment and the guidance of a national terrorism strategy. For example, the intelligence community has not always agreed upon the list of biological agents the US is most likely to confront. Thus, the priority list of biological agents for which vaccines and antibiotics should be developed changed repeatedly. The implications of these changes are that it is very difficult to know what vaccines and antidotes should be developed if there is not a solid consensus on the most likely agents we may face. The research and development for these prevention and response tools could take many years, if not decades. Thus, these spending decisions require considerable care and scrutiny.

At the other end of the task spectrum for HHS is mental health response to terrorist incidents, both real and threatened, which has not received the support it should. How to manage the problem of the "worried well" and the mental trauma American society might experience in the event of a catastrophic terrorist attack deserves greater priority and financial support. The Tokyo subway attack and other mass casualty terrorist attacks suggest that hospitals will need to deal with many multiples more people with psychosomatic disturbances than physical injuries. How to manage the onslaught of the psychosomatic

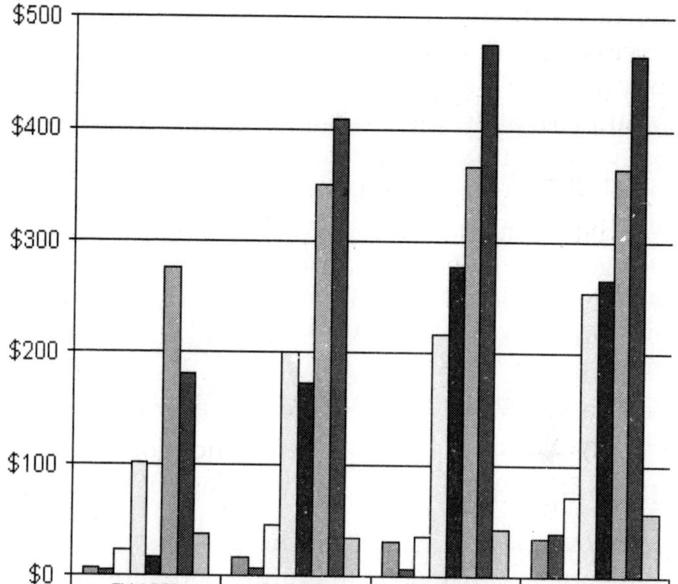

	FY 1998	FY 1999	FY 2000	FY 2001 - Req
FEMA	$5.9	$17.6	$30.8	$34.5
Agriculture	$5.2	$6.7	$7.3	$39.8
State	$23.0	$46.0	$37.0	$72.0
Justice	$100.8	$201.2	$217.2	$254.7
HHS	$15.9	$173.1	$277.6	$265.4
Energy	$275.8	$350.8	$366.3	$364.2
National Security Community	$180.6	$408.2	$475.8	$467.2
Other	$38.2	$34.9	$41.8	$57.2

Figure: Funding to Combat WMD Terrorism - By Agency ($ in Millions)

and psychologically injured public must be addressed if the health system has any chance of treating the physically wounded.

Our official communication about the threat of terrorism, particularly WMD terrorism, has increased rather than reduced concern. Anthrax hoaxes dramatically increased in the United States after the initial Nunn-Lugar-Domenici local responders training sessions began, as Secretary of Defense Cohen held up a bag of sugar at a news conference to indicate how little anthrax would be needed to kill thousands in a city, and as a result of the government's poorly handled detention of Larry Wayne Harris, who had anthrax vaccine in the back of his car. More sober official communications about the potential danger of WMD terrorism and our preparations might have limited the tremendous increase in unconventional weapons threats and hoaxes. The vastly different strategies in New Jersey and New York for dealing with the West Nile virus suggest that effective communication with the public about the nature of an outbreak can mean the difference between creating public concern and maintaining public order and confidence.

R&D Spending

R&D spending poses the greatest long-term policy challenge. The search for future tools to address the full range of terrorist threats, particularly those stemming from the use biological weapons, is critical. But given the time required for new technologies to mature, special care must be taken to ensure that each yearly research dollar contributes to future technological advancements.

The R&D spending related to weapons of mass destruction (WMD) deserves special attention. There are significant differences in how the OMB annual reports depicted R& D spending from one year to another. The 1999 OMB Annual Report, for example, lists very different figures for the Department of Energy R&D spending than those listed in the 2000 OMB Annual Report for the same years.

Finally, the R&D spending category of "Other" has consistently outpaced all other mission categories. Some means of characterizing the variety of activities covered by the "Other" R&D category must be found. Proper oversight of the R&D budget is difficult without greater detail.

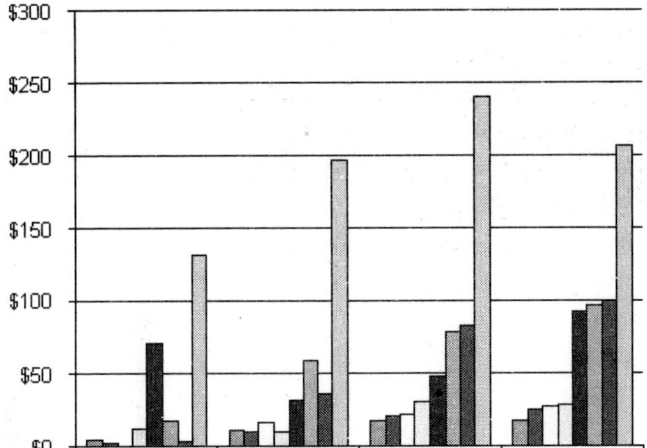

	FY1998	FY1999	FY2000	FY2001 - Req
Modeling, Simulation, Systems Analyses	$3.6	$10.6	$16.7	$16.7
Personal/Environmental Decontamination	$1.8	$9.3	$20.3	$24.2
Therapeutics/Treatments	$0.0	$16.0	$20.9	$26.6
Personal/Collective Protection	$12.0	$10.0	$30.0	$28.2
Basic Research, incl. Gene Sequencing	$70.5	$31.0	$48.0	$92.3
Detection/Diagnostics	$17.8	$59.0	$78.3	$97.0
Vaccines	$2.9	$35.7	$82.6	$99.2
Other	$131.2	$197.2	$240.3	$205.8

Figure: R & D for Defense against WMD Terrorism ($ in Millions)

Managing Rapid Budget Increases

The President and the Congress responded rapidly to the prospect of an increase in terrorist activity on American soil and the potential use of unconventional weapons materials. In several instances, government departments and agencies received significant budget increases to "stand up" important programs. The Departments of Health and Human Services has received enormous increases in budget authority for antiterrorism and counterterrorism programs in the last few years. Managing such rapid increases in funding is bound to present formidable challenges.

A thorough review of the three or four government programs that received the most significant percentage increases is important to the integrity of the government's overall effort. Challenges about the propriety of the increases and their effective allocation could stall important programs at a crucial stage of development. Alternatively, if fast growing programs have gone off track, it is important to identify these problems before sunk costs drive spending decisions more than wise policy.

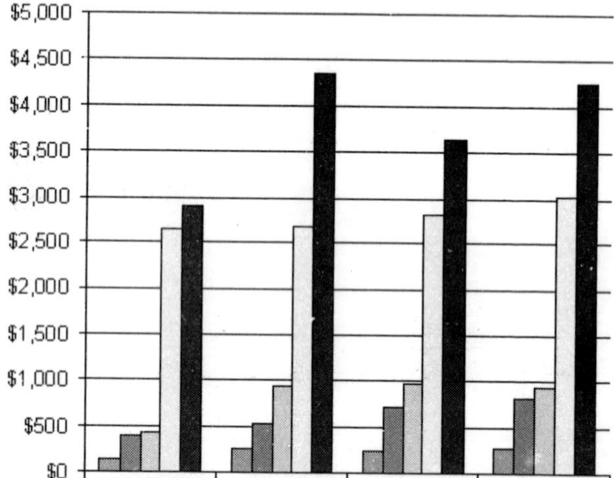

	FY1998	FY1999	FY2000	FY2001 - Req
Physical protection of national population/infrastructure	$146.7	$256.8	$249.9	$266.8
Research and Development	$403.1	$527.0	$727.9	$812.8
Preparing for & responding to terrorist acts	$417.8	$930.2	$984.4	$947.0
Law enforcement & investigative activities	$2,654.7	$2,686.8	$2,820.0	$3,025.5
Physical security of govt facilities/employees	$2,893.7	$4,356.4	$3,637.5	$4,259.2

Figure: Funding to Combat Terrorism, Including WMD - By Mission Area ($ in Millions)

Funding the Department of Justice's National Domestic Preparedness Office

PDD-62 designates the Department of Justice (DOJ) as the lead agency for handling domestic terrorism crisis. While allocation of financial resources is not the only way to indicate policy priorities, the lack of support for DOJ's terrorism offices is conspicuous by its absence. The 2000 OMB Annual Report does not discuss the National Domestic Preparedness Office (NDPO) in any

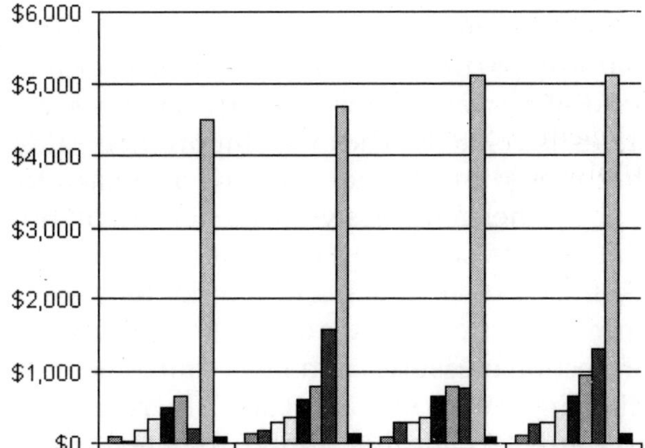

	FY 1998	FY 1999	FY 2000	FY 2001 - Req
General Services Admin	$89.6	$133.5	$92.8	$117.0
HHS	$15.9	$173.1	$277.6	$265.4
Transportation	$169.3	$270.8	$277.2	$298.2
Treasury	$341.4	$368.0	$348.0	$440.2
Energy	$499.0	$611.1	$647.6	$663.5
Justice	$647.1	$794.0	$782.0	$949.3
State	$186.0	$1,579.0	$781.0	$1,312.0
National Security Community	$4,493.1	$4,682.5	$5,117.2	$5,124.1
Other	$67.7	$135.3	$85.8	$130.6

Figure: Funding to Combat Terrorism, Including WMD - By Agency ($ in Millions)

meaningful detail. Appropriately, the task of local and state responder training will transition from the military as designated by earlier Nunn-Lugar-Domenici legislation to the DOJ's NDPO. Based on questions regarding the NDPO's funding and its operational pace, neither the executive branch nor the Congress seems to have fully endorsed the mission of this new office. This sends exactly the wrong signal to State and Local officials at precisely the moment they look to the Federal government to bring some leadership to this daunting new challenge.

Other Nations' Approaches to Combat Terrorism

The GAO's report on other nation's approaches to combating terrorism is a valuable contribution to improve the formulation and implementation of a national terrorism policy. Examining the policies and practices of other nations, particularly those with experience who have suffered a greater number of terrorist attacks than the United States, is valuable. The most important finding of the report that should inform our national approach to the problem is how other countries view the terrorism threat in context. The nations survey by the GAO all took into account the likelihood of an attack and did not focus as intensively on vulnerabilities. They adapt their intelligence, physical protection measures, and law enforcement activities to the changing nature of the threat. Vulnerabilities are taken into account, but the likelihood that terrorists will exploit vulnerabilities is a significant component of their preparation.

Given the greater historical experience with terrorism on their national territory, the publics of the countries surveyed accept periodic casualties without a significant loss in public confidence of the government. In the United States, we aim as a society to take whatever measures deemed appropriate to protect our entire territory, every citizen, and all public and private facilities from any and all malicious and intentional attack. Our national desire for protection against ballistic missiles is another expression of this desire that is not shared to the same degree by other nations, including many of our key allies. Furthermore, more Americans die from alcohol related traffic accidents or food-borne illness than terrorist incidents. Political support has not surged to ensure that the government takes meaningful actions to reduce these casualty rates.

Taking note of the limitations of such an analysis will help American policy put this international comparison in perspective. While the GAO clearly indicates that they did not conduct a comparative study, the value of their findings lies in the potential for comparison with the United States. At this moment, the United States stands as the preeminent power with global influence and responsibilities. The countries considered in the GAO analysis are regional powers. As the sole global power the United States attracts admiration, envy and antipathy. Periodically, the US government, American companies and American citizens may be a terrorist target for no other reasons than the perception of the country's global power.

Second, two of the countries included in the GAO analysis, Israel and the United Kingdom, struggle with acute terrorism problems stemming from their presence on disputed territories. American forces stationed abroad face a somewhat similar threat environment, but it is not nearly as acute or as constant. The security environments in the Middle East and Northern Ireland have changed in the last few years due to improvements in the political dialogues of the parties concerned. The United States does not face any analogous circumstances that could lead to a significant lessening of the terrorist threat.

A comprehensive threat assessment that integrates information on both domestic and international terrorist threats is an essential baseline tool for informing a national strategy on terrorism, which the US currently lacks. At the moment, far too much of the government's policy on terrorism is driven by perceptions of vulnerability and planning for worst-case scenarios. Inordinate attention to vulnerabilities and worst-case scenarios may be skewing resources in ways that do not effectively add to the government's effort to protect our personnel and facilities, private businesses, and citizens at home and abroad. Producing a comprehensive and integrated national threat assessment that takes into account vulnerabilities to attack as well as the capabilities and motivations of terrorists will improve our national understanding of the threat and should inform the President and the Congress as they decide upon investments in short and long term programs to combat terrorism.

3

The Counterterrorist Allegory

The United States has spent billions of dollars on counterterrorism since the U.S. embassy bombings in Tanzania and Kenya, in August of 1998. Tens of millions have been spent on covert operations specifically targeting Usama bin Ladin and his terrorist organization, al-Qa'ida. Senior U.S. officials boldly claim—even after the suicide attack last October on the USS Cole, in the port of Aden—that the Central Intelligence Agency and the Federal Bureau of Investigation are clandestinely "picking apart" bin Ladin's organization "limb by limb." But having worked for the CIA for nearly nine years on Middle Eastern matters (I left the Directorate of Operations because of frustration with the Agency's many problems), I would argue that America's counterterrorism program in the Middle East and its environs is a myth.

Peshawar, the capital of Pakistan's Northwest Frontier, is on the cultural periphery of the Middle East. It is just down the Grand Trunk Road from the legendary Khyber Pass, the gateway to Afghanistan. Peshawar is where bin Ladin cut his teeth in the Islamic jihad, when, in the mid-1980s, he became the financier and logistics man for the Maktab al-Khidamat, The Office of Services, an overt organization trying to recruit and aid Muslim, chiefly Arab, volunteers for the war against the Soviets in Afghanistan.

The friendships and associations made in The Office of Services gave birth to the clandestine al-Qa'ida, The Base, whose explicit aim is to wage a *jihad* against the West, especially the United States.

According to Afghan contacts and Pakistani officials, bin Ladin's men regularly move through Peshawar and use it as a hub for phone, fax, and modem communication with the outside world. Members of the embassy-bombing teams in Africa probably planned to flee back to Pakistan. Once there they would likely have made their way into bin Ladin's open arms through al-Qa'ida's numerous friends in Peshawar. Every tribe and region of Afghanistan is represented in this city, which is dominated by the Pathans, the pre-eminent tribe in the Northwest Frontier and southern Afghanistan. Peshawar is also a power base of the Taliban, Afghanistan's fundamentalist rulers. Knowing the city's ins and outs would be indispensable to any U.S. efforts to capture or kill Bin Ladin and his closest associates. Intelligence collection on al-Qa'ida can't be of much real value unless the agent network covers Peshawar.

During a recent visit, at sunset, when the city's cloistered alleys go black except for an occasional flashing neon sign, I would walk through Afghan neighborhoods. Even in the darkness I had a case officer's worst sensation—eyes following me everywhere. To escape the crowds I would pop into carpet, copper, and jewelry shops and every cybercafé I could find. These were poorly lit one- or two-room walk-ups where young men surfed Western porn. No matter where I went, the feeling never left me. I couldn't see how the CIA as it is today had any chance of running a successful counterterrorist operation against bin Ladin in Peshawar, the Dodge City of Central Asia.

Westerners cannot visit the cinder-block, mud-brick side of the Muslim world—whence bin Ladin's foot soldiers mostly come—without announcing who they are. No case officer stationed in Pakistan can penetrate either the Afghan communities in Peshawar or the Northwest Frontier's numerous religious schools, which feed manpower and ideas to bin Ladin and the Taliban, and seriously expect to gather useful information about radical Islamic terrorism—let alone recruit foreign agents.

Even a Muslim CIA officer with native-language abilities (and the Agency, according to several active-duty case officers, has very few operatives from Middle Eastern backgrounds) could do little more in this environment than a blond, blue-eyed all-American. Case officers cannot long escape the embassies and consulates in which they serve. A U.S. official overseas, photographed and registered with the local intelligence and security services, can't travel much, particularly in a police-rich country like Pakistan, without the "host" services' knowing about it. An officer, who tries to go native, is pretending to be a true-believing radical Muslim searching for brothers in the cause, will make a fool of him quickly.

In Pakistan, where the government's Inter-Services Intelligence Agency and the ruling army are competent and tough, the CIA can do little if these institutions are against it. And they are against it. Where the Taliban and Usama bin Ladin are concerned, Pakistan and the United States aren't allies. Relations between the two countries have been poor for years, owing to American opposition to Pakistan's successful nuclear-weapons program and, more recently, Islamabad's backing of Muslim Kashmiri separatists. Bin Ladin's presence in Afghanistan as a "guest" of the Pakistani-backed Taliban has injected even more distrust and suspicion into the relationship.

In other words, American intelligence has not gained and will not gain Pakistan's assistance in its pursuit of bin Ladin. The only effective way to run offensive counterterrorist operations against Islamic radicals in more or less hostile territory is with "non-official-cover" officers—operatives who are in no way openly attached to the U.S.

government. Imagine James Bond minus the gadgets, the women, the Walther PPK, and the Aston Martin. But as of late 1999 no program to insert NOCs into an Islamic fundamentalist organization abroad had been implemented, according to one such officer who has served in the Middle East. "NOCs haven't really changed at all since the Cold War," he told me recently. "We're still a group of fake businessmen who live in big houses overseas. We don't go to mosques and pray."

A former senior Near East Division operative says, "The CIA probably doesn't have a single truly qualified Arabic-speaking officer of Middle Eastern background who can play a believable Muslim fundamentalist who would volunteer to spend years of his life with shitty food and no women in the mountains of Afghanistan. For Christ's sake, most case officers live in the suburbs of Virginia. We don't do that kind of thing." A younger case officer boils the problem down even further: "Operations that include diarrhea as a way of life don't happen."

Behind-the-lines counterterrorism operations are just too dangerous for CIA officers to participate in directly. When I was in the Directorate of Operations, the Agency would deploy a small army of officers for a meeting with a *possibly* dangerous foreigner if he couldn't be met in the safety of a U.S. embassy or consulate. Officers still in the clandestine service say that the Agency's risk-averse, bureaucratic nature—which mirrors, of course, the growing physical risk-aversion of American society—has only gotten worse.

A few miles from Peshawar's central bazaar, near the old Cantonment, where redcoats once drilled and where is the U.S. consulate and the American Club, a traditional hangout for international-aid workers, diplomats, journalists, and spooks. Worn-out Western travelers often stop here on the way from Afghanistan to decompress; one can buy a drink, watch videos, and order a steak. Security warnings from the American embassy are posted on the club's hallway bulletin board.

The bulletins I saw last December advised U.S. officials and their families to stay away from crowds, mosques, and anyplace else devout Pakistanis and Afghans might gather. The U.S. embassy in Islamabad, a fortress surrounded by roadblocks, Pakistani soldiers, and walls topped with security cameras and razor wire, strongly recommended a low profile—essentially life within the Westernized, high-walled Cantonment area or other spots where diplomats are unlikely to bump into fundamentalists.

Such warnings accurately reflect the mentality inside both the Department of State and the CIA. Individual officers may venture out, but their curiosity isn't encouraged or rewarded. Unless one of bin Ladin's foot soldiers walks through the door of a U.S. consulate or embassy, the odds that a CIA counterterrorist officer will ever see one are extremely poor.

The Directorate of Operations' history of success has done little to prepare the CIA for its confrontation with radical Islamic terrorism. Perhaps the DO's most memorable victory was against militant Palestinian groups in the 1970s and 1980s. The CIA could find common ground with Palestinian militants, who often drink, womanize, and spend time in nice hotels in pleasant, comfortable countries. Still, it's "penetrations" of the PLO—delightfully and kindly rendered in David Ignatius's novel *Agents of Innocence* (1987)—were essentially emissaries from Yasir Arafat to the U.S. government.

Difficulties with fundamentalism and mud-brick neighborhoods aside, the CIA has stubbornly refused to develop cadres of operatives specializing in one or two countries. Throughout the Soviet-Afghan war (1979-1989) the DO never developed a team of Afghan experts. The first case officer in Afghanistan to have some proficiency in an Afghan language didn't arrive until 1987, just a year and a half before the war's end. Robert Baer, one of the most talented Middle East case officers of the past twenty years (and the only operative in the 1980s to collect consistently first-rate intelligence on the Lebanese Hizbollah and the Palestinian Islamic Jihad), suggested to headquarters in the early 1990s that the CIA might want to collect intelligence on Afghanistan from the neighboring Central Asian republics of the former Soviet Union.

Headquarters' reply: Too dangerous, and why bother? The Cold War there was over with the Soviet withdrawal in 1989. Afghanistan was too far away, internecine warfare was seen as endemic, and radical Islam was an abstract idea. Afghanistan has since become the brain center and training ground for Islamic terrorism against the United States, yet the CIA's clandestine service still usually keeps officers on the Afghan account no more than two or three years.

Until October of 1999 no CIA official visited Ahmad Shah Mas'ud in Afghanistan. Mas'ud is the ruler of northeastern Afghanistan and the leader of the only force still fighting the Taliban. He was the most accomplished commander of the anti-Soviet mujahideen guerrillas; his army now daily confronts Arab military units that are under the banner of bin Ladin, yet no CIA case officer has yet debriefed Mas'ud's soldiers on the front lines or the Pakistani, Afghan, Chinese-Turkoman, and Arab holy warriors they've captured.

The CIA's Counterterrorism Center, which now has hundreds of employees from numerous government agencies, was the creation of Duane "Dewey" Clarridge, an extraordinarily energetic bureaucrat-spook. In less than a year in the mid-1980s Clarridge converted a three-man operation confined to one room with one TV set broadcasting CNN into a staff that rivaled the clandestine service's Near East Division for primacy in counterterrorist operations. Yet the Counterterrorism Center didn't alter the CIA's methods overseas at all. "We didn't really think about the details of operations—how we would penetrate this or that group," a former senior counterterrorist official says. "Victory for us meant that we stopped [Thomas] Twetten [the chief of the clandestine service's Near East Division] from walking all over us." In my years inside the CIA, I never once heard case officers overseas or back at headquarters discuss the ABCs of a recruitment operation against any Middle Eastern target that took a case officer far off the diplomatic and business-conference circuits. Long-term seeding operations simply didn't occur.

George Tenet, who became the director of the CIA in 1997, has repeatedly described America's counterterrorist program as "robust" and in most cases successful at keeping bin Ladin's terrorists "off-balance" and anxious about their own security. The Clinton Administration's senior director for counterterrorism on the National Security Council, Richard Clarke, who has continued as the counterterrorist czar in the Bush Administration, is sure that bin Ladin and his men stay awake at night "around the campfire" in Afghanistan, "worried stiff about who we're going to get next."

If we are going to defeat Usama bin Ladin, we need to openly side with Ahmad Shah Mas'ud, who still has a decent chance of fracturing the tribal coalition behind Taliban power. That, more effectively than any clandestine counterterrorist program in the Middle East, might eventually force al-Qa'ida's leader to flee Afghanistan, where U.S. and allied intelligence and military forces cannot reach him.

4

Improving Counterterrorism Operations

In the last 3 years, many government agencies have conducted several successful interagency operations overseas, including some in which suspected terrorists have been returned to the United States to stand trial. In addition, federal agencies have deployed personnel and equipment to prepare for many special events such as the Atlanta Olympic Games. However, federal agencies have not completed interagency guidance and resolved command and control issues. Proposed interagency Domestic Guidelines have not been completed, nor coordinated with all federal agencies with domestic counterterrorism roles. For example, the Federal Bureau of Investigation (FBI) has not coordinated the proposed Domestic Guidelines with the Department of the Treasury even though it could have a significant role in an actual terrorist incident.

Furthermore, approval of proposed interagency International Guidelines has been delayed because the Department of State, the Department of Justice, and the FBI have not reached agreement on the level of State participation in highly sensitive missions to arrest suspected terrorists overseas. In addition, some interagency and intergovernmental command and control issues regarding domestic counterterrorist operations have not been fully resolved. To improve their preparedness to respond to terrorist incidents, federal agencies have conducted over 200 exercises, of which about half included three or more federal agencies and about one third included state and local participants. However, agencies have not fully achieved the interagency counterterrorist exercise program directed in a June 1995 Presidential Directive because an interagency Exercise Subgroup has not prepared and submitted, and senior agency officials have not approved, an interagency programme.

As a result, some complex transfers of command and control between agencies have not been exercised. International counter terrorism exercises, sponsored for many years by the Department of Defense (DOD), are relatively comprehensive in that they include many federal agencies and test tactical units along with State Department's leadership role and DOD's command and control. In contrast, domestic exercises sponsored by the FBI and the Federal Emergency Management Agency (FEMA)—the lead federal agencies for domestic operations—are not as comprehensive. The FBI exercise program focuses on its regional and field offices' tactical capabilities to respond and generally has not included the Bureau's full interagency leadership role that is expected to be critical during a domestic terrorist incident.

Recently, the FBI has made significant progress and taken steps to enhance its program in this regard. The FEMA counterterrorism exercise program consists of tabletop exercises and does not include field exercises that would deploy personnel and equipment, and practice roles and responsibilities in realistic settings. DOD, the Department of Energy (DOE), and FEMA have requirements and processes in place to capture lessons learned from counterterrorist operations and exercises. These agencies, however, did not capture lessons learned for all the exercises they led or all the field exercises they participated in. Other federal agencies had less rigorous requirements and processes for capturing lessons learned. There is also no requirement or process to capture lessons learned at the interagency level. Establishing a process to record and share the lessons learned of counterterrorism operations and exercises would be beneficial and could improve future operations.

In our classified report, we made several recommendations to enhance interagency guidance, command and control, exercises, and processes to capture and share lessons learned. The U.S. policy and strategy on combating terrorism have been evolving since the 1970s and are articulated in Presidential Directives and implementing guidance. These guidance documents divide activities to combat terrorism into three elements: preventing and deterring terrorism; responding to a terrorist crisis, and managing the consequences after a terrorist attack. One of the highest priorities in the federal government is to prevent and prepare for terrorist attacks that use weapons of mass destruction (WMD).

Crisis management includes efforts to stop a terrorist attack, arrest terrorists, and gather evidence for criminal prosecution. Consequence management includes efforts to provide medical treatment and emergency services, evacuate people from dangerous areas, and restore government services. When terrorist attacks occur without adequate threat warning, crisis response and consequence management will be concurrent activities. In the post-Cold War world, the multi-faceted phenomenon of transnational terrorism has replaced the monolithic Soviet menace as the preeminent threat to our safety and sovereignty as a nation. The issues you will confront over the next two days lie at the heart of national security policy as we enter the 21st century. The National Governors Association and the National Emergency Management Association play an integral role in shaping national counterterrorism policies and programs because terrorism strikes first in the buildings, the streets, the farms, the factories and public places that are your domains.

No early warning satellites will alert us to an attack. No command post in a Colorado mountain will direct the critical, early response. Against so insidious an enemy, who relies upon surprise and mass fear as primary weapons, the federal government and states must work as partners in unprecedented ways to prevent the next attack, and failing that, be prepared to deal with the consequences. In my view, we are not prepared. By all accounts, we are particularly vulnerable to the use of biological agents in the type of "low probability, high consequence" scenario you are modeling here.

After spending ten years and more than $50 billion to fashion a coherent federal counterterrorism program, only slow progress can be claimed against an insidious and adaptable foe. In the event of a major, multi-site attack involving the effective release of a contagious pathogen, current response capabilities would be quickly overwhelmed, washed away like a sand castle at high tide. Today, more than forty federal departments and agencies operate programs to deter, detect, prepare for, and respond to terrorist attacks. While some inter-agency cooperation and information sharing has begun, substantial barriers – including congressional mandates – still prevent a fully coordinated counterterrorism effort. As the organizational chart gets more complex, the effort inevitably becomes less cohesive.

In the course of 19 National Security Subcommittee hearings on these issues over the past three years, we have found the fight against terrorism remains fragmented and unfocused primarily because no overarching national strategy guides planning, directs spending or disciplines bureaucratic balkanization. A national strategy should be developed with a high-level statement of national objectives.

This strategy should be coupled logically to a statement of the means that will be used to achieve these objectives. Federal and state agencies should use the strategy as a roadmap in developing plans and programs to counter terrorism.

Essential to a sound strategy is a clear understanding of the threat. We found no formal assessment of domestic-origin threats that could be combined with existing assessments of the foreign-origin threat to establish the priorities required to determine allocation of funds. The General Accounting Office recommends the use of established risk assessment criteria. It is a deliberate, analytical approach to identify which threats can exploit known vulnerabilities. Variables are ranked according to predetermined criteria, such as the probability of a threat targeting a specific asset or the impact of vulnerabilities being exploited by a specific threat. The process results in a ranked list of risks used to select safeguards to reduce vulnerabilities and create a certain level of protection.

A formal assessment of the domestic-origin threat, combined with existing assessments of the foreign-origin threat, should be developed to provide an authoritative, comprehensive and intelligence-based overview. It should be updated regularly and it should be shared with state and local authorities to the fullest extent possible. And, as you know, there is no central office, or designated individual appointed by the president and confirmed by the Senate, with budget authority over federal efforts to counter terrorism. Clearer leadership is required. Someone or some office needs to be in charge to provide leadership and insure monies are spent properly.

A central office for combating terrorism should be established with program and budget authority over all federal efforts to combat terrorism to ensure compliance with established priorities. When pressed for a national strategy, the previous administration pointed to a pastiche of event-driven presidential decision directives and the Justice Department's five-year plan. Reactive in vision and scope, that "strategy" changed only as we lurched from crisis to crisis, from Khobar to the Cole, from Oklahoma City to Dar e Salaam. When confronted with the need for government-wide coordination, President Clinton appointed a National Coordinator to the National Security Council staff. That person had no authority to influence budgets and no power to terminate obsolete or duplicative programs.

The Bush Administration is reviewing government-wide preparation to counter terrorism, focusing mainly on domestic preparedness. But, the new administration does not need to reinvent the wheel. The work Congress and expert groups like this have done on this issue is extensive. Those findings and recommendations generally concur with our Subcommittee findings and provide the new administration a roadmap to use in preparing the United States and its citizens for the next terrorist attack.

The Second Annual Report of the Advisory Panel to Assess Domestic Response Capabilities For Terrorism Involving Weapons of Mass Destruction concluded, "the United States has no coherent, functional national strategy for combating terrorism, and the next President should establish a National Office for Combating Terrorism."

The Phase III Report of the US Commission on National Security/21st Century (the Hart-Rudman panel) recommended, "The President should develop a comprehensive strategy to heighten America's ability to prevent and protect against all forms of attacks on the homeland, and to respond to such attacks if prevention and protection fail."

The National Commission on Terrorism (created by Public Law 105-277) advocated enhancing planning and preparation to respond to terrorist attacks and creating stronger mechanisms to ensure funding for individual agency counterterrorism programs. The Center for Strategic and International Studies' report, Combating Chemical, Biological, Radiological and Nuclear Terrorism: A Comprehensive Strategy stated, "The United States currently lacks a comprehensive strategy for countering the threat of terrorism...."

Bruce Hoffman, Director of Rand Corporation's Washington office, in a study of terrorism stated, "A prerequisite to ensuring US resources are focused where they can have the most effect is a sober and empirical understanding of the terrorist threat, coupled with comprehensive and coherent strategy." Dr. Amy E. Smithson, a researcher on chemical and biological weapons at the Henry L. Stimson Center in Washington, concluded in a recent report entitled Ataxia, that the federal government has wasted large sums of money by mismanaging an array of domestic preparedness programs.

The specific effects of this strategic and organizational vacuum will become apparent as you work through your exercise today and tomorrow. I hope you will share your findings with our Subcommittee. Let me share a similar experience with you. On March 27, 2000, we held a tabletop exercise and field hearing in Connecticut. The event was sponsored and organized by the Connecticut Department of Emergency Management. Together, we wanted to assess the impact of federal programs at the state and local levels, and to ask what needs to be done to improve their focus, their reach, and their effectiveness. That scenario involved an Amtrak train that pulled into the Bridgeport station spewing thick black smoke. Local police, fire and emergency response personnel had been alerted by a 911 call from aboard the train. Only after the injured had been transported to local hospitals was it learned the smoke contained an intentionally introduced toxic chemical.

From that exercise we learned some clear lessons:

- Communications quickly break down or clog.
- Detection capabilities are too dispersed and take too long to arrive at the scene of a suspected incident.
- Decontamination equipment is limited.
- Many first responders lack access to full training and standard equipment.
- Federal and local emergency management procedures don't always mesh effectively.
- Already overtaxed health care facilities are not prepared to diagnose or treat mass casualties.

All the participants in that exercise agreed that more exercises were sorely needed. Many also expressed frustration and confusion over the jumble of federal counterterrorism agencies and programs, and the complexity of applying for help. Another recent exercise ominously named "Dark Winter" was designed to simulate US reaction to the deliberate introduction of smallpox virus in three states during the winter of 2002. The players included former Senator Sam Nunn as President, David Gergen, as National Security Advisor, Governor Frank Keating as himself, and William Sessions as Director of the Federal Bureau of Investigation. Meeting as the National Security Council as the scenario played out, they faced many of the issues you will face today and tomorrow.

Initially, one smallpox case was reported in Oklahoma City. Additional cases were soon identified in Georgia and Pennsylvania. More cases appeared in Oklahoma. The source of the infection was still unknown. Due to the lengthy incubation period of smallpox, exposure had probably taken place at least nine days earlier. Consequently, exposed individuals likely traveled far from the epicenter of what was presumed to be a biological attack.

That exercise illustrated several important points I offer for your consideration here:

- An attack on the United States with biological weapons could threaten vital national security interests.
- Massive civilian casualties, breakdown in essential institutions, violation of democratic processes, civil disorder, loss of confidence in government and reduced US strategic flexibility abroad are among the ways a biological attack might compromise US security.
- Current organizational structures and capabilities are not well suited for the management of a biological weapons attack. Major fault lines exist between different levels of government.
- There is no surge capability in the US health care and public health systems, or the pharmaceutical and vaccine industries.
- Dealing with the media during a crisis such as a biological weapons attack will be a major challenge for all levels of government.
- Should a contagious biological weapon be used, containing the spread of disease will present significant ethical, political, cultural, operational, and legal challenges.

Lessons from the "Dark Winter" exercise will be subject of a hearing of the National Security Subcommittee on July 23. Many of the key players will testify on the role of first responders, assistance to state governments, National Guard capabilities, the use of military assets, maintaining civil order and protecting public health in a biological outbreak. What you learn here will add to the growing body of national knowledge about our increasingly likely, but still unthinkable, future. Terrorists willing to die for their cause will not wait while we rearrange bureaucratic boxes on the organizational chart. Their strategy is clear, their focus keen, their resources efficiently deployed. Our national security demands greater strategic clarity, shaper focus and unprecedented coordination to confront the threat of terrorism today.

U.S. Policy, Lead Agencies, and Guidance

U.S. policy to combat terrorism was formalized in 1986 with the issuance of National Security Decision Directive 207, which primarily focused on terrorist incidents overseas. After the bombing of a federal building in Oklahoma City, Oklahoma, the President issued Presidential Decision Directive (PDD) 39 in June 1995, which enumerated responsibilities for federal agencies in combating terrorism, including domestic incidents. In May 1998, the President issued PDD 62 that reaffirmed PDD 39 and further articulated responsibilities for specific agencies. PDD 62 also established a National Coordinator for Security, Infrastructure Protection, and Counterterrorism, within the National Security Council, to coordinate agencies' programs. These directives, and the guidelines and contingency plans that implement them, call for robust, tailored and rapidly deployable interagency teams to conduct well-coordinated and highly integrated operations.

PDDs 39 and 62 assigned or reaffirmed the lead and supporting roles to various federal agencies and established interagency support teams. The State Department is the lead agency for international terrorist incidents. An interagency Foreign Emergency Support Team (FEST) was established to provide advice and support to U.S. ambassadors, Washington decision- makers, and host governments. Similarly, the FBI is the lead federal agency for domestic crisis response. An interagency Domestic Emergency Support Team (DEST) was established to provide advice and support to FBI on- scene commanders. Both the FEST and DEST consist of rapidly deployable interagency teams tailored to the specific terrorist incident. For example, experts from DOD, DOE, the Department of Health and Human Services (HHS) or the Environmental Protection Agency (EPA) might be part of the teams if the incident involved WMD. The State Department and the FBI determine the composition of the FEST and DEST, respectively.

The PDDs also affirmed FEMA as the lead agency for coordinating consequence management in domestic incidents. Other agencies have important support roles in combating terrorism. For example, DOD could provide significant support to other agencies, both for international incidents and for domestic incidents involving WMD. DOE provides support and technical expertise related to nuclear devices and radiological events. EPA provides expertise and support in incidents involving certain hazardous chemicals. The U.S. Secret Service designs and implements operational security at designated special events provides protection against the terrorist attacks. Lead federal agencies drafted interagency guidance to provide operational details for implementing PDD 39.

The State Department, as the lead federal agency for international incidents, drafted "Coordinating Subgroup Guidelines for the Mobilization, Deployment, and Employment of U.S. Government Elements in Response to an Overseas Terrorist Incident" (also known as the International Guidelines). The International Guidelines outline procedures for deploying the FEST and otherwise coordinating federal operations overseas. The FBI, as lead federal agency for domestic crisis response, drafted "Guidelines for the Mobilization, Deployment, and Employment of U.S. Government Agencies in Response to a Domestic Terrorist Threat or Incidence in Accordance With Presidential Decision Directive 39" (also known as the Domestic Guidelines) and the "United States Government Interagency Domestic Terrorism Concept of Operations Plan" (also known as the CONPLAN).

The Domestic Guidelines describe specific procedures and responsibilities of deploying the DEST, particularly in WMD incidents, while the CONPLAN provides overall guidance to federal, state, and local officials on how the federal government is structured to respond to a terrorist threat or incident in the United States. FEMA, the lead federal agency for domestic consequence management, coordinated and completed an interagency annex to the Federal Response Plan that discusses how the federal government would assist state and local authorities in managing the consequences of a terrorist attack in the United States. Support agencies developed their own guidance to be used to support an interagency terrorism response. For example, DOD developed a detailed contingency plan to guide its actions in deploying and responding to a terrorist incident and HHS developed a plan to deal with the health and medical consequences of terrorist attacks.

Issues Identified

In 1996, a congressional committee held hearings to provide oversight of counterterrorism programs, highlighting interagency operational and coordination challenges and issues. In 1996, the Nunn-Lugar hearings focused on the preparedness of the federal government to conduct counterterrorist operations at the agency, interagency, and intergovernmental levels (i.e., with state and local governments). Some of the issues highlighted in the hearings were as follows:

- Domestic interagency counterterrorism exercises should be more comprehensive and held more often and should go beyond tabletop exercises to field exercises where personnel and equipment rapidly deploy to a location and practice their activities.
- The FBI and FEMA needed to exercise their operations together when crisis response and consequence management was concurrent.
- Domestic interagency counterterrorism exercises should include the full array of federal, state, and local agencies.
- Individual agencies should capture lessons learned from counterterrorism exercises, disseminate such lessons both internally and externally, and track corrective actions.

- There should be an interagency process to capture lessons learned and track corrective actions.

Following the Nunn-Lugar hearings, Congress passed the Defense Against Weapons of Mass Destruction Act of 1996 (commonly known as the Nunn- Lugar-Domenici Act). The act designated DOD as the lead agency to enhance domestic preparedness for WMD terrorism by providing federal, state, and local emergency response personnel with, among other things, training and advice. The legislation led to the creation of the Nunn-Lugar-Domenici Domestic Preparedness Program, which was intended to be an interagency and intergovernmental effort among key agencies with responsibilities for crisis and consequence management in the event of a terrorist incident. We reported separately on the implementation of this programme.

Agencies Operate

We found that federal agencies worked together and generally coordinated their counterterrorist activities. For example, federal agencies carried out several overseas operations and prepared for domestic special events. However, interagency guidance for coordinating federal operations—both overseas and domestically—has not been approved or fully coordinated. In addition, several command and control issues related to domestic operations have not been resolved.

Agencies Successfully Performed Operations and Prepared for Special Events [h] In the 3 years following PDD 39, federal agencies successfully participated in many counterterrorist activities. In actual operations and special events, agencies generally coordinated their activities. For example, we examined several overseas counterterrorist operations and found that agencies generally followed the draft interagency International Guidelines. DOD, the FBI, and the Central Intelligence Agency (CIA) performed their respective roles in military planning, law enforcement, and intelligence gathering under the oversight of the State Department (e.g., the ambassador). Minor interagency tensions or conflicts during these operations were resolved and did not appear to have posed risk to the missions. Examples of these overseas operations include several overseas arrests to bring suspected terrorists back to the United States for trial outside of normal extradition channels. Interagency teams consisting of the FBI, the State Department, DOD, and CIA conducted these missions.

These arrests included those of Ayyad Najim in July 1995, Wahli Khan in December 1995, Tsutomo Shirasaki in September 1996, Matwan Al-Safadi in November 1996, Mir Aimal Kansi in June 1997, and Mohamed Said Rasheed in June 1998. Key agencies have also prepared for and deployed personnel in advance to many special events. Special events are high visibility events in which federal agencies initiate contingency measures. For recent major special events, such as the 50th anniversary of the United Nations in 1995, the Atlanta Olympic Games in 1996, and the Presidential Inauguration in 1997, federal agencies prepared contingency plans for a possible terrorist attack and provided protection to the President and other dignitaries.

For example, federal agencies sending advance or contingency teams to the Atlanta Olympics included Secret Service, the FBI, FEMA, DOD, DOE, HHS, EPA, CIA, the State Department's Bureau of Diplomatic Security, the Bureau of Alcohol Tobacco and Firearms (ATF), the U.S. Customs Service, the Internal Revenue Service, and the Nuclear Regulatory Commission (NRC). Federal agencies also exercised their personnel together in advance of these events against various counterterrorism scenarios. For example, before the Atlanta Olympics, federal agencies conducted eight exercises with scenarios specific to the games. Our review of these special events indicated that most agencies involved gained valuable experience in coordinating their activities. Agency officials cited special events as successful efforts to integrate personnel and assets across federal agencies. In preparing for such events, federal agencies also worked closely with state and local agencies and nongovernmental organizations. These operations and special events enhanced federal agencies' abilities to coordinate and integrate their activities.

Interagency Guidance Not Approved or Fully Coordinated

With the exception of FEMA, lead federal agencies have not completed interagency guidance on counterterrorist operations more than 3 ½ years after PDD 39 directed them to do so. The FBI, which drafted the Domestic Guidelines and CONPLAN, coordinated drafts of these documents with five other federal agencies (FEMA, DOD, DOE, HHS, and EPA) that could have major operational roles in a domestic terrorist incident. These federal agencies have still not given their final approval to either document. Further, the FBI has not coordinated the Domestic Guidelines or the CONPLAN with other federal agencies that would have counterterrorist roles in certain circumstances, such as Treasury Department, the NRC, and the Departments of Transportation and Agriculture. Of the agencies omitted, the Treasury Department is the most significant, due to its special capabilities that have been called upon and could be needed in a variety of possible terrorist incidents. For example, the Secret Service protects the President and other designated protectees from terrorist attacks and plays a key counterterrorist security role at major special events.

The U.S. Customs Service provides aircraft at special events to detect and monitor aircraft activity and to perform interception if necessary. ATF supports FBI investigations of terrorist crimes involving explosives. In addition, the Treasury Department has numerous field personnel who could support FBI crisis management efforts. The NRC would provide expertise and technical support in a terrorist incident involving facilities, materials, and activities that it licenses (e.g., nuclear power plants). The Department of Transportation includes the Federal Aviation Administration, which has jurisdiction over aircraft hijackings in certain circumstances, and the Coast Guard, which has jurisdiction over hazardous materials (e.g., WMD) in U.S. waterways. The Department of Agriculture is responsible for providing emergency food assistance.

Department of Agriculture officials said they would monitor and ensure the safety of the food supply where a WMD agent is released, potentially contaminating crops or livestock or food processing facilities. FBI officials said that they coordinated the Domestic Guidelines and CONPLAN with the five other agencies (FEMA, DOD, DOE, HHS and EPA) because those agencies were cited most prominently in PDD 39. However, PDD 39 also cited Treasury as having an important role in counterterrorism. These officials told us that they plan to coordinate the Domestic Guidelines and CONPLAN with other agencies once the FBI and the five other agencies agree on the documents.

FBI officials did not have an estimate on when the five agencies would approve either document or when these documents would be coordinated with other appropriate agencies. We believe that the FBI, as lead federal agency for crisis management in domestic terrorist incidents, would better serve that role by fully coordinating both documents with all federal agencies that have counterterrorist roles. The International Guidelines have also not been approved as final. These guidelines, which were drafted by the State Department and provide procedures for overseas incidents and operations, had not been approved because of differences among agencies about overseas arrests. Specifically, the Departments of State and Justice have not reached agreement on specific operational issues related to these missions. Since our classified report was issued, a State Department official told us the Department deleted procedures for these arrests from the International Guidelines to expedite their approval, but the different views on operational matters continue. He stated that the guidelines are in the final coordination stage.

Command and Control Issues Require Resolution

The FBI and the Secret Service were not always coordinating their command and control structures or contingency plans with each other in the period we reviewed. FBI and Secret Service officials acknowledged that the two agencies had not worked well together, and cited efforts underway to improve coordination and cooperation between the two agencies for special events. Specifically, the Directors of the FBI and Secret Service mutually agreed to a command and control plan and signed the agreement in October 1998. This agreement has been submitted to the Attorney General and the Secretary of the Treasury for final approval. The two agencies also stated that they recently had conducted a joint tabletop exercise to test their command and control relationship. DOD needs to clarify its internal command and control structure for domestic operations.

Although not a lead federal agency, DOD could have a major supporting role in any federal response to terrorist incidents in the United States, particularly those involving WMD. In reviewing DOD's participation in domestic support operations, special events, and exercises, we found several command and control issues where guidance was either confusing or conflicting. To resolve these issues, DOD is undertaking a high-level review of its support to civilian authorities, generally under the rubric of "homeland defense." The National Defense Panel recommended that DOD emphasize homeland defense more, and use military assets to assist law enforcement agencies in combating terrorism and incorporate its forces into all levels of government to manage the consequences of a WMD-type attack.

The Chairman of the Joint Chiefs of Staff has chartered a study called "UCP 21," which is reviewing these issues and may recommend changes to the Unified Command Plan—the overall command structure for military forces. There are also unresolved issues of intergovernmental command and control (i.e., whether the federal, state, or local government is in charge) in certain circumstances. For consequence management, federal guidance— the Federal Response Plan and its Terrorism Incident Annex— indicates that state and local authorities are in overall charge of recovery efforts and that the federal government is in a support role. For crisis management, the overall leadership of the response at the incident site is not as clear. The FBI has recently taken some steps to work with state and local governments to better define their respective lead and support roles in managing a terrorist crisis.

Strengths and Weaknesses in Counterterrorist Exercises

PDD 39 required key federal agencies to ensure that their counterterrorist capabilities were well exercised. We found that federal agencies had conducted a number of counterterrorist exercises following PDD 39. However, while agencies were exercising together, there was no formal interagency program as envisioned in PDD 39. We also found that international crisis management exercises were more comprehensive than domestic crisis exercises, though neither included scenarios of no-warning terrorist attacks. Consequence management exercises sponsored by FEMA were not comprehensive, but other federal agencies were making progress exercising their capabilities.

Agencies Conducted Many Exercises Since PDD 39

Federal agencies conducted 201 exercises to improve their preparedness for counterterrorist operations in the past 3 years. In general, exercises test and validate policies and procedures, test the effectiveness of response capabilities, and increase the confidence and skill level of personnel. In addition, exercises identify strengths and weaknesses before they arise in an actual incident. Exercises further allow agencies to apply operational lessons learned from past exercises and actual deployments. In counterterrorism, where federal operations are inherently interagency matters, exercises also allow the various departments' and agencies' personnel to become familiar with each others' missions and procedures and learn to coordinate and operate together. Interagency exercises can help identify aspects of cooperation that work well and problems and conflicts that require interagency resolution. Table 1 shows the number of federal Counterterrorism exercises that different agencies participated in and led.

The agencies conducted a mixture of tabletop exercises in which agency officials discuss scenarios around a table or other similar setting, and field exercises where agency leadership and operational units actually deploy to practice their skills and coordination in a realistic field setting. Of the total 201 exercises, 85 (or 42 percent) were tabletop exercises and 116 (or 58 percent) were field exercises. Counterterrorism included both conventional and WMD scenarios to prepare federal agencies for a wide variety of possible situations. In many of the exercises, federal agencies gained experience working together. Of the 201 federal counterterrorist exercises, 140 (or 70 percent) were interagency exercises—involving more than one federal department or independent agency. Exercises and included three or more departments or independent agencies. In some of the exercises, federal agencies also gained experience working with state and / or local authorities, and nongovernmental organizations. Specifically, 69 (or 34 percent) of the 201 exercises were intergovernmental, and 18 (or 9 percent) included nongovernmental or other private organizations. Four exercises included foreign government participation to simulate federal agency integration in international incidents.

Interagency Exercise Program Has Not Been Fully Achieved

We found that there was no formal interagency exercise program as envisioned in PDD 39. The National Security Council established an interagency Exercise Subgroup co-chaired by the State Department (for international exercises) and the FBI (for domestic exercises) that also included FEMA, DOD, HHS, DOE, EPA, CIA, NRC, and the Departments of Transportation and Agriculture as members. The purpose of the Exercise Subgroup is to promote interagency discussions of exercises, but it has not implemented PDD 39 requirements to prepare or receive approval for interagency exercise objectives and a schedule of exercises. Interagency field exercises occur when individual agencies, particularly DOD and DOE, invite other agencies to participate. Because individual agencies that sponsor or participate in exercises tend to focus on their own roles, some complex transfers of command and control between agencies have not been exercised, particularly in domestic scenarios.

We believe that without interagency exercises objectives set by the Exercise Subgroup, agencies are not likely to exercise these key scenarios. As a result, the federal government will be less prepared to respond in a tailored, synchronized manner if an incident occurs. Officials from State, FBI, DOD, DOE, EPA, and HHS said that the Exercise Subgroup has fallen short of achieving its full objectives. These officials cited a number of obstacles to full implementation of the group as envisioned in PDD 39 and in the group's charter. Despite the incomplete implementation of an interagency exercise program as envisioned in PDD 39, in the 3 years since PDD 39, there were 96 counterterrorist field and tabletop exercises involving 3 or more agencies. These interagency exercises occurred because individual sponsoring agencies, such as DOD, invited other agencies to participate in their exercises. For example, DOD's Domestic Preparedness Program tabletop exercises form the core of interagency exercises with a focus on domestic consequence management and intergovernmental participation.

International Crisis Exercises More Comprehensive Than Domestic Crisis Exercises

International crisis management exercises are more comprehensive than domestic exercises. DOD's and DOE's well-developed international field exercise programs have enhanced the preparedness of the federal government to conduct counterterrorist operations overseas. The State Department uses DOD-led and DOE-led exercises to practice its leadership role in international terrorist incidents. Each year, DOD and DOE sponsor several international interagency field exercises. Commanders and exercise planners take several steps to challenge participants in these exercises. For example, these exercises test rapid and no-notice deployment of command elements and tactical units to locations worldwide. In addition, these exercises also frequently test the FEST, so rapid and no-notice deployments also can be practiced by the full cadre of interagency players.

While exercises do not guarantee success, they have resulted in a high degree of preparedness of federal agencies to operate overseas in a terrorist crisis. Domestic crisis response exercises are led by law enforcement agencies and primarily provide tactical training to their crisis response teams. Many of these exercises center on the response capabilities of the lead agency, rather than coordinating an interagency response and therefore do not include many of the federal, state, and local agencies that would be needed to effectively respond, or the entire range of activities required to respond to a terrorist crisis. The FBI's domestic crisis response program is well developed with regularly scheduled field exercises that test regional and field office capabilities at the tactical level.

But the program generally does not exercise the broader interagency leadership role that the Bureau would play in a major terrorist incident. Some aspects of this leadership role have been tested in selected exercises, such as FBI-led exercises done in preparation for the Atlanta Olympics. The FBI has begun taking steps to enhance its program and it played a significant interagency leadership role in a June 1998 exercise sponsored by DOD. FBI officials noted that the Bureau had increased this program's budget resources—which they had previously cited as an impediment to a more robust program. The Secret Service conducts a variety of counterterrorist exercises for its special agents related to its mission to protect the President. The exercises generally involve continuity of operations of the White House or protecting the President or other officials. Some of the exercises included other federal agencies (generally DOD), state and local police, and fire and rescue authorities.

The Secret Service generally did not conduct exercises with the FBI, although the two agencies have overlapping responsibilities at special events. In the few cases in which both agencies participated in the same exercise, they did not exercise how they would interact in a terrorist incident. The Secret Service plans to increase the agency's counterterrorism exercise program to reflect its new role in certain special events. For example, in preparing for the World Energy Council in Houston in September 1998, the Secret Service conducted a tabletop exercise that included

FBI and state and local authorities. In its comments on our classified report, the Secret Service stated that it planned to conduct the exercises with the FBI on scenarios where the two agencies need to work together.

ATF conducts exercises that test its crisis response and investigation roles in terrorist bombings. These exercises do not involve tests of ATF's supporting role in an interagency response led by the FBI. ATF generally does not exercise with FBI, although the two agencies have potentially overlapping responsibilities, such as in cases where the sources of bombings are unknown. ATF is developing a crisis management exercise program similar to the FBI program. ATF exercises feature its Critical Incident Management Response Team and involve its regional Special Response Teams. FBI exercises feature its Critical Incident Response Group and involve its Hostage Rescue Team and regional Special Weapons and Tactics teams. The ATF and FBI scenarios that we reviewed were similar, and ATF officials were unable to make any distinction between their program and the FBI's program.

Based upon our analysis of the ATF's program, it appears that ATF is exercising its lead in incidents in which the FBI, not ATF, would lead. The lack of coordination on exercises between these two law enforcement agencies could reduce the effectiveness of the total federal response to a terrorist incident and lead to duplication of effort. In addition, crisis management exercises, both international and domestic, always end in the successful tactical resolution of the incidents and do not include more likely scenarios where terrorist attacks are successful, or occur without adequate threat warning. Thus, the full gamut of interagency crisis management activities is not tested. For example, in the 3 years following PDD 39, the FBI did not conduct or participate in a field exercise that simulated the concurrence of crisis response and consequence management to deal with a major terrorist incident.

Consequence Management Exercises Not Comprehensive

Domestic consequence management exercises are not well developed. PDD 39 designated FEMA as the lead federal agency for consequence management in domestic terrorist events. In addition, the fiscal year 1995 Emergency Supplemental Appropriations tasked FEMA to develop exercises to focus on the consequences of terrorist incidents as part of its exercise program. In response to these tasking, FEMA sponsored a series of interagency counterterrorism tabletop exercises that focused on interagency and intergovernmental issues. However, FEMA has not planned or sponsored an interagency field exercise to test its consequence management leadership role.

Tabletop exercises are useful to the extent they identify important policy and operational issues that need to be resolved. However, tabletop exercises are not a substitute for field exercises that test the federal government's ability to use and coordinate personnel and assets in a realistic setting. FEMA officials told us that they lack the resources to manage an interagency field exercise program. They also stated that they are reluctant to commit resources to field exercises because the Domestic Guidelines and CONPLAN are still not approved and that they do not want to exercise their staff using procedures that may nct be correct because of additional changes in these guidance documents. Commenting on our classified report, FEMA noted that numerous other disaster-related operations (which were outside the scope of our review) significantly improved the federal government's overall response capabilities to conduct consequence management in terrorist incidents.

Federal agencies or entities other than FEMA have sponsored some consequence management field exercises. The Department of Veterans Affairs (VA) sponsored four recent domestic field exercises that dealt with the medical aspects of consequence management in a terrorist attack using WMD. For example, in March 1997, VA sponsored an exercise, in conjunction with the state of Minnesota that simulated a terrorist attack on a federal building with explosives laced with radioactive material, and the subsequent decontamination and treatment of hundreds of casualties. Commenting on our classified report, VA stated that numerous other disaster-related exercises (which were outside the scope of our review) also improved VA's consequence management capabilities. DOD sponsored two recent domestic field exercises that also dealt with the medical aspects of consequence management in a terrorist attack using WMD.

For example, in September 1997, DOD sponsored a field exercise (co-sponsored by VA) to practice providing medical care to victims of a terrorist WMD attack. That exercise, which had over 2,000 participants, also included state and local responders, and local community hospitals. In addition, some states and cities have sponsored field exercises on consequence management, some of them in conjunction with the DOD Domestic Preparedness Program. For example, in November 1997, New York City sponsored a field exercise based on a scenario where terrorists released chemical agents. The objectives of this exercise were to test first responder's ability to appropriately evaluate and respond to a chemical attack and fully integrate the city's incident command system.

DOD, in conjunction with cities, plans to conduct more than 100 Domestic Preparedness Program field exercises in the next several years. Better Processes to Capture Lessons Learned Could Improve Future Operations Lessons learned processes are practices that allow an agency to learn from its successes and mistakes to improve its performance. We found that DOD, DOE, and FEMA had relatively good processes in place to capture and share lessons learned, while other agencies had less rigorous processes. There was also no interagency process in place to capture and share lessons learned, but agencies were starting to implement a process at the end of our review.

DOD, DOE, and FEMA Have Requirements and Processes to Capture Lessons Learned

A key part of any lessons learned process is preparing an After Action Report (AAR) or other evaluation that provides an official description of the results of an operation, special event, or exercise. An AAR typically includes a summary of objectives, operational limitations, and major participants, a description of strengths and weaknesses, and recommended actions. Effective follow-up and validation also are important parts of a lessons learned process, as they are the only means to ensure that problems have been corrected. Another important feature of a lessons learned process is the dissemination within an organization and, where appropriate, to other organizations, of aspects of operations that worked well and those that need further improvement or development.

For counterterrorism operations, which are inherently interagency matters, the lessons learned process should also address the interaction between different agencies to highlight problems for resolution in interagency forums or by top national leadership. The DOD and DOE processes for capturing lessons learned had several positive characteristics in comparison to the other agencies' processes we reviewed. DOD and DOE had requirements to produce AARs and their officials or contractors wrote AARs, made specific recommendations, disseminated AARs to different organizational units, and produced AARs for some exercises and events led by other agencies.

For example, we observed DOE contractors as they entered lessons learned data "real time" during a June 1998 exercise led by DOD. Some DOD field exercises included data evaluation plans in advance to ensure that lessons were learned on the specific exercise objectives. In addition, DOD and DOE officials included interagency issues in their AARs and sometimes disseminated them to other agencies. DOD and DOE officials cited the value of a sound AAR process to improving their performance and said that on the basis of issues identified in earlier AARs, they had improved operations. For example, DOD exercises helped determine and refine policy and procedures on the final disposition of WMD devices. Policy issues on this topic were identified in AARs going back to 1993. In the intervening years, DOD continued to include this issue in its tabletop exercises. In 1996, a new policy was incorporated into a formal contingency plan.

The new policy was further tested in tabletop exercises in 1997 and finally in field exercises in 1998. While there are remaining issues to be resolved on the final disposition of a WMD device, DOD officials were able to track their progress on this issue. DOE reorganized its Nuclear Emergency Search Team on the basis of lessons learned from a series of exercises. We were able to track the evolution of the Nuclear Emergency Search Team through past evaluations and AARs written by DOE. Although the DOD and DOE lessons learned processes were good in comparison to the other agencies we reviewed, we did note some weaknesses in their processes. DOD and DOE did not write AARs for all of the counterterrorism operations, special events, or exercises that they participated in. Both DOD and DOE officials stated that emerging crises or the tempo of operations did not always allow staff to write AARs.

In addition, dissemination of lessons learned was sometimes limited because of security classifications. Finally, our prior report, which included a broader and more detailed review of DOD's lessons learned programs, discussed weaknesses in the collection, analysis, dissemination, and ultimate use of lessons learned. FEMA also had relatively sound lessons learned requirements and processes as part of its Comprehensive Exercise Program for designing, conducting, and evaluating exercises. For several years, FEMA had been developing computer software to record lessons learned from exercises and monitor corrective actions. FEMA produced AARs on the tabletop exercises it led but not for exercises led by other agencies.

Contractors usually wrote AARs and FEMA officials reviewed and approved them. FEMA disseminated its AARs both internally and externally. FEMA's AARs generally included interagency issues for those exercises that included other agencies. For example, the AAR on FEMA's June 1996 "Cirrus Wind" exercise stressed the need for FEMA and FBI to work together to understand their responsibilities for consequence and crisis management.

Other Agencies' Lessons Learned Processes Not Well Developed

Federal agencies other than DOD, DOE, and FEMA had less rigorous processes for capturing lessons learned and producing AARs. The other agencies did not have a written policy that required that they produce AARs or a formal process to capture lessons learned. The production of AARs by some of these other agencies was sporadic, particularly for operations, special events, and exercises led by other agencies. In addition, few of these other agencies included discussions of interagency issues in their AARs. Finally, the dissemination of AARs was limited at many agencies, which minimized the benefits of lessons learned. These limitations make it more difficult for the agencies to capture the strengths and weaknesses shown in operations or exercises so they can continue or expand good practices or take corrective actions when necessary to improve future performance.

Many agencies did not produce AARs even in cases where they led an exercise. Agencies lead exercises because they have specific objectives to achieve, and one purpose of exercises is to capture lessons that might improve future operations. Nevertheless, we found many cases where agencies devoted their resources to develop exercise objectives and conduct an exercise, yet did not write AARs. For example, the FBI has sponsored the Weapons of Mass Destruction Interagency Support Exercise series, which includes numerous federal agencies and has the objective to advance interagency coordination for terrorist attacks. However, FBI has not produced AARs on any of the four tabletop exercises.

Many agencies also did not produce AARs when they participated in a field exercise. Field exercises are very resource intensive because they require a great deal of advance planning and because agency personnel and equipment actually deploy to another location. Again, we found cases where agencies led or otherwise participated in field exercises but did not produce AARs. For example, in a recent DOD-sponsored field exercise, FEMA developed specific objectives and tasks to be accomplished and sent several staff to planning meetings and to the week-long exercise itself, yet it did not produce an AAR. Table 4 given in chapter-2, shows the extent to which agencies produced AARs for field exercises that they participated in.

Officials from these agencies generally cited a lack of dedicated staff or the tempo of ongoing operations or exercises as reasons they did not write AARs or otherwise capture lessons learned. In our view, agencies that devote the resources to lead exercises or to participate in other agencies' field exercises should also devote the resources to writing AARs to capture lessons learned. Some officials noted that they hold a "hotwash" (i.e., an oral AAR discussion) after an exercise which, they said, served the purpose of capturing lessons learned. Hotwashes are valuable because they are held immediately after exercises; however, their value is limited to the participants that attend. Written AARs, on the other hand, provide accountability because they identify and document problems or issues and can be used to track the progress of corrective action. By not producing written AARs, agencies are forfeiting many of the benefits of participating in exercises. In commenting on our classified report, several agencies cited efforts underway to develop or improve processes for capturing lessons learned at their individual agencies.

Interagency Lessons Learned Process Being Developed

The 1996 Nunn-Lugar hearings highlighted that, although some agencies wrote AARs and made recommendations, there were recurrent interagency problems because there was no central place where officials assembled and analyzed AARs together to discuss interagency problems. During our review, we also found no AAR or lessons learned process at the interagency level. The Exercise Subgroup charter included the discussion of lessons learned and AARs. While this interagency forum had been used to discuss specific exercises, there was no process to review individual agency AARs that raise interagency issues. For more than 2 years, the group has discussed developing a formal interagency process and has looked specifically at the processes being used by DOD and DOE.

The State Department has been a repository for various agencies' AARs for international exercises, but Department officials there said they lacked the staff and standing to analyze them, separate out the interagency issues, and prepare related evaluations or make recommendations. At the time of our review, the FBI was in charge of developing an interagency AAR process, but no decisions had been made. In commenting on our classified report, several agencies noted that the Exercise Subgroup had recently adopted an interagency AAR process and was starting to implement it. During the last 3 years, federal agencies have worked together in many operations and special events and have generally coordinated their activities.

However, issues of interagency guidance and command and control remain that need to be addressed to enhance the federal government's ability to effectively respond to terrorist incidents. Federal agencies have participated in many interagency counterterrorism exercises in the last 3 years. However, an interagency exercise program, as directed in PDD 39, has not been fully achieved, so exercises have not generally practiced key transfers of authority among responding federal agencies. International field exercises, generally led by DOD, include the full cadre of interagency players in demanding scenarios and some are done with no notice. In contrast, domestic counterterrorism exercises are not as demanding in testing the interagency ability to respond.

The FBI's crisis management field exercises have provided good practice for its tactical response units but have generally not exercised the Bureau's interagency leadership role and rapid deployments for no-warning terrorist attacks. FEMA's consequence management exercises have been limited to tabletop exercises that do not fully test the federal government's ability to provide a rapid interagency response in a realistic exercise environment. Although agencies can benefit most from counterterrorism exercises if they produce AARs and have a process to capture lessons learned, most of the agencies that we reviewed did not do so. Although counterterrorism is inherently an interagency response, there was also no interagency process to capture lessons learned. At the close of our review, agencies said they were adopting several measures to address these issues at both the agency and interagency level.

Recommendations

This report makes no recommendations. However, in our classified report, we made several recommendations to enhance interagency guidance, command and control, exercises, and processes to capture and share lessons learned. DOD classified these recommendations as a result of its security review of our classified report.

Scope and Methodology

We focused our examination on counterterrorist activities in the 3-year period following the issuance of PDD 39 in June 1995. We obtained documents and interviewed officials at the Departments of Justice, State, Treasury (including the Secret Service and ATF), DOD, DOE, HHS, VA, CIA, EPA, FEMA, NRC, and the U.S. Capitol Police. We also obtained information on matters pertaining to intergovernmental counterterrorist operations (e.g., those involving federal, state, and local entities) from state and local officials and selected federal field offices in the course of our related work on DOD's Domestic Preparedness Program. We compiled a list of 230 counterterrorism activities that included operations, special events, and exercises that were conducted from June 1995 to June 1998. In some cases, we discussed counterterrorist activities before and after that period, but we did not include them in the statistics we compiled and analyzed. We did not review covert activities or law enforcement cases (e.g., criminal investigations and arrests of terrorists) except in the cases of overseas arrests, which are interagency operations.

We also did not include aircraft hijackings or related exercises, where the Federal Aviation Administration is generally the lead federal agency. To ensure the accuracy of our list of activities, appropriate federal agencies reviewed it for completeness and accuracy. We also examined policy guidelines, contingency plans, AARs, and other documents from actual operations, special events, and exercises. Further, we attended and observed interagency meetings, planning sessions, and exercises. We performed our work in accordance with generally accepted government auditing standards between November 1997 and September 1998.

As agreed with your offices, unless you publicly announce the contents of this report earlier, we plan no further distribution of this report until 30 days after its issue date. At that time we will send copies to appropriate congressional committees, the federal agencies discussed in this report, and to the Director of the Office of Management and Budget. We also will make copies available to other interested parties upon request.

5

Networks of Terrorism, Netwar, and Information Age

The rise of network forms of organization is a key consequence of the ongoing information revolution. Business organizations are being newly energized by networking, and many professional militaries are experimenting with flatter forms of organization. In this chapter, we explore the impact of networks on terrorist capabilities, and consider how this development may be associated with a move away from emphasis on traditional, episodic efforts at coercion to a new view of terror as a form of protracted warfare. Seen in this light, the recent bombings of U.S. embassies in East Africa, along with the retaliatory American missile strikes, may prove to be the opening shots of a war between a leading state and a terror network. We consider both the likely context and the conduct of such a war, and offer some insights that might inform policies aimed at defending against and countering terrorism.

A New Terrorism

The age-old phenomenon of terrorism continues to appeal to its perpetrators for three principal reasons. First, it appeals as a weapon of the weak—a shadowy way to wage war by attacking asymmetrically to harm and try to defeat an ostensibly superior force. This has had particular appeal to ethno-nationalists, racist militias, religious fundamentalists, and other minorities who cannot match the military formations and firepower of their "oppressors"—the case, for example, with some radical Middle Eastern Islamist groups *vis-à-vis* Israel, and, until recently, the Provisional Irish Republican Army (PIRA) *vis-à-vis* Great Britain.

Countering the New Terrorism

Second, terrorism has appealed as a way to assert identity and command attention—rather like proclaiming, "I bomb, therefore I am." Terrorism enables a perpetrator to publicize his identity, project it explosively, and touch the nerves of powerful distant leaders. This kind of attraction to violence transcends its instrumental utility. Mainstream revolutionary writings may view violence as a means of struggle, but terrorists often regard violence as an end in itself that generates identity or damages the enemy's identity. Third, terrorism has sometimes appealed as a way to achieve a new future order by willfully wrecking the present. This is manifest in the religious fervor of some radical Islamists, but examples also lie among millenarian and apocalyptic groups, like Aum Shinrikyo in Japan, who aim to wreak havoc and rend a system asunder so that something new may emerge from the cracks.

The substance of the future vision may be only vaguely defined, but its moral worth is clear and appealing to the terrorist. In the first and second of these motivations or rationales, terrorism may involve retaliation and retribution for past wrongs, whereas the third is also about revelation and rebirth, the coming of a new age. The first is largely strategic; it has a practical tone, and the objectives may be limited and specific. In contrast, the third may engage a transcendental, unconstrained view of how to change the world through terrorism. Such contrasts do not mean the three are necessarily at odds; blends often occur. Presumptions of weakness (the first rationale) and of willfulness (in the second and third) can lead to peculiar synergies.

For example, Aum's members may have known it was weak in a conventional sense, but they believed that they had special knowledge, a unique leader, invincible willpower, and secret ways to strike out. These classic motivations or rationales will endure in the information age. However, terrorism is not a fixed phenomenon; its perpetrators adapt it to suit their times and situations. What changes is the conduct of terrorism—the operational characteristics built around the motivations and rationales. These chapter addresses, often in a deliberately speculative manner, changes in organization, doctrine, strategy, and technology that, taken together, speak to the emergence of a "new terrorism" attuned to the information age.

Our principal hypotheses are as follows:

- **Organization.** Terrorists will continue moving from hierarchical toward information-age network designs. Within groups, "great man" leaderships will give way to flatter decentralized designs. More effort will go into building arrays of transnationally internetted groups than into building stand-alone groups.
- **Doctrine and strategy.** Terrorists will likely gain new capabilities for lethal acts. Some terrorist groups are likely to move to a "war paradigm" that focuses on attacking U.S. military forces and assets. But where terrorists suppose that "information operations" may be as useful as traditional commando-style operations for achieving their goals, systemic 'disruption' may become as much an objective as target 'destruction.' Difficulties in coping with the new terrorism will mount if terrorists move beyond isolated acts toward a new approach to doctrine and strategy that emphasizes campaigns based on swarming.

- **Technology.** Terrorists are likely to increasingly use advanced information technologies for offensive and defensive purposes, as well as to support their organizational structures.

Despite widespread speculation about terrorists using cyberspace warfare techniques to take "the Net" down, they may often have stronger reasons for wanting to keep it up (e.g., to spread their message and communicate with one another). In short, terrorism is evolving in a direction we call netwar. Thus, after briefly reviewing terrorist trends, we outline the concept of netwar and its relevance for understanding information-age terrorism.

In particular, we elaborate on the above points about organization, doctrine, and strategy, and briefly discuss how recent developments in the nature and behaviour of Middle Eastern terrorist groups can be interpreted as early signs of a move toward netwar-type terrorism. Given the prospect of a netwar-oriented shift in which some terrorists pursue a war paradigm, we then focus on the implications such a development may have for the U.S. military. We use these insights to consider defensive antiterrorist measures, as well as proactive counterterrorist strategies. We propose that a key to coping with information-age terrorism will be the creation of interorganizational networks within the U.S. military and government, partly on the grounds that it takes networks to fight networks.

Recent View about Terrorism

Terrorism remains a distinct phenomenon while reflecting broader trends in irregular warfare. The latter has been on the rise around the world since before the end of the Cold War. Ethnic and religious conflicts, recently in evidence in areas of Africa, the Balkans, and the Caucasus, for awhile in Central America, and seemingly forever in the Middle East, attest to the brutality that increasingly attends this kind of warfare. These are not conflicts between regular, professional armed forces dedicated to warrior creeds and Geneva Conventions. Instead, even where regular forces play roles; these conflicts often revolve around the strategies and tactics of thuggish paramilitary gangs and local warlords. Some leaders may have some professional training; but the foot soldiers are often people who, for one reason or another, get caught in a fray and learn on the job.

Adolescents and children with high-powered weaponry are taking part in growing numbers. In many of these conflicts, savage acts are increasingly committed without anyone taking credit—it may not even be clear which side is responsible. The press releases of the protagonists sound high-minded and self-legitimizing, but the reality at the local level is often about clan rivalries and criminal ventures (e.g., looting, smuggling, or protection rackets). Thus, irregular warfare has become endemic and vicious around the world. A decade or so ago, terrorism was a rather distinct entry on the spectrum of conflict, with its own unique attributes. Today, it seems increasingly connected with these broader trends in irregular warfare, especially as waged by nonstate actors.

As Martin Van Creveld warns: In today's world, the main threat to many states, including specifically the U.S., no longer comes from other states. Instead, it comes from small groups and other organizations which are not states. Either we make the necessary changes and face them today, or what is commonly known as the modern world will lose all sense of security and will dwell in perpetual fear. Meanwhile, for the past several years, terrorism experts have broadly concurred that this phenomenon will persist, if not get worse. General agreement that terrorism may worsen parses into different scenarios.

For example, Walter Laqueur warns that religious motivations could lead to "superviolence," with millenarian visions of a coming apocalypse driving "postmodern" terrorism. Fred Iklé worries that increased violence may be used by terrorists to usher in a new totalitarian age based on Leninist ideals. Bruce Hoffman raises the prospect that religiously-motivated terrorists may escalate their violence in order to wreak sufficient havoc to undermine the world political system and replace it with a chaos that is particularly detrimental to the United States—a basically nihilist strategy. The preponderance of U.S. conventional power may continue to motivate some state and nonstate adversaries to opt for terror as an asymmetric response.

Technological advances and underground trafficking may make weapons of mass destruction (WMD—nuclear, chemical, biological weapons) ever easier for terrorists to acquire. Terrorists' shifts toward looser, less hierarchical organizational structures, and their growing use of advanced communications technologies for command, control, and coordination, may further empower small terrorist groups and individuals who want to mount operations from a distance. There is also agreement about an emergence of two tiers of terror: one characterized by hard-core professionals, the other by amateur cut-outs. The deniability gained by terrorists operating through willing amateurs, coupled with the increasing accessibility of ever more destructive weaponry, has also led many experts to concur that terrorists will be attracted to engaging in more lethal destruction, with increased targeting of information and communications infrastructures.

Some specialists also suggest that "information" will become a key target—both the conduits of information infrastructures and the content of information, particularly the media. While these target sets may involve little lethal activity, they offer additional theaters of operations for terrorists. Laqueur in particular foresees that, "If the new terrorism directs its energies toward information warfare, its destructive power will be exponentially greater than any it wielded in the past—greater even than it would be with biological and chemical weapons." New planning and scenario-building is needed to help think through how to defend against this form of terrorism. Such dire predictions have galvanized a variety of responses, which range from urging the creation of international control regimes over the tools of terror (such as WMD materials and advanced encryption capabilities), to the use of coercive diplomacy against state sponsors of terror. Increasingly, the liberal use of military force against terrorists has also been recommended. Caleb Carr in particular espoused this theme, sparking a heated debate.

Against this background, experts have begun to recognize the growing role of networks—of networked organizational designs and related doctrines, strategies, and technologies—among the practitioners of terrorism. The growth of these networks is related to the spread of advanced information technologies that allow dispersed groups, and individuals, to conspire and coordinate across considerable distances. Recent U.S. efforts to investigate and attack the bin Laden network (named for the central influence of Osama bin Laden) attest to this. The rise of networks is likely to reshape terrorism in the information age, and lead to the adoption of netwar—a kind of information- age conflict that will be waged principally by nonstate actors. Our contribution to this volume is to present the concept of netwar and show how terrorism is being affected by it.

The Advent of Netwar—Analytical Background

The information revolution is altering the nature of conflict across the spectrum. Of the many reasons for this, we call attention to two in particular. First, the information revolution is favoring and strengthening network forms of organization, often giving them an advantage over hierarchical forms. The rise of networks means that power is migrating to nonstate actors, who are able to organize into sprawling multi-organizational networks (especially all-channel networks, in which every node is connected to every other node) more readily than can traditional, hierarchical, state actors. Nonstate-actor networks are thought to be more flexible and responsive than hierarchies in reacting to outside developments, and to be better than hierarchies at using information to improve decision making. Second, as the information revolution deepens, conflicts will increasingly depend on information and communications matters.

More than ever before, conflicts will revolve around "knowledge" and the use of "soft power." Adversaries will emphasize "information operations" and "perception management"—that is, media-oriented measures that aim to attract rather than coerce, and that affect how secure a society, a military, or other actor feels about its knowledge of itself and of its adversaries. Psychological disruption may become as important a goal as physical destruction. Thus, major transformations are coming in the nature of adversaries, in the type of threats they may pose, and in how conflicts can be waged. Information-age threats are likely to be more diffuse, dispersed, multidimensional, and ambiguous than more traditional threats. Metaphorically, future conflicts may resemble the Oriental game of *Go* more than the Western game of chess. The conflict spectrum will be molded from end to end by these dynamics:

- Cyberwar—a concept that refers to information-oriented military warfare—is becoming an important entry at the military end of the spectrum, where the language has normally been about high intensity conflicts (HICs).
- Netwar figures increasingly at the societal end of the spectrum, where the language has normally been about low-intensity conflict (LIC), operations other than war (OOTW), and nonmilitary modes of conflict and crime. Whereas cyberwar usually pits formal military forces against each other, netwar is more likely to involve nonstate, paramilitary, and irregular forces—as in the

case of terrorism. Both concepts are consistent with the views of analysts such as Van Creveld, who believe that a "transformation of war" is under way. Neither concept is just about technology; both refer to 'comprehensive' approaches to conflict—comprehensive in that they mix organizational, doctrinal, strategic, tactical, and technological innovations, for offense and defense.

Definition of Netwar

To be more precise, netwar refers to an emerging mode of conflict and crime at societal levels, involving measures short of traditional war, in which the protagonists use network forms of organization and related doctrines, strategies, and technologies attuned to the information age. These protagonists are likely to consist of dispersed small groups who communicate, coordinate, and conduct their campaigns in an internetted manner, without a precise central command. Thus, information-age netwar differs from modes of conflict and crime in which the protagonists prefer formal, standalone, hierarchical organizations, doctrines, and strategies, as in past efforts, for example, to build centralized movements along Marxist lines.

The term is meant to call attention to the prospect that networkbased conflict and crime will become major phenomena in the decades ahead. Various actors across the spectrum of conflict and crime are already evolving in this direction. To give a string of examples, netwar is about the Middle East's Hamas more than the Palestine Liberation Organization (PLO), Mexico's Zapatistas more than Cuba's Fidelistas, and the American Christian Patriot movement more than the Ku Klux Klan. It is also about the Asian Triads more than the Sicilian Mafia and Chicago's Gangsta Disciples more than the Al Capone Gang.

This spectrum includes familiar adversaries who are modifying their structures and strategies to take advantage of networked designs, such as transnational terrorist groups, black-market proliferators of WMD, transnational crime syndicates, fundamentalist and ethnonationalist movements, intellectual property and high-sea pirates, and smugglers of black-market goods or migrants. Some urban gangs, back-country militias, and militant single-issue groups in the United States are also developing netwar-like attributes. In addition, there is a new generation of radicals and activists who are just beginning to create information-age ideologies, in which identities and loyalties may shift from the nation-state to the transnational level of global civil society. New kinds of actors, such as anarchistic and nihilistic leagues of computer-hacking "cyboteurs," may also partake of netwar.

Many—if not most—netwar actors will be nonstate. Some may be agents of a state, but others may try to turn states into their agents. Moreover, a netwar actor may be both subnational and transnational in scope. Odd hybrids and symbioses are likely. Furthermore, some actors (e.g., violent terrorist and criminal organizations) may threaten U.S. and other nations' interests, but other netwar actors (e.g., peaceful social activists) may not. Some may aim at destruction, others at disruption. Again, many variations are possible. The full spectrum of netwar proponents may thus seem broad and odd at first glance. But there is an underlying pattern that cuts across all variations: the use of network forms of organization, doctrine, strategy, and technology attuned to the information age.

More about Organizational Design

The notion of an organizational structure qualitatively different from traditional hierarchical designs is not recent; for example, in the early 1960s Burns and Stalker referred to the *organic* form as "a network structure of control, authority, and communication," with "lateral rather than vertical direction of communication." In organic structure, omniscience [is] no longer imputed to the head of the concern; knowledge about the technical or commercial nature of the here and now task may be located anywhere in the network; [with] this location becoming the ad hoc centre of control authority and communication. In the business world, virtual or networked organizations are being heralded as effective alternatives to bureaucracies—as in the case of Eastman Chemical Company and the Shell-Sarnia Plant—because of their inherent flexibility, adaptiveness, and ability to capitalize on the talents of all members of the organization.

What has long been emerging in the business world is now becoming apparent in the organizational structures of netwar actors. In an archetypal netwar, the protagonists are likely to amount to a set of diverse, dispersed "nodes" who share a set of ideas and interests and who are arrayed to act in a fully internetted "all-channel" manner.

Networks come in basically three types (or topologies):

- The *chain* network, as in a smuggling chain where people, goods, or information move along a line of separated contacts, and where end-to-end communication must travel through the intermediate nodes.
- The *star*, hub, or wheel network, as in a franchise or a cartel structure where a set of actors is tied to a central node or actor, and must go through that node to communicate and coordinate.
- The *all-channel* network, as in a collaborative network of militant small groups where every group is connected to every other.

The nodes may be large or small, tightly or loosely coupled, and inclusive or exclusive in membership. They may be segmentary or specialized—that is, they may look alike and engage in similar activities, or they may undertake a division of labour based on specialization. The boundaries of the network may be well defined, or blurred and porous in relation to the outside environment. All such variations are possible. Each type may be suited to different conditions and purposes, and all three may be found among netwar-related adversaries—e.g., the chain in smuggling operations, the star at the core of terrorist and criminal syndicates, and the all-channel type among militant groups that are highly internetted and decentralized.

There may also be hybrids. For example, a netwar actor may have an all-channel council at its core, but use stars and chains for tactical operations. There may also be hybrids of network and hierarchical forms of organization, and hierarchies may exist inside particular nodes in a network. Some actors may have a hierarchical organization overall, but use networks for tactical operations; other actors may have an all channel network design, but use hierarchical teams for tactical operations. Again, many configurations are possible, and it may be difficult for an analyst to discern exactly what type of networking characterizes a particular actor.

Of the three network types, the all-channel has been the most difficult to organize and sustain historically, partly because it may require dense communications. However, it gives the network form the most potential for collaborative undertakings, and it is the type Chain network Star or hub network All-channel network that is gaining strength from the information revolution. Pictorially, an all-channel netwar actor resembles a geodesic "Bucky ball" (named for Buckminster Fuller); it does not resemble a pyramid. The design is flat. Ideally, there is no single, central leadership, command, or headquarters—no precise heart or head that can be targeted.

The network as a whole (but not necessarily each node) has little to no hierarchy, and there may be multiple leaders. Decision making and operations are decentralized, allowing for local initiative and autonomy. Thus the design may sometimes appear acephalous (headless), and at other times polycephalous (Hydra-headed). The capacity of this design for effective performance over time may depend on the presence of shared principles, interests, and goals—at best, an overarching doctrine or ideology—that spans all nodes and to which the members wholeheartedly subscribe. Such a set of principles, shaped through mutual consultation and consensus-building, can enable them to be "all of one mind," even though they are dispersed and devoted to different tasks.

It can provide a central ideational, strategic, and operational coherence that allows for tactical decentralization. It can set boundaries and provide guidelines for decisions and actions so that the members do not have to resort to a hierarchy—"they know what they have to do." The network design may depend on having an infrastructure for the dense communication of functional information. All nodes are not necessarily in constant communication, which may not make sense for a secretive, conspiratorial actor. But when communication is needed, the network's members must be able to disseminate information promptly and as broadly as desired within the network and to outside audiences.

In many respects, then, the archetypal netwar design corresponds to what earlier analysts called a "segmented, polycentric, ideologically integrated network" (SPIN): By segmentary I mean that it is cellular, composed of many different groups. By polycentric I mean that it has many different leaders or centers of direction. By networked I mean that the segments and the leaders are integrated into reticulated systems or networks through various structural, personal, and ideological ties. Networks are usually unbounded and expanding. This acronym [SPIN] helps us picture this organization as a fluid, dynamic, expanding one, spinning out into mainstream society.

Caveats about the Role of Technology

To realize its potential, a fully interconnected network requires a capacity for constant, dense information and communications flows, more so than do other forms of organization (e.g., hierarchies). This capacity is afforded by the latest information and communications technologies—cellular telephones, fax machines, electronic mail (email), World Wide Web (WWW) sites, and computer conferencing. Moreover, netwar agents are poised to benefit from future increases in the speed of communication, dramatic reductions in the costs of communication, increases in bandwidth, vastly expanded connectivity, and integration of communication with computing technologies. Such technologies are highly advantageous for a netwar actor whose constituents are geographically dispersed. However, caveats are in order. First, the new technologies, however enabling for organizational networking, may not be the only crucial technologies for a netwar actor.

Old means of communications such as human couriers, and mixes of old and new systems, may suffice. Second, netwar is not simply a function of the Internet; it does not take place only in cyberspace or the infosphere. Some key 'battles' may occur there, but a *war's* overall conduct and outcome will normally depend mostly on what happens in the real world. Even in information- age conflicts, what happens in the real world is generally more important than what happens in the virtual worlds of cyberspace or the infosphere. Netwar is not Internet war.

Swarming and the Blurring of Offense and Defense

This distinctive, often ad-hoc design has unusual strengths, for both offense and defense. On the offense, networks are known for being adaptable, flexible, and versatile *vis-à-vis* opportunities and challenges. This may be particularly the case where a set of actors can engage in swarming. Little analytic attention has been given to swarming, yet it may be a key mode of conflict in the information age. The cutting edge for this possibility is found among netwar protagonists. Swarming occurs when the dispersed nodes of a network of small (and perhaps some large) forces converge on a target from multiple directions.

The overall aim is the 'sustainable pulsing' of force or fire. Once in motion, swarm networks must be able to coalesce rapidly and stealthily on a target, then dissever and redisperse, immediately ready to recombine for a new pulse. In other words, information-age attacks may come in "swarms" rather than the more traditional "waves." In terms of defensive potential, well-constructed networks tend to be redundant and diverse, making them robust and resilient in the face of adversity. Where they have a capacity for interoperability and shun centralized command and control, network designs can be difficult to crack and defeat as a whole. In particular, they may defy counter leadership targeting—attackers can find and confront only portions of the network.

Moreover, the deniability built into a network may allow it to simply absorb a number of attacks on distributed nodes, leading the attacker to believe the network has been harmed when, in fact, it remains viable, and is seeking new opportunities for tactical surprise. The difficulties of dealing with netwar actors deepen when the lines between offense and defense are blurred, or blended. When 'blurring' is the case, it may be difficult to distinguish between attacking and defending actions, particularly when an actor goes on the offense in the name of self-defense. The 'blending' of offense and defense will often mix the strategic and tactical levels of operations. For example, guerrillas on the defensive strategically may go on the offense tactically; the war of the 'mujahideen' in Afghanistan provides a modern example.

The blurring of offense and defense reflects another feature of netwar: it tends to defy and cut across standard boundaries, jurisdictions, and distinctions between state and society, public and private, war and peace, war and crime, civilian and military, police and military, and legal and illegal. A government has difficulty assigning responsibility to a single agency—military, police, or intelligence—to respond. Thus, the spread of netwar adds to the challenges facing the nationstate in the information age.

Nation-state ideals of sovereignty and authority are traditionally linked to a bureaucratic rationality in which issues and problems can be neatly divided, and specific offices can be charged with taking care of specific problems. In netwar, things are rarely so clear. A protagonist is likely to operate in the cracks and gray areas of society, striking where lines of authority crisscross and the operational paradigms of politicians, officials, soldiers, police officers, and related actors get fuzzy and clash.

Networks versus Hierarchies: Challenges for Counternetwar

Against this background, we are led to a set of four policy-oriented propositions about the information revolution and its implications for netwar and counternetwar. Hierarchies have a difficult time fighting networks. There are examples across the conflict spectrum. Some of the best are found in the failings of governments to defeat transnational criminal cartels engaged in drug smuggling, as in Colombia. The persistence of religious revivalist movements, as in Algeria, in the face of unremitting state opposition, shows the robustness of the network form. The Zapatista movement in Mexico, with its legions of supporters and sympathizers among local and transnational nongovernmental organizations (NGOs), shows that social netwar can put a democratizing autocracy on the defensive and pressure it to continue adopting reforms.

It takes networks to fight networks. Governments that would defend against netwar may have to adopt organizational designs and strategies like those of their adversaries. This does not mean mirroring the adversary, but rather learning to draw on the same design principles of network forms in the information age. These principles depend to some extent upon technological innovation, but mainly on a willingness to innovate organizationally and doctrinally, and by building new mechanisms for interagency and multijurisdictional cooperation. Whoever masters the network form first and best will gain major advantages. In these early decades of the information age, adversaries who have adopted networking (be they criminals, terrorists, or peaceful social activists) are enjoying an increase in their power relative to state agencies.

Counternetwar may thus require effective interagency approaches, which by their nature involve networked structures. The challenge will be to blend hierarchies and networks skillfully, while retaining enough core authority to encourage and enforce adherence to networked processes. By creating effective hybrids, governments may better ccnfront the new threats and challenges emerging in the information age, whether generated by terrorists, militias, criminals, or other actors. The U.S. Counterterrorist Center, based at the Central Intelligence Agency (CIA), is a good example of a promising effort to establish a functional interagency network, although its success may depend increasingly on the strength of links with the military services and other institutions that fall outside the realm of the intelligence community.

Middle Eastern Terrorism and Netwar

Terrorism seems to be evolving in the direction of violent netwar. Islamic fundamentalist organizations like Hamas and the bin Laden network consist of groups organized in loosely interconnected, semi independent cells that have no single commanding hierarchy. Hamas exemplifies the shift away from a hierarchically oriented

The netwar concept is consistent with patterns and trends in the Middle East, where the newer and more active terrorist groups appear to be adopting decentralized, flexible network structures. The rise of networked arrangements in terrorist organizations is part of a wider move away from formally organized, state-sponsored groups to privately financed, loose networks of individuals and subgroups that may have strategic guidance but enjoy tactical independence.

Related to these shifts is the fact that terrorist groups are taking advantage of information technology to coordinate the activities of dispersed members. Such technology may be employed by terrorists not only to wage information warfare, but also to support their own networked organizations. While a comprehensive empirical analysis of the relationship between (a) the structure of terrorist organizations and (b) group activity or strength is beyond the scope of this paper, a cursory examination of such a relationship among Middle Eastern groups offers some evidence to support the claim that terrorists are preparing to wage netwar. The Middle East was selected for analysis mainly because terrorist groups based in this region have been active in targeting U.S. government facilities and interests, as in the bombings of the Khobar Towers, and most recently, the American embassies in Kenya and Tanzania.

Middle Eastern Terrorist Groups: Structure and Actions

Terrorist groups in the Middle East have diverse origins, ideologies, and organizational structures, but can be roughly categorized into traditional and new-generation groups. Traditional groups date back to the late 1960s and early 1970s, and the majority of these were (and some still are) formally or informally linked to the PLO. Typically, they are also relatively bureaucratic and maintain a nationalist or Marxist agenda. In contrast, most new-generation groups arose in the 1980s and 1990s, have more fluid organizational forms, and rely on Islam as a basis for their radical ideology. The traditional, more-bureaucratic groups have survived to this day partly through support from states such as Syria, Libya, and Iran.

The groups retain an ability to train and prepare for terrorist missions; however, their involvement in actual operations has been limited in recent years, partly because of successful counterterrorism campaigns by Israeli and Western agencies. In contrast, the newer and less hierarchical groups, such as Hamas, the Palestinian Islamic Jihad (PIJ), Hizbullah, Algeria's Armed Islamic Group (GIA), the Egyptian Islamic Group (IG), and Osama bin Laden's Arab Afghans, have become the most active organizations in and around the Middle East. Traditional terrorist groups in the Middle East include the Abu Nidal Organization (ANO), the Popular Front for the Liberation of Palestine (PFLP), and three PFLP-related splinters—the PFLP-General Command (PFLP-GC), the Palestine Liberation Front (PLF), and the Democratic Front for the Liberation of Palestine (DFLP).

The ANO was an integral part of the PLO until it became independent in 1974. It has a bureaucratic structure composed of various functional committees. The activism it displayed in the 1970s and 1980s has lessened considerably, owing to a lessening of support from state sponsors and to effective counterterrorist campaigns by Israeli and Western intelligence services. The very existence of the organization has recently been put into question, given uncertainty as to the whereabouts and fate of Abu Nidal, the leader of the group. The PFLP was founded in 1967 by George Habash as a PLO-affiliated organization. It has traditionally embraced a Marxist ideology, and remains an important PLO faction. However, in recent years it has suffered considerable losses from Israeli counterterrorist strikes.

The PFLP-General Command split from the PFLP in 1968, and in turn experienced a schism in the mid-1970s. This splinter group, which called itself the PLF, is composed of three subgroups, and has not been involved in high-profile acts since the 1985 hijacking of the Italian cruise ship *Achille Lauro*. The PFLP was subjected to another split in 1969, which resulted in the Democratic Front for the Liberation of Palestine. The DFLP resembles a small army more than a terrorist group—its operatives are organized in battalions, backed by intelligence and Special Forces. DFLP strikes have become less frequent since the 1970s, and since the late 1980s it has limited its attacks to Israeli targets near borders. What seems evident here is that this old generation of traditional, hierarchical, bureaucratic groups is on the wane.

The reasons are varied, but the point remains—their way of waging terrorism is not likely to make a comeback, and is being superseded by a new way that is more attuned to the organizational, doctrinal, and technological imperatives of the information age.

The new generation of Middle Eastern groups is the most active groups and their organisation has been active both in and outside the region in recent years. In Israel and the occupied territories, Hamas, and to a lesser extent the Palestinian Islamic Jihad, have shown their strength over the last four years with a series of suicide bombings that have killed more than one hundred people and injured several more. Exploiting a strong presence in Lebanon, the Shi'ite Hizbullah organization has also staged a number of attacks against Israeli Defense Forces troops and Israeli cities in Galilee.

The al-Gama'a al-Islamiya, or Islamic Group (IG), is the most active Islamic extremist group in Egypt. In November 1997 IG carried out an attack on Hatshepsut's Temple in Luxor, killing 58 tourists and 4 Egyptians. The Group has also claimed responsibility for the bombing of the Egyptian embassy in Islamabad, Pakistan, which left 16 dead and 60 injured. In Algeria, the Armed Islamic Group (GIA) has been behind the most violent, lethal attacks in Algeria's protracted civil war. Approximately 70,000 Algerians have lost their lives since the domestic terrorist campaign began in 1992. Recently, the loosely organized group of Arab Afghans—radical Islamic fighters from several North African and Middle Eastern countries who forged ties while resisting the Soviet occupation of Afghanistan—has come to the fore as an active terrorist outfit.

One of the leaders and founders of the Arab Afghan movement, Osama bin Laden, a Saudi entrepreneur who bases his activities in Afghanistan, is suspected of sending operatives to Yemen to bomb a hotel used by U.S. soldiers on their way to Somalia in 1992, plotting to assassinate President Clinton in the Philippines in 1994 and Egyptian President Hosni Mubarak in 1995, and of having a role in the Riyadh and Khobar blasts in Saudi Arabia that resulted in the deaths of 24 Americans in 1995 and 1996. U.S. officials have pointed to bin Laden as the mastermind behind the U.S. embassy bombings in Kenya and Tanzania, which claimed the lives of more than 260 people, including 12 Americans.

To varying degrees, these groups share the principles of the networked organization—relatively flat hierarchies, decentralization and delegation of decision-making authority, and loose lateral ties among dispersed groups and individuals. For instance, Hamas is loosely structured, with some elements working openly through mosques and social service institutions to recruit members, raise funds, organize activities, and distribute propaganda. Palestinian security sources indicate that there are ten or more Hamas splinter groups and factions with no centralized operational leadership. The Palestine Islamic Jihad is a series of loosely affiliated factions, rather than a cohesive group.

The pro-Iranian Hizbullah acts as an umbrella

organization of radical Shiite groups, and in many respects is a hybrid of hierarchical and network arrangements; Although the formal structure is highly bureaucratic, interactions among members are volatile and do not follow rigid lines of control. According to the U.S. Department of State, Egypt's Islamic Group is a decentralized organization that operates without a single operational leader, while the GIA is notorious for the lack of centralized authority. Unlike traditional terrorist organizations, Arab Afghans are part of a complex network of relatively autonomous groups that are financed from private sources forming "a kind of international terrorists' Internet." The most notorious element of the network is Osama bin Laden, who uses his wealth and organizational skills to support and direct a multinational alliance of Islamic extremists.

At the heart of this alliance is his own inner core group, known as Al-Qaeda ("The Base"), which sometimes conducts missions on its own, but more often in conjunction with other groups or elements in the alliance. The goal of the alliance is opposition on a global scale to perceived threats to Islam, as indicated by bin Laden's 1996 declaration of a holy war against the United States and the West. In the document, bin Laden specifies that such a holy war will be fought by irregular, light, highly mobile forces using guerrilla tactics.

Even though bin Laden finances Arab Afghan activities and directs some operations, he apparently does not play a direct command and control role over all operatives. Rather, he is a key figure in the coordination and support of several dispersed activities. For instance, bin Laden founded the "World Islamic Front for Jihad Against Jews and Crusaders." And yet most of the groups that participate in this front (including Egypt's Islamic Group) remain independent, although the organizational barriers between them are fluid.

From a netwar perspective, an interesting feature of

bin Laden's Arab Afghan movement is its ability to relocate operations swiftly from one geographic area to another in response to changing circumstances and needs. Arab Afghans have participated in operations conducted by Algeria's GIA and Egypt's IG. Reports in 1997 also indicated that Arab Afghans transferred training operations to Somalia, where they joined the Islamic Liberation Party (ILP). The same reports suggest that the Arab Afghan movement has considered sending fighters to Sinkiang Uighur province in western China, to wage a holy war against the Chinese regime. This group's ability to move and act quickly (and, to some extent, to swarm) once opportunities emerge hampers counterterrorist efforts to predict its actions and monitor its activities.

The fact that Arab Afghan operatives were able to strike the U.S. embassies in Kenya and Tanzania substantiates the claim that members of this network have the mobility and speed to operate over considerable distances. Although the organizational arrangements in these groups do not match all the basic features of the network ideal, they stand in contrast to more traditional groups. Another feature that distinguishes the newer generation of terrorist groups is their adoption of information technology.

Middle Eastern Terrorist Groups and the Use of Information Technology

Information technology (IT) is an enabling factor for networked groups; terrorists aiming to wage netwar may adopt it not only as a weapon, but also to help coordinate and support their activities. Before exploring how Middle Eastern terrorist groups have embraced the new technology, we posit three hypotheses that relate the rise of IT to organization for netwar:

- The greater the degree of organizational networking in a terrorist group, the higher the likelihood that IT is used to support the network's decision-making.

- Recent advances in IT facilitate networked terrorist organizations because information flows are becoming quicker, cheaper, more secure, and more versatile.
- As terrorist groups learn to use IT for decision-making and other organizational purposes, they will be likely to use the same technology as an offensive weapon to destroy or disrupt.

Middle Eastern terrorist groups provide examples of information technology being used for a wide variety of purposes. As discussed below, there is some evidence to support the claim that the most active groups—and therefore the most decentralized groups—have embraced information technology to coordinate activities and disseminate propaganda and ideology. At the same time, the technical assets and know-how gained by terrorist groups as they seek to form into multi-organizational networks can be used for offensive purposes—an Internet connection can be used for both coordination and disruption.

The anecdotes provided here are consistent with the rise in the Middle East of what has been termed 'techno-terrorism,' or the use by terrorists of satellite communications, e-mail, and the World Wide Web. Arab Afghans appear to have widely adopted information technology. According to reporters who visited bin Laden's headquarters in a remote mountainous area of Afghanistan, the terrorist financier has computers, communications equipment, and a large number of disks for data storage. Egyptian "Afghan" computer experts are said to have helped devise a communication network that relies on the World Wide Web, e-mail, and electronic bulletin boards so that the extremists can exchange information without running a major risk of being intercepted by counterterrorism officials.

Hamas is another major group that uses the Internet to share operational information. Hamas activists in the United States use chat rooms to plan operations and activities. Operatives use e-mail to coordinate activities across Gaza, the West Bank, and Lebanon. Hamas has realized that information can be passed securely over the Internet because it is next to impossible for counterterrorism intelligence to monitor accurately the flow and content of Internet traffic. Israeli security officials have difficulty in tracing Hamas messages and decoding their content. During a recent counterterrorist operation, several GIA bases in Italy were uncovered, and each was found to include computers and diskettes with instructions for the construction of bombs.

It has been reported that the GIA uses floppy disks and computers to store and process instructions and other information for its members, who are dispersed in Algeria and Europe. Furthermore, the Internet is used as a propaganda tool by Hizbullah, which manages three World Wide Web sites—one for the central press office, another to describe its attacks on Israeli targets. The presence of Middle Eastern terrorist organizations on the Internet is suspected in the case of the Islamic Gateway, a World Wide Web site that contains information on a number of Islamic activist organizations based in the United Kingdom. British Islamic activists use the World Wide Web to broadcast their news and attract funding; they are also turning to the Internet as an organizational and communication tool. While the vast majority of Islamic activist groups represented in the Islamic Gateway are legitimate, one group—the Global Jihad Fund—makes no secret of its militant goals.

The appeal of the Islamic Gateway for militant groups may be enhanced by a representative's claim, in an Internet Newsnet article in August 1996 that the Gateway's Internet Service Provider review this patterns and trends in the Middle East substantiates our speculations that the new terrorism is evolving in the direction of netwar, along the following lines:

- An increasing number of terrorist groups are adopting networked forms of organization and relying on information technology to support such structures.

- Newer groups (those established in the 1980s and 1990s) are more networked than traditional groups.
- A positive correlation is emerging between the degree of activity of a group and the degree to which it adopts a networked structure.
- Information technology is as likely to be used for organizational support as for offensive warfare.
- The likelihood that young recruits will be familiar with information technology implies that terrorist groups will be increasingly networked and more computer-friendly in the future than they are today.

Terrorist Doctrines—The Rise of a "War Paradigm"

The evolution of terrorism in the direction of netwar will create new difficulties for counterterrorism. The types of challenges, and their severity, will depend on the kinds of doctrines that terrorists develop and employ. Some doctrinal effects will occur at the operational level, as in the relative emphasis placed on disruptive information operations as distinct from destructive combat operations. However, at a deeper level, the direction in which terrorist netwar evolves will depend upon the choices terrorists make as to the overall doctrinal paradigms that shape their goals and strategies.

At least three terrorist paradigms are worth considering: terror as coercive diplomacy, terror as war, and terror as the harbinger of a "new world." These three engage, in varying ways, distinct rationales for terrorism—as a weapon of the weak, as a way to assert identity, and as a way to break through to a new world—discussed earlier in this chapter. While there has been much debate about the overall success or failure of terrorism, the paradigm under which a terrorist operates may have a great deal to do with the likelihood of success. Coercion, for example, implies distinctive threats or uses of force, whereas norms of "war" often imply maximizing destruction.

The Coercive-Diplomacy Paradigm

The first paradigm is that of coercive diplomacy. From its earliest days, terrorism has often sought to persuade others, by means of symbolic violence, either to do something, stop doing something, or undo what has been done. These are the basic forms of coercive diplomacy, and they appear in terrorism as far back as the Jewish Sicarii Zealots who sought independence from Rome in the first century AD, up through the Palestinians' often violent acts in pursuit of their independence today. The fact that terrorist coercion includes violent acts does not make it a form of war—the violence is exemplary, designed to encourage what Alexander George calls "forceful persuasion," or "coercive diplomacy as an alternative to war." In this light, terrorism may be viewed as designed to achieve specific goals, and the level of violence is limited, or proportional, to the ends being pursued.

Under this paradigm, terrorism was once thought to lack a "demand" for WMD; as such tools would provide means vastly disproportionate to the ends of terror. This view was first elucidated over twenty years ago by Brian Jenkins—though there was some dissent expressed by scholars such as Thomas Schelling—and continued to hold sway until a few years ago.

The War Paradigm Caleb

Carr, surveying the history of the failures of coercive terrorism and the recent trends toward increasing destructiveness and deniability, has elucidated what we call a "war paradigm." This paradigm, which builds on ideas first considered by Jenkins, holds that terrorist acts arise when weaker parties cannot challenge an adversary directly and thus turn to asymmetric methods. A war paradigm implies taking a strategic, campaign-oriented view of violence that makes no specific call for concessions from, or other demands upon, the opponent. Instead, the strategic aim is to inflict damage, in the context of what the terrorists view as an ongoing war.

In theory, this paradigm, unlike the coercive diplomacy one, does not seek a proportional relationship between the level of force employed and the aims sought. When the goal is to inflict damage generally, and the terrorist group has no desire or need to claim credit, there is an attenuation of the need for proportionality—the worse the damage, the better. Thus, the use of WMD can be far more easily contemplated than in a frame of reference governed by notions of coercive diplomacy. A terrorist war paradigm may be undertaken by terrorists acting on their own behalf or in service to a nation-state. In the future, as the information age brings the further empowerment of nonstate and transnational actors, "stateless" versions of the terrorist war paradigm may spread.

At the same time, however, states will remain important players in the war paradigm; they may cultivate their own terrorist-style commandos, or seek cut-outs and proxies from among nonstate terrorist groups. Ambiguity regarding a sponsor's identity may prove a key element of the war paradigm. While the use of proxies provides an insulating layer between a state sponsor and its target, these proxies, if captured, may prove more susceptible to interrogation and investigative techniques designed to winkle out the identity of the sponsor. On the other hand, while home-grown commando-style terrorists may be less forthcoming with information if caught, their own identities, which may be hard to conceal, may provide undeniable evidence of state sponsorship.

These risks for states who think about engaging in or supporting terrorism may provide yet more reason for the war paradigm to increasingly become the province of nonstate terrorists—or those with only the most tenuous linkages to particular states. Exemplars of the war paradigm today are the wealthy Saudi jihadist, Osama bin Laden, and the Arab Afghans that he associates with. As previously mentioned, bin Laden has explicitly called for war-like terrorism against the United States, and especially against U.S. military forces stationed in Saudi Arabia. President Clinton's statement that American retaliation for the U.S. embassy bombings in East Africa represented the first shots in a protracted war on terrorism suggests that the notion of adopting a war paradigm to counter terror has gained currency.

The New-World Paradigm

A third terrorist paradigm aims at achieving the birth of what might be called a "new world." It may be driven by religious mania, a desire for totalitarian control, or an impulse toward ultimate chaos. Aum Shinrikyo would be a recent example. The paradigm harks back to the dynamics of millennialist movements that arose in past epochs of social upheaval, when 'prophetae' attracted adherents from the margins of other social movements and led small groups to pursue salvation by seeking a final, violent cataclysm.

This paradigm is likely to seek the vast disruption of political, social, and economic order. Accomplishing this goal may involve lethal destruction, even a heightened willingness to use WMD. Religious terrorists may desire destruction for its own sake, or for some form of "cleansing." But the ultimate aim is not so much the destruction of society as a rebirth after a period of chaotic disruption.

The Paradigms and Netwar

All three paradigms offer room for netwar. Moreover, all three paradigms allow the rise of "cybotage"—acts of disruption and destruction against information infrastructures by terrorists who learn the skills of cyberterror, as well as by disaffected individuals with technical skills who are drawn into the terrorist milieu. However, we note that terrorist netwar may also be a battle of ideas—and to wage this form of conflict some terrorists may want the Net up, not down. Many experts argue that terrorism is moving toward ever more lethal, destructive acts. Our netwar perspective accepts this, but also holds that some terrorist netwars will stress disruption over destruction.

Networked terrorists will no doubt continue to destroy things and kill people, but their principal strategy may move toward the nonlethal end of the spectrum, where command and control nodes and vulnerable information infrastructures provide rich sets of targets. Indeed, terrorism has long been about "information"—from the fact that trainees for suicide bombings are kept from listening to international media, through the ways that terrorists seek to create disasters that will consume the front pages, to the related debates about countermeasures that would limit freedom of the press, increase public surveillance and intelligence gathering, and heighten security over information and communications systems.

Terrorist tactics focus attention on the importance of information and communications for the functioning of democratic institutions; debates about how terrorist threats undermine democratic practices may revolve around freedom of information issues. While netwar may be waged by terrorist groups operating with any of the three paradigms, the rise of networked groups whose objective is to wage war may be the one most relevant to and dangerous from the standpoint of the military. Indeed, if terrorists perceive themselves as warriors, they may be inclined to target enemy military assets or interests.

Information-Age Terrorism and the U.S. Air Force

Terrorists, especially those operating under a war paradigm, have every reason to seek out and target U.S. military personnel, installations, and equipment. The inability to pose direct opposition to American power may stimulate ethno-nationalist and religious revivalist movements—both types of actors may feel inherently threatened by the preeminent position of the United States in current world politics. Using a war paradigm allows terrorists an easy rationale for striking at American power, even in the absence of specific demands and without the need to claim credit for actions.

Further, the high profile of the Air Force suggests that attacks upon it will be a way to grab worldwide public attention and strike at what is perceived, by some, to be a "conditionally fragile" American public ability to accept losses and casualties. The U.S. Air Force, which in many ways epitomizes American power—as the Royal Navy did in the heyday of British Empire—has symbolic value as a target of terror. It also has expensive and sophisticated equipment that increases its attractiveness to the terrorist. Further, air assets are a quintessential element of the balance of power in any region of the world, as they are an available form of American military power that may be exercised in support of U.S. interests.

Given a U.S. air mastery that precludes direct challenges, a terrorist commando strategy against U.S. air assets might prove an attractive option for potential adversaries. This option poses the prospect of a campaign with low costs and risks—much like the British use of the Special Air Service (SAS) in North Africa during World War II. In that campaign, British commandos were sent against Luftwaffe airbases, destroying over 400 aircraft between 1941 and 1943 and helping to mitigate the effects of German air superiority early in the desert war with deep strikes of up to 400 miles behind the front. This irregular approach to weakening an enemy's air power has remained a vibrant strand in British strategic thought, and the SAS would reprise its role in the 1982 Falklands War, most notably by destroying 11 Argentine ground-attack aircraft in the raid on Pebble Island.

The potential of this type of threat to USAF bases has been acknowledged, and mitigation measures explored, in recent studies on ground-based threats to airbases. For the USAF, the prospect of terrorist attack exists across the spectrum of operations and across the types of asset—from personnel to equipment, and, increasingly, against command and control nodes. In peacetime, for example, the USAF plays a key role in maintaining a sense of American presence around the world. It is often a part of shows of force, and is an element in the American grand strategy of being open to the world regarding its military prowess—an important part of extending deterrent protection to U.S. friends and allies. Small-scale contingencies (SSC) range, on lower-intensity end of the spectrum, from humanitarian aid delivery to peace enforcement (e.g., of "no fly" zones).

Finally, the USAF will always play a key role in major theater wars (MTW), shoring up indigenous forces and multiplying the strength of other American military forces arriving in theater. U.S. air power, in this last category, may be the only viable hope of slowing down a numerically superior aggressor—and the aggressor may realize this, raising his interest in a terrorist commando strategy against the USAF.

Toward a New USAF Strategy for Coping with Information-Age Terrorism

At the most basic level, USAF strategy needs to have both defensive (antiterrorist) and proactive (counter-terrorist) components. Measures must be devised to protect forces stationed at home and abroad, to strike targets belonging to groups or their sponsors, and to gather intelligence on imminent attacks or other terrorist group activities. More specifically, the USAF strategy against terrorism should encompass four generic missions:

- General, "political" deterrence
- Interdiction and strike
- Intelligence gathering
- Force protection.

General deterrence relates to the USAF's ability to prevent further terrorist actions by striking (or threatening to strike) those targets of most value to the political supporters of a given group; interdiction and strike refer to the tactical use of USAF assets in the pursuit of terrorist attackers, as well as for retaliatory response. Intelligence gathering finds information about imminent terrorist attacks and identifies terrorist group weaknesses. As its name suggests, force protection concerns the security and safety of USAF personnel, plants, and equipment. Each mission has different implications for how the Air Force responds to the terrorist threat.

Greater emphasis on force protection, for instance, would place more weight on defensive antiterrorism. The deterrence and strike missions are inherently more proactive, while intelligence gathering can serve the causes of both anti- and counterterrorism. The foregoing suggests that the USAF should adopt a balanced approach that emphasizes all four missions to achieve an offensive/ defensive blend that can defend against and counter information age terrorism.

Mitigation Measures

The USAF must devise measures to protect personnel, equipment and installations, and C2 nodes. First, in the face of a significant increase in terrorist attacks (conventional or WMD) on USAF personnel and assets overseas, the USAF might consider shifting away from forward basing as much as possible, returning to forces based in the continental United States (CONUS) but with a wide network of dormant bases in the regions of interest. The principle here is similar to that articulated by Albert Wohlstetter et al. in their classic study of forward-based bomber vulnerability to surprise attack—the further forward, the more vulnerable the bombers. In the future, if the terrorist threat grows substantially, a similar basing solution might be applicable. Such an option would dovetail neatly with emerging USAF doctrine regarding the surging forward of air expeditionary forces in crisis and war.

While it may be difficult to secure access to a large number of bases, the redundancy created by this option would make it difficult for terrorists to predict which dormant bases to target prior to a deployment, and would help the USAF to remain engaged in key regions through "virtual presence." As attractive as moving to a preponderantly CONUS-based force might be under some circumstances, it would present a number of problems. First, there would be costs and risks to regional stability engendered by a lack of U.S. presence. For example, the USAF has been the principal stabilizer for Kuwait in the Persian Gulf region since the end of the war. Air assets are often crucial for deterrence and defense; when deterrence fails, it takes time to muster American ground and naval forces for a response. Therefore, when forward basing is deemed absolutely necessary for crisis stability, or for peace operations (e.g., "no fly" zones), the host nation must be made aware of USAF security requirements and allow the USAF an active role in preparing its antiterrorist defenses.

Also, the USAF might explore developing standardized doctrine regarding antiterrorism—perhaps along the lines of the general guidance that is provided by the Joint Staff. Clearly, different regional settings impose differing security requirements, but the USAF can develop a body of generalizable thought to impart to base commanders and others charged with securing USAF assets and personnel overseas. Our research has revealed a wide variance in views about base and personnel security, as well as widely differing levels of concern about the problem. With regard to forward basing, one must consider the risk of terrorist attack on prepositioned supplies and ordnance. The simplest solution is to move as much prepositioned equipment out to sea as possible, a step that the USAF has already partially taken.

However, this approach then subjects the USAF to the same problem that the U.S. Navy has in terms of response time—the need to wait for the arrival of ships, which will, generally, take some days to reach the region in question. Depending on the weakness of the American ally in the regional setting, a delay of days can be critical. Maritime prepositioning squadrons will not provide an overall solution, but they may provide a useful hedge in a prepositioning scheme that includes both ground-based materials and those kept afloat. The second deficiency with CONUS-basing as a solution lies in the nature of terrorist IW, which is not limited by geographical concerns.

Indeed, in some respects, the highly internetted U.S. information infrastructure might make access to USAF C2 nodes easier than if an airbase were located in the northern desert of Saudi Arabia. How, then, should the terrorist information warfare threat be defended against? A simple solution is to avoid becoming too interconnected to the global information infrastructure. The USAF currently retains the robust, dedicated C2 system that it needed to operate under the most trying conditions (i.e., protracted nuclear war), so perhaps the answer lies in *not* interconnecting all sensitive communications as rapidly as possible. Paradoxically, less modernization may make for more security in some cases. Moving toward more advanced electronic interconnectivity might undermine the security and safety of the current system, opening up a window of opportunity for cyberterror. The problem of increasing modernization and complexity is noted by Perrow and Sagan.

Proactive Counterterrorism and the USAF

If terrorists are moving toward a war paradigm, then it may be appropriate for the targeted to move to a war paradigm of their own. Indeed, President Clinton deliberately invoked the language and imagery of a war paradigm in his public comments on the reasons for retaliating with missile attacks against the terrorists responsible for the 1998 U.S. embassy bombings in East Africa. The adoption of a war paradigm by the U.S. armed forces would carry deep political and security implications, especially in terms of how other countries and terrorist groups view American power. For instance, one could argue that a war paradigm would result in more unilateral U.S. actions to counter terrorism, and that increased reliance on unilateral force might create tension with allies.

Also, more frequent "acts of war" against terrorism may only embolden terrorists, and encourage an increasingly destructive action-reaction process. Examining the full impact of the adoption of a war paradigm is beyond our scope here, and a recommendation for a war paradigm must be backed by further analysis. What we are proposing is that the USAF considers adopting some principles of the war paradigm in how it defends against and counters terrorism. If we assume—and this is an uncertain assumption—that terrorist targets can be indisputably identified, and then the USAF would be suited to key missions should the United States adopt a war paradigm? Air power offers a flexible, timely strike capability, including a new generation of highly discriminate weapons.

It also affords the least politically risky of the military options for striking back at terror, because it does not entail putting troops on the ground or moving significant naval assets in harm's way. Moreover, the high speed of response associated with air power will become increasingly important as terrorists acquire the capabilities to move swiftly from one theater to another and to attack with little or no warning. Thus, the USAF, with the strike capabilities afforded by air-launched cruise missiles and other smart munitions, should be considered a natural, leading element in any proactive strategy for countering terror. Beyond direct bombardment, the USAF can provide tactical mobility for special forces teams—and give them close support—should they be called upon to strike directly at key terrorist nodes. There are three fundamental ways in which air power could support a counterterrorist war paradigm.

First, the USAF could play a major role in coercive diplomatic campaigns against state sponsors of terror, along the lines of the use of air power against Qaddafi in the 1986 air raid on Tripoli or the 1998 Tomahawk strikes in Sudan and Afghanistan. Another possibility is that, instead of being used for coercive diplomacy, the USAF could be employed for either preemptive or preventive strikes against terrorist or state-sponsored sites that foment terror (such as deep underground facilities where WMD might be produced). Finally, the USAF could be the key link, along with Special Forces, in an information war against the terrorists in terms of both striking at the key telecommunications nodes of terrorists, and gaining information about them via IW means. The last point merits some discussion.

It is commonly argued that national technical means (NTM) of intelligence gathering are aimed at Cold War-era targets (i.e., tanks, planes, silos, etc.), and are therefore poorly suited to the needs of counterterrorism. This has led to calls for greater reliance upon human intelligence (humint) in dealing with terror. Humint is carried out by human operatives often working under cover or as double agents. Unfortunately, there are two principal limitations on the usefulness of humint regarding terrorists. First, organizations such as Hamas frequently recruit members when they are quite young, precluding infiltration of seasoned agents and making it more difficult to sway existing members or convince them to give up information.

Second, advancing in a terrorist organization may require committing violent acts, including murder, which are incompatible with accepted Western intelligence practices. The source's reliability will always be in question, both in terms of the inherent risks of dealing with double agents and the likelihood that views expressed by the source are skewed by personal hatreds, rivalries, or mental instability. For these reasons, it is ill-advised to pin significant hopes on the development of sufficient humint sources to wage an effective counterterrorist campaign. Instead, it may prove optimal to tailor NTM to the new needs of countering terror, relying less on satellite surveillance and perhaps rather more on drones and other pilotless craft capable of listening in on terrorists' increasingly advanced telecommunications.

Coupling this with a joint IW capability for penetrating terrorist C2 nodes might well create a form of "virtual humint" that will prove a key to counterterrorist strategy—and provide a new concept for the intelligence community. The approach will emphasize intelligence gathering by orbital assets or by human assets on the ground. But beyond the technological aspects of this form of counterterrorism, it will be crucial to rethink how to target terrorist groups. We next discuss how U.S. strategy might evolve.

Targeting Terrorists in the Information Age

The transition from hierarchical to networked terrorist groups is likely to be uneven and gradual. The netwar perspective suggests that, for the foreseeable future, various networked forms will emerge, coexisting with and influencing traditional organizations. Such organizational diversity implies the need for a counterterrorism strategy that recognizes the differences among organizational designs and seeks to target the weaknesses associated with each. Counter leadership strategies or retaliation directed at state sponsors may be effective for groups led by a charismatic leader who enjoys the backing of sympathetic governments, but are likely to fail if used against an organization with multiple, dispersed leaders and private sources of funding.

Networked organizations rely on information flows to function, and disruption of the flows cripples their ability to coordinate actions. It is no coincidence, for instance, that while the separation between Hamas political and military branches is well documented, this terrorist group jealously guards information on the connections and degree of coordination between the two. At the same time, the two-way nature of connectivity for information networks such as the Internet implies that the dangers posed by information warfare are often symmetric—the degree to which a terrorist organization uses information infrastructure for offensive purposes may determine its exposure to similar attacks by countering forces.

While it is true that terrorist organizations will often enjoy the benefit of surprise, the IW tactics available to them can also be adopted by counterterrorists. The key task for counterterrorism, then, is the identification of organizational and technological terrorist networks. Once such structures are identified, it may be possible to insert and disseminate false information, overload systems, misdirect message traffic, preclude access, and engage in other destructive and disruptive activities to hamper and prevent terrorist operations.

Policy Implications

The USAF can take various steps to effectively defend against and counter terrorism that is guided by a war paradigm. Defensive ideas and options might include:

1. *Do not modernize all communications nodes.* The USAF's C2 system is robust—it is designed to withstand the strains of protracted nuclear war—and full interconnectivity may in fact allow cyberterrorists to enter where they could not in the old C2 structure.
2. *Develop defensive antiterror standards for all operating bases and across mission types.* The standards should guarantee safety without constraining flexibility in varied settings; the standards may be more rigid in peacetime and in OOTW than in wartime.
3. *If terrorism worsens, increase reliance on CONUS basing and a wide network of dormant bases to reduce vulnerability of forward based elements to a terrorist commando strategy.* While likely to make terrorism against USAF personnel and equipment more difficult, increased CONUS basing will be controversial because it entails military and political costs. First, general (i.e., ongoing peacetime) deterrence stability may suffer from the diminution of USAF presence abroad. With decreased deterrence there may be political fallout resulting from a dramatic withdrawal from key regions such as Europe.

Third, terrorists might portray such redeployments as a "retreat" that they had caused, and a great victory over American power. Fourth, CONUS basing does not limit exposure to terrorist information warfare and the risk of suffering delays in the "just in time" deployment process may increase. These downside factors may be mitigated, however, by negotiating with friendly countries in key regions for access to bases that would be used only in times of crisis or for occasional engagement activities. Such an option would allow for prompt demonstration or deployment of USAF assets in crisis to shore up deterrence; and regular exercises in forward areas would show that

USAF reach remains extensive and that terrorism has in no way forced a retreat. Finally, defense against terrorist information warfare would both enable and support CONUS basing.

For proactive counterterrorism, the USAF might consider the following: At the doctrinal level, consider development of a war paradigm to counter the activities of groups that see themselves as waging war against the United States. This implies extending the list of what the USAF considers targets, to include more new-generation targets such as key nodes and the network itself. The adoption of a war paradigm may extend to the need for weapons designed to disrupt terrorist information flows, especially high-energy radio-frequency (HERF) and high-power microwave (HPM) weapons. The political and security implications of the adoption of such a paradigm would be profound, perhaps profoundly controversial—and need to be factored into future analyses. At the organizational level, deepen interservice and interagency networking.

The USAF is a principal actor in a counterterrorist war paradigm, and it should be a key node in an intergency network. As noted earlier, it may take networks to fight networks—and whoever masters the network form of organization will gain the greatest advantages. Countering terror will require the formation of highly effective interagency and interservice mechanisms and command structures. In the intelligence realm, develop requirements for counterterrorist operations. The USAF has a unique operating position in the area between orbital intelligence assets and humint, neither of which is likely to be effective against information-age terror.

The Air Force might develop a form of "virtual humint" based on both hacking into Continue planning for traditional operations such as raiding key terrorist nodes (in particular, deep underground [DUG] facilities that might produce weapons of mass destruction). This, a key element of an eventual counterterrorist war paradigm, would require careful nodal analysis of terrorist groups to inform the campaign planning process. These policy recommendations affect all the USAF missions, so that a balanced approach is achieved. A comprehensive counterterrorism policy ensures that the USAF can leverage its capabilities to the greatest extent while targeting the "soft spots" of information-age terrorist groups. However, the rise of networked terrorist organizations calls for a change in the analysis of terrorist groups.

Analysts should no longer assume that terrorist groups are bureaucratic, hierarchical, stand-alone organizations. In closing, we note that the history of the 20th century has demonstrated the crucial importance of air power to the outcome of land and naval warfare. Now, with the coming of the information age, it may well be that the history of the 21st century will show that air power proved equally useful in determining the outcome of the struggle against terrorism.

6

Human Rights and Counterterrorism

The United Nations unequivocally condemns terrorism in all its forms as a violation of human rights. However, finding a rights-based approach to fighting it has been less obvious. The anti-terrorism debate hinges on finding the right balance between human rights protection and effective security measures – measures taken as a precaution against theft or espionage or sabotage etc. Are effective counter-terrorism measures compatible with the full respect for fundamental freedoms? Is it necessary for States to make compromises and infringe on the rule of law in order to better protect their population from the threat of terrorism?

In November 2002, Secretary-General Kofi Annan (born April 8, 1938) is a Ghanaian diplomat who served as the seventh Secretary-General of the United Nations from January 1 1997 to January 1 2007, serving two five-year terms. He was the co-recipient of the Nobel Peace Prize in 2001. Noted that the 11 September 2001 terrorist attacks have acerbated the dilemma, "where an understandable focus on preventing still more terrible terrorist acts has increased concerns about the price we must pay in terms of cherished rights and liberties". He added: "We face a nearly unsolvable conflict between two imperatives of modern life—protecting the traditional civil liberties of our citizens, and at the same time ensuring their safety from terrorist attacks with catastrophic consequences." Particular attention needed to be given to balancing anti-terrorism measures and the observance of human rights standards, Mr. Annan said; otherwise the fight against terrorism would be "self-defeating".

For the United Nations, respect for human rights remains an integral part of any comprehensive counter-terrorism strategy. UN guidelines to help States strike a balance between human rights and combating terrorism including antiterrorism (defensive measures taken to reduce vulnerability to terrorist acts) and counterterrorism (offensive measures taken to prevent, deter, and respond to terrorism), taken to oppose terrorism throughout the entire threat spectrum. Also called CBT have been established in a number of resolutions adopted by the General Assembly, Security Council and Commission on Human Rights. These resolutions stress that "States must ensure that any measures taken to combat terrorism comply with all their obligations under international law and should adopt such measures in accordance with international law".

The International Commission of Jurists - The International Commission of Jurists (ICJ) is an international human rights non-governmental organisation. The Commission itself is a standing group of 60 eminent jurists (judges and lawyers), including members of the senior judiciary in Australia, Canada, and South Africa and International Court of Justice), noting that counter-terrorism measures should not "undermine the human rights law that Member States have themselves painstakingly built up over fifty years", has listed a number of fundamental rights that have been violated in the pursuit of counter-terrorism efforts: freedom from torture; the right to life; freedom from arbitrary detention; the right to a fair trial. The Right to a fair trial is an essential right in all countries respecting the rule of law. It is explicitly proclaimed in Article Ten of the Universal Declaration of Human Rights, the Sixth Amendment of the US Constitution, and Article Six of the European Convention of Human by an independent and impartial tribunal established by law; freedom of association and expression; and the rights to asylum and non-discrimination.

The protection of fundamental freedoms while countering terrorism is no new concern to the General Assembly. In 1997, the Sub-Commission on the Promotion and Protection of Human Rights (before 1999, known as the Sub-Commission on Prevention of Discrimination and Protection of Minorities) was the main subsidiary body of the United Nations Commission on Human Rights recommended the appointment of a Special Rapporteur. It is a title given to individuals working on behalf of various regional and international organizations who bear specific mandates to investigate, monitor and recommend solutions to specific human rights problems to conduct a comprehensive study on human rights and terrorism.

Special Rapporteur Kalliopi Koufa noted that her work needed to be reviewed in light of the events of 11 September and submitted a series of reports. In her progress report presented in July 2002, she reviewed international anti-terrorist actions, as well as comments, observations and decisions adopted by international human rights bodies and mechanisms. The issue of terrorism and human rights has become more urgent with the global surge in terrorism. While recognizing the importance of the fight against terrorism, some UN bodies have expressed concern that countermeasures may infringe on human rights.

In July 2004, the ICJ noted that "in some countries the 'war against terrorism' has given greater legitimacy to long-standing human rights violations carried out in the name of national security", leading to a worrying erosion of **International humanitarian law** (IHL), also known as the law of war, the laws and customs of war or the law of armed conflict, is the legal corpus "comprised of the Geneva Conventions and the Hague Conventions, as well as subsequent treaties, case law, and refugee law.

Refugee law is the branch of international law which deals with the rights and protection of related to, but distinct from, international human rights law and international humanitarian law, which deal respectively with human rights in general, and the conduct of war in particular, particularly through the "increasingly militarizing judicial functions", transferring "substantial judicial police powers from the 10th Amendment to the Constitution, which reserves to the states the rights and powers "not delegated to the United States" which include protection of the welfare, safety, health and even morals of the public to the armed forces without any judicial control".

The UN system has emphasized that human rights norms must be rigorously respected, even in states of emergency. For the **Office of the High Commissioner for Human Rights** (OHCHR) United Nations, protecting human rights in the context of counter-terrorism measures has high priority. It has voiced "profound concern at the multiplication of policies, legislation and practices increasingly being adopted by many countries in the name of the fight against terrorism, which affect negatively the enjoyment of virtually all human rights".

Drawing attention to the dangers inherent in the indiscriminate use of the term "terrorism" and the resulting new categories of discrimination, OHCHR has stressed that, in accordance with the **International Covenant on Civil and Political Rights** is a United Nations treaty based on the Universal Declaration of Human Rights, created in 1966 and entered into force on 23 March 1976 and pursuant to the Convention against Torture and Other Cruel, Inhuman or Degrading Treatment or Punishment, certain rights are non-derogable, meaning they cannot be suspended, not even in times of emergency. However, threats to national security may, under very specific and exceptional conditions, lead to a state of emergency under which certain rights are subject to derogation- the partial repeal of a law, usually by a subsequent act that in some way diminishes its Original Intent or scope.

The Digest of Jurisprudence of the UN and Regional Organizations on the Protection of Human Rights while Countering Terrorism, published by OHCHR in 2003, makes several important contributions, clarifying the concept of non-derogable rights. Its leading task is to establish a framework in which terrorism can be effectively countered without adversely affecting fundamental freedoms and to address the core principles of necessity and proportionality, fundamental to lawful counter-terrorism measures. In 2003, the General Assembly adopted without a vote resolution 57/219, "Protecting human rights and fundamental freedoms while countering terrorism", under which OHCHR is mandated to analyze counter-terrorism laws and measures and make recommendations concerning the obligation to promote and protect human rights and fundamental freedoms of States, including in their implementation of relevant Security Council resolutions.

Security Council efforts to protect fundamental human rights while countering terrorism are guided by its resolution 1456 (2003), which declared that "States must ensure that any measure taken to combat terrorism comply with all their obligations under international law and should adopt such measures in accordance with international law, in particular international human rights, refugee and humanitarian law".

Briefing the Council on 18 January 2002, the Chairman of the **Counter-Terrorism Committee,** an organ of the Security Council of the United Nations The Security Council Committee established pursuant to resolution 1373 (2001) concerning counter-terrorism will hold its fifth special meeting with international, regional and subregional organizations, on the theme stated that the Cornell Theory Center (CTC) is mandated to monitor the implementation of resolution 1373 (2001). Monitoring performance against other international conventions, including human rights law, is outside the scope of the Committee's mandate.

The major challenge is finding a balance between counter-terrorism monitoring and full respect for human rights. Recommendation 16 of the Report of the Policy Working Group on the United Nations and Terrorism proposes that security cannot be achieved by sacrificing human rights: "Together with the United Nations High Commissioner for Human Rights, a dialogue should be maintained with the Counter-Terrorism Committee on the importance of ensuring respect for human rights during the implementation of legislation, policies and practices to combat terrorism."

While the CTC has been willing to receive information on human rights issues, it has not yet developed a systematic approach to monitoring anti-terrorism measures in compliance with human rights norms. In October 2003, at a Conference organized by the ICJ, Deputy High Commissioner for Human Rights Dr. Bertrand G. Ramcharan, from Guyana, a former United Nations (UN) official who once held functional diplomatic status, is Chancellor of the University of Guyana, Senior Fellow at the Ralph Bunche Institute for International Studies and currently Visiting Professor of pointed out that terrorism must be fought "within the framework of the law and with respect for the principle of proportionality".

Fighting Terrorism in the Security Council

In the aftermath of the 11 September 2001 terrorist attacks, the Security Council, acting under Chapter VII of the UN Charter, adopted resolution 1373 (2001), condemning terrorist acts and incriminating:

1. To accuse of a crime or other wrongful act.
2. All parties who support or participate in the financing, planning and preparation of these acts.

It also said that such acts are serious criminal offences in domestic law and asked all Member States to submit to the Counter Terrorism Committee (CTC) a report listing their anti-terrorism initiatives. Established in 1999, the CTC monitors compliance with resolution 1373 and the twelve other terrorism-related conventions and protocols adopted by the General Assembly. Over 500 reports had been submitted as of the middle of 2004. But CTC experts argue that the mere documentation of anti-terrorist actions does little in terms of aiding enforcement, because the effectiveness of any international resolution depends on its implementation. However, support for resolution 1373 is not universal; some 71 countries have not met the submission deadline.

Responding to the need for CTC reform, the Council on 26 March adopted resolution 1535 (2004) establishing a new structure which does not alter the Committee's mandate but enhances its operational capacity. The revitalized CTC comprises a plenary of all Council members, focusing on strategic and policy decisions, and a bureau, which includes the Chair, Vice-Chairs and consolidated expert and secretariat staff.

Expert Joel Sollier explained that while structural and operational changes might be helpful, "it will not change anything if political will remains so low". The verification system, he noted, remained stalled because it involved so "many politically sensitive fields", including monetary systems, police, immigration -entrance of a person (an alien) into a new country for the purpose of establishing permanent residence. Motives for immigration, like those for migration generally, are often economic, although religious or political factors may be very important.

Limitation of the development, testing, production, deployment, proliferation, or use of weapons through international agreements and arms control did not arise in international diplomacy until the first Hague Convention (1899) and money laundering. It is the process of taking the proceeds of criminal activity and making them appear legal. Laundering allows criminals to transform illegally obtained gain into seemingly legitimate funds, leaving "countries afraid of evaluation from the CTC".

The Challenge of Defining Terrorism

Fighting terrorism has been a long-standing concern of the General Assembly. Beginning in 1963, the United Nations has focused on building a legal framework to eliminate international terrorism. **Noun 1. international terrorism** - terrorism practiced in a foreign country by terrorists who are not native to that country act of terrorism, terrorism, terrorist act - the calculated use of violence (or the threat of violence) against civilians in order to attain and, to date, there are twelve major multilateral conventions about terrorism that constitute the main element of international law. However, despite this progress, one of the central challenges facing the Assembly has been the definition of terrorism .Few words are as politically or emotionally charged as terrorism.

A 1988 study by the US Army counted 109 definitions of terrorism that covered a total of 22 different definitional elements. Each of the twelve conventions relies on an "operational" definition, based on specific terrorist "activities". Thus, separate treaties exist to address issues such as bombings, hijackings; hostage-taking and covert financing of terrorist activities, but a universal definition has yet to be adopted.

Since 1996, the Assembly's Sixth (Legal) Committee has worked on drafting a **Comprehensive Convention on International Terrorism** is a convention which the United

Nations is deliberating as of October 2006. However, negotiations remain stalled due to disagreements between States on how to distinguish liberation movements from terrorist cells. Thus, until States resolve the adage that "one man's terrorist "**One Man's Terrorist**" is the seventeenth episode of season one of the fictional CBS drama *Jericho*. Synopsis Gray and Roger face off over the refugee problem is another man's freedom fighter", the debate over a universal definition of terrorism will continue.

Panel on counter-terrorism and human rights

With continuing widespread fear of terrorist attacks and a security- dominated agenda, governments are redefining and seeking to bypass well-established human rights and rule of law principles. Terrorism itself puts human rights in peril and states have a duty to protect people from terrorist acts. However, new and old counter-terrorism measures worldwide threaten the rule of law and human rights. The legal and human rights community is struggling to meet this global challenge in an effective and coordinated way. Policy-makers dismiss general statements of human rights principles as unrealistic and the public in many countries seems ready to accept an erosion of rights.

Some states have faced cycles of terrorism and counter-terrorism for decades, yet policy-makers are not listening to the lessons of history. Despite signs of an emerging rhetorical acceptance by democratic states that their fight against terrorism should not jeopardize democratic values, there is still little agreement on what this means in practice for the work of the police, the military, anti- terror units and the courts. There is a need to move from principle to a more sophisticated and detailed exploration of the issues. What are the acceptable limits of counter-terrorism measures? What is the nature of today's security threats and how different are they to past threats? Do these threats justify changing existing rules of international human rights and humanitarian law? How should laws and policies change if they are both to confront terrorism effectively and respect human rights and the rule of law?

The legal community worldwide must now take a leadership role in articulating how the rule of law can be respected in addressing terrorism in its many complex global and local forms. To meet this challenge, the ICJ has launched in October 2005 a major 18-month initiative: the Eminent Jurists Panel on Terrorism, Counter-terrorism and Human Rights.

The human rights price of excessive counter-terrorism measures

- Detainees tortured to extract information and torture "outsourced"
- Suspects transferred to countries where they are at risk of torture
- Indefinite or secret detentions, often without charge or trial
- Protective reach of the courts cut down, detainees held without habeas corpus.
- Fair trial guarantees ignored, rights of defence cut down and rights of appeal removed
- Criminalization of political and social dissent
- Freedom of expression threatened
- Erosion of democratic checks and balances
- Discrimination against minority communities
- Vague definitions of terrorism misused

The Eminent Jurists Panel

The Eminent Jurists Panel is composed of eight internationally renowned jurists from all regions and legal traditions, chaired by Arthur Chaskalson, Former Chief Justice of South Africa and the first President of South Africa's new Constitutional Court. The Panel is considering the nature of today's terrorist threats and the impact of new and old counter-terrorism measures on human rights. It is also exploring how counter-terrorism laws and policies can be both effective and respect human rights and the rule of law. A small team in the ICJ Secretariat in Geneva is coordinating the work of the Panel.

Over 18 months the Panel will:

- Listen to past and present experiences of cycles of terrorism and counter-terrorism in a series of national and regional hearings in different parts of the world
- Meet three times in plenary
- Seek meetings with government and security officials who shape or implement counter-terrorism policies
- Invite submissions from non-governmental organizations, lawyers, judges, academics, national human rights institutions, governmental authorities and inter-governmental organizations
- Engage in discussions with ICJ's global network of judges, lawyers, prosecutors and human rights defenders
- Stimulate public debate on critical issues through the media in different languages
- Produce a final, detailed report with recommendations, which the ICJ will seek to have translated into French, Spanish, Arabic and Russian and which will guide ICJ advocacy for the next phase of its Global Security and Rule of Law Programme.

The national and regional hearings

At the heart of the Eminent Jurists Panel initiative is a series of public hearings in countries and regions around the world (see list of proposed hearings below) that have in the past faced cycles of terrorism and counter-terrorism or still face threats today. Lawyers, judges, government officials, NGOs, human rights defenders, academics and victims will be approached to identify the lessons that today's policy-makers should learn from their experiences. They will be asked to identify problems with contemporary counter-terrorism measures in their countries and the most difficult unresolved legal and policy challenges. They will consider the impact in their region of the current "war on terror" and how to fight terrorism within the rule of law.

They will reflect on the role of the legal and judicial communities in ensuring respect for the principles the ICJ laid down in 2004 in its Berlin Declaration. The hearings will stimulate critical domestic debate and expand the Panel's source of first-hand information and legal and policy analysis. The hearings will be timed and organized to support local initiatives that seek to ensure counter-terrorism measures respect human rights and the rule of law. At some hearings participants may decide to adopt recommendations to support subsequent advocacy in their own country and region. ICJ sections, affiliates or other legal and human rights organizations in each country are working with the ICJ Secretariat to organize these hearings. At least one member of the Panel will attend each hearing. Background papers will be prepared before each hearing and the organizers will submit a report of the hearing to the Panel.

Legal and policy issues:

- Should terrorism be fought by military means or should it be tackled through the criminal justice system?
- Do we need to have intrusive surveillance of public places and transports, data on travel, phone calls and Internet use in order to protect people from terrorism?
- How can we criminalize incitement to violence without eroding freedom of speech, the press and religion?
- How to increase security without discriminating, alienating and marginalizing minority communities?
- Does human rights law prevent effective international legal cooperation in fighting terrorism?

- Should suspected terrorists be tried by special, even military, courts and should trial procedures be relaxed?
- How can intelligence services both be effective and accountable? How can intelligence information be used fairly in court?
- What is the role of the Security Council in fighting terrorism? What due process should persons have when their names are put on international terrorist lists?
- Are targeted killings a legitimate act of a state?
- What are the rights of victims of counter-terrorism?

National hearings

Australia

Canada

Colombia

India

Indonesia

Malaysia

Pakistan

Philippines

Russian Federation/CIS

Sri Lanka

Spain

Thailand

United Kingdom

United States

Sub-regional hearings

East Africa

North Africa

Middle East

South America

Founded in Berlin in 1952, the ICJ is a global network of judges, lawyers and human rights defenders united by international law and rule of law principles that advance human rights. Using our expertise in law, justice systems and advocacy, we work for victims to obtain remedies, for those responsible for abuses to be held accountable and for justice systems to be independent and active protectors of human rights. We work to change law and policy at the national and international levels when they do not adequately protect people from human rights violations. The ICJ's greatest asset is its network of 60 Commissioners, 37 National Sections and 45 Affiliated Organizations.

Having as its members many of the world's most prominent judges, lawyers and human rights defenders, the ICJ is able to mobilize authoritative and practical expertise on most rule of law and human rights issues. The ICJ network crosses linguistic, cultural and legal frontiers, spread across all regions of the world. It can command attention at the highest levels of the judiciary, legislature and executive.

The Berlin Declaration: A commitment to act

In August 2004, the ICJ brought together 160 jurists of all regions in the city of its birth, Berlin, and adopted the Berlin Declaration on Upholding Human Rights and the Rule of Law in Combating Terrorism. The Declaration sets out 11 principles that states should respect when countering terrorism. In addressing today's rule of law challenges, judges and lawyers have a responsibility to play a critical leadership role. With its reliable legal approach to the protection and promotion of human rights and its strong network, the ICJ is in a unique position to inform and mobilize the legal community around the world and to act as a catalyst for change.

Recent ICJ initiatives on terrorism, counter-terrorism and human rights

- Two-volume study on Terrorism and Human Rights
- Three-year advocacy leading to the establishment of a UN Special Rapporteur on counter-terrorism and human rights
- Global monitoring of counterterrorism measures and interventions on domestic legislation, including Bahrain, Colombia, Nepal, Thailand and the United Kingdom
- Bi-monthly E-Bulletin on Counter-terrorism and human rights
- Preparation of a series of round-table policy dialogues

7

The War on Terrorism

Let me begin by saying a few words about the nature of our ongoing war on terrorism. September 11 dramatically changed the way Americans view the world and their own security. We learned that we are vulnerable, and we learned that tensions and instability abroad can have catastrophic consequences on American interests and American lives. The U.S. is now focused on combating the threat of terrorism and has launched a global campaign against terrorists and those who support them. One of the first questions to ask in assessing our war on terrorism is: What is terrorism?

Terrorism is difficult to define because terrorist attacks have different meanings for different people. Some people condemn the targeting of civilians; others exempt national liberation movements and resistance to foreign occupation. In my view, terrorism is the premeditated, politically motivated targeting of innocent people, whether through hijackings, hostage-taking, assassination, bombing, the use of weapons of mass destruction, or other means.

The terrorist organization that inflicted such a terrible wound on the U.S. one year ago is al Qaeda. Al Qaeda has a unique set of strengths that allows it to inflict terror on a global scale. Al Qaeda has the leadership and popular appeal of Osama bin Laden, extensive and widely disbursed financial assets, a sophisticated organizational capacity, and determined members who have been highly trained in camps and cells. Al Qaeda brings together fundamentalist Muslims from around the world who share certain radical political views and religious fervor. They are united in hating the United States and its policies, and they are committed to striking American targets and civilians.

A question that many Americans asked in the immediate aftermath of September 11 was: Why do they hate us? It seemed inconceivable that people would train for years to fly airplanes into buildings, killing themselves and thousands of innocent civilians. While nothing justifies terrorism, there are several factors that have contributed to the rise of groups such as al Qaeda. Many militant radicals oppose or are jealous of the extent of American power in today's world, and reject our secular and open society. Fundamentalist Muslims are threatened by the spread of American culture – the respect for women's rights, materialism, and the tolerance of free expression.

They apparently believed that Americans had become self-indulgent, weak, and incapable of responding. Our support for Israel, our perceived indifference to the suffering of Palestinians and other Muslims, our support for despotic rulers, our military presence in the Persian Gulf and Saudi Arabia, and the embargo in Iraq have also led to widespread anger and resentment in the Islamic world. Many Muslims live under poor and repressive governments. They are angry and frustrated by the desperation of their own lives and the stagnation of their societies. They are looking for someone to blame and the U.S., as the only superpower, is the biggest target. Radical fundamentalists tap into that anger and frustration and turn it into terrorism. Osama bin Laden does not draw followers because he is a true warrior for Islam; he draws followers because many Muslims hate America, and bin Laden are seen as the only one in the Islamic world who will take America on.

The Nature of the Threat

Osama bin Laden and his followers could never defeat the U.S. on a traditional battlefield; that is why they resort to the shadowy world of terrorism. They are an unseen enemy – often living and plotting among us. They have come at us from the edges of the world, right into our centers of strength. There are no clear battle lines or enemy armies as there were in America's previous wars. Instead, this conflict takes place in the shadows, with terrorists scattered in small cells in over eighty countries around the world.

The terrorists have a variety of methods at their disposal. They are, above all, opportunistic, selecting targets based on weaknesses that they observe in our defenses. They have performed a wide range of conventional attacks: car bombs, assassinations, kidnappings, and suicide attacks. The use of civilian aircraft as missiles on September 11 demonstrated the versatility of the conventional terrorist threat. Even more horrifying is the possibility that terrorists will strike with weapons of mass destruction. It is clear from intelligence reports and material found in Afghanistan that al Qaeda has been seeking chemical, biological and radiological weapons that, if deployed, could inflict catastrophic damage. The worst-case scenario is that terrorists acquire or build a nuclear warhead

In addition to having a variety of methods, terrorists have an endless list of targets that they can attack. For instance, in the past decade, al Qaeda has struck a diverse list of American targets: U.S. embassies in Africa, military barracks in Saudi Arabia, and the U.S.S. Cole in Yemen, as well as the World Trade Center and the Pentagon. Since September 11, we have seen attacks on a synagogue in Tunisia, a U.S. consulate in Pakistan, and the recent attempted assassination of President Hamid Karzai of Afghanistan. Terrorists will strike at targets that they believe are vulnerable. On September 11 they exploited weaknesses in our air travel security. In the future, we should expect attacks to come in other forms and places.

Terrorism is a consistent and ever-changing threat, with methods and targets that change, and operations that are planned out of visibility. Given the uncertain nature of the terrorist threat, we should prepare ourselves for a sustained campaign against terrorism. It is likely to be long, complex, nasty and brutish. The war will not have a clear end. I think it will go on indefinitely. There will be no V-E Day or V-J Day, no unconditional surrender, no one grand moment of victory. It is simply not possible to eliminate all terrorism. There have always been political and religious fanatics and there always will be. But if we remain resolute we can achieve certain victories: making Americans safer and less fearful, denying terrorist's access to the world's most dangerous weapons, disrupting and destroying terrorist networks, and curbing the instability that allows terrorists to flourish.

Right now, there is much discussion about what the next phase of the war on terrorism should be. The Bush administration is beginning to make its case to the American people, Congress and our allies that Saddam Hussein is a dangerous threat that needs to be dealt with. The coming months will bring more debate as to the urgency of the threat, and how we should deal with it. Right now the CIA says that al Qaeda is still the greatest present danger to the U.S. In my view, al Qaeda should remain our primary target and our first priority. We need to crush the forces that are responsible for September 11.

That means we go where the terrorist trail leads, whether it's to the remaining hideouts in Afghanistan, the Islamic schools in Pakistan, the remote islands of Indonesia, the mountains of Georgia, the charitable institutions of Saudi Arabia, the slums of Somalia, or the neighborhoods of New York, Chicago, Paris and Rome. Al Qaeda may lack its home base in Afghanistan, but it still has leaders, supporters and trained operatives in many countries – they are alive and plotting, and we must not be deterred from the goal of rooting out this terrorist network that continues to plan direct attacks on the U.S.

A lot has happened in one year, a year that was filled with triumphs and tragedies, violence and liberation. Much of what happened was good:

- The U.S. did not retreat after September 11; it became more engaged in the world;
- Americans rediscovered their faith, patriotism and resolve;
- The U.S. did not lash out indiscriminately; instead, it deliberately built a remarkable global coalition of nations to combat terrorism;
- The U.S. prevailed in Afghanistan, eliminating the terrorist base and freeing the Afghan people from one of the world's most vile and repressive regimes. Few of us will forget the pictures of Afghans celebrating in the streets and Afghan girls going back to school;
- We have become a major, active power in Central Asia – an area too big and important to ignore – and overall Central Asia is in better shape than it was a year ago;
- Osama bin Laden, though not yet captured or confirmed dead, has been driven from his stronghold and is surely less able to wage terror;
- No mass movement in the Islamic world has moved against the U.S., despite chilling predictions of a clash of civilizations;
- While underlying differences still exist, our relations with China and Russia have been improved;
- Globalization has not reversed; it has expanded;
- Our economy has not been devastated by the terrorist attacks. Indeed, it is telling that the Enrons, World Coms and Arthur Andersens were more damaging to the U.S. economy than Osama bin Laden or al Qaeda.

We now know that our economy can come back from catastrophic terrorist attacks.

But in addition to these notable successes, the past year has seen some troubling developments and disappointments:

- We became aware of the magnitude of the failure of American intelligence that preceeded 9/11;
- We discovered further evidence of how terrorists are exploiting technology to develop weapons of mass destruction;
- At times, we have acted is if we were confused. The formula or "you are either with us or against" proved unworkable in a complex world – for example, we have a hard time explaining our close alliance with Saudi Arabia in relation to the stark, moral clarity or "you're either with us or against us."
- Little progress has been made to resolve some of the most intractable conflicts. In Kashimir, the Indians and Pakistanis still have hundreds of thousands of troops mobilized on the border and nuclear weapons pointed at one another. In the Middle East, violence between the Israelis and Palestinians has escalated to horrific levels, and a peace settlement seems like a more and more distant hope.
- To win the support of strategic allies in Central Asia we have embraced, too closely I think, certain unsavory leaders – most notably, we have gained some unpleasant friends in Uzbekistan and Krygizstan. And, of course, to win the support of Pakistan we have soft-pedaled our convictions on democracy and human rights, as Mushurraf has consolidated power.
- While we liberated Afghanistan, the stability of the new government no longer seems to be a priority. Prominent aid has not been delivered, the international peacekeeping force has been confined to Kabul, re-development has not begun, and warlords maintain

power in certain regions. Recent bombings in Kabul and the assassination attempt on President Karzai indicate the minimal effect that our half-hearted engagement is having.

– Our relations with our closest friends are being severely tested. Our European allies are increasingly concerned with American policies of "going it alone," and worry about the doctrine of preemptive action. Other allies in Asia and Latin America worry that we have forgotten their interests, and are focused too narrowly on the threat.

– We have seen an erosion of our civil liberties. Immigrants have been deported in secret, American citizens have been detained and labeled 'enemy combatants' without access to lawyers or judges, and surveillance has increased with e-mail monitoring, wiretaps, and the Attorney General's exhortation that Americans spy on one another. All of this has taken place without much of a public or Congressional outcry.

It has indeed been a trying year – sometimes inspirational, sometimes disheartening. It started with an attack that shattered a sense of isolation that had rested upon centuries of experience and oceans on either coast, and it ends with America proposing the most aggressive and extensive international engagement in its history. We have much to learn from the positive developments of the last year – the strength and resolve of all Americans, the might of our armed forces, the success of our multilateral coalition building, the hope we can bring to places such as Afghanistan, the constructive relations we can forge with former adversaries Russia and China, and the potential for recreating our relations with the Islamic world.

There is also much we can learn from the negative developments of the last year – the need to improve our intelligence, anticipation, and preparedness for terrorist attacks, the urgency of resolving the world's most intractable conflicts, the danger of allowing countries such as Afghanistan to slip into instability, the fragility of even our closest alliances, and the need to guard our rights and liberties at home as closely as we pursue our interests abroad.

As we have taken action to fight terrorism abroad, we have also begun a massive effort to change the way we protect our homeland.

A. Organization

September 11 profoundly altered our sense of security in our homes, businesses and communities, and Americans now live in fear of future attacks. The federal government has responded with a national strategy for homeland security, declaring that "the U.S. government has no more important mission than protecting the homeland from further terrorist attacks."

The largest reorganization of the federal government in fifty years will produce a new Department of Homeland Security, charged with defending the homeland from attack. The department will oversee an enormous budget and well over 150,000 employees, while coordinating the efforts of twenty-two federal agencies. The Department will include security agencies such as the Customs Service and Coast Guard, emergency agencies such as the Federal Emergency Management Agency (FEMA), and biological, chemical and nuclear research programs and information centers.

In addition to the new Department of Homeland Security, the new national strategy calls for better coordination between the federal government and state and local governments, as well as the participation of the private sector and the American people. The reorganization of our homeland security is a good idea, but the long-term task of governmental reorganization must not divert our attention from guarding against terrorism today and the new efforts and more spending do not automatically equal results.

B. Prevention

Homeland security must have three critical components: prevention, protection, and response. Preventing a potential attack is quite clearly everybody's first priority. In order to prevent possible attacks, we need to substantially improve our intelligence and counter-terrorism activities.

Intelligence

September 11 was a systemic failure of American intelligence. Everything broke down – CIA-FBI coordination, immigration controls, law enforcement and airport security. The biggest failure was that our intelligence community did not piece together bits of information from multiple sources suggesting that a major attack was in the works. The CIA Director repeatedly warned during the summer that it was highly likely that a significant al Qaeda attack would take place in the near future, and he told President Bush in August that al Qaeda had discussed hijacking airplanes.

Around the same time, FBI agents were suspicious of some Middle Eastern men training at U.S. flight schools. And in the days before the attacks, the National Security Agency (NSA) intercepted messages referring to "the big match" and "zero hour." But the government intelligence and counter-terrorism apparatus was too fragmented to grasp the emerging pattern – they had the dots, but did not connect them and present them to the President.

The problem in intelligence is sifting through large amounts of information dispersed at various agencies so that you can then get the right information to the right person at the right time. We have the technological capacity to collect infinite information, but we have to better utilize that information to prevent attacks. Since September 11, steps have been taken to improve our intelligence capabilities. The FBI has increased its activity overseas and shifted its focus at home to counter-terrorism.

The CIA has expanded its budget and increased domestic surveillance. Under the new national strategy for homeland security, the new Department would examine intelligence provided by the FBI and CIA and get the information to the proper agency. But more needs to be done to prepare our intelligence agencies to prevent the new threat of terrorist attacks. We should make the following changes in intelligence:

— We need to change priorities to pay more attention to the threat of terrorism and dissemination of information before attacks take place. Prosecuting terrorists after the fact is not good enough. Prevention must be the goal.

— We need to hire more spies. We need to be committed to putting people on the ground that can detect and alert us to potential terrorist plots. Technology alone will not make us secure – clandestine work is necessary to crack terrorist networks.

— We need to improve the talent pool so that we are hiring the most qualified people for our intelligence agencies. We should invest more in language and professional training, and hire more officers familiar with foreign cultures and religions so that they can detect broad trends and patterns.

— We need to improve the organization of our intelligence community. Right now intelligence gathering is splintered among many agencies, including the CIA, NSA, FBI and Department of Defense. Turf wars and competition often keep agencies from sharing information or working together.

— We need a center in the government for all intelligence foreign and domestic – to come together. One person should be responsible for coordinating all elements of the intelligence community. This person should not be the Director of the CIA or Secretary of Defense, who has a natural bias from being the head of a particular agency or department. Only by establishing an independent center for intelligence can we solve the problems of scattered information and infighting that have plagued our intelligence efforts.

– We need to improve cooperation with foreign countries. We cannot be everywhere at once, so we must develop relationships with other countries that can help us get critical information. Countries such as Pakistan and Yemen have already been helpful in the war on terrorism.

Intelligence will be the most significant tool we have in preventing future attacks. It will take years to implement these changes, but we must be determined to avoid another breakdown on the scale of 9/11.

Redefine Law Enforcement

We must also be committed to redefining certain elements of law enforcement to face the new threat of terrorism. There needs to be a priority in domestic law enforcement on preventing attacks. In the past, the FBI has emphasized law enforcement, not counter-terrorism. The FBI is trying to change this by making the mission of counter-terrorism its priority – targets will now be al Qaeda instead of Bonnie and Clyde. We must be careful to avoid weakening the FBI's crime-fighting capabilities, but clearly changes in the FBI's structure and priorities are in order. The FBI must reduce the layers of bureaucracy in its headquarters. It is simply too difficult to get information through the chain of command – the FBI needs to cut layers from its command structure and restore accountability. Only then can it transform itself from a police force into an effective counter-terrorism force.

More effective law enforcement will enable more aggressive prosecution of prospective terrorists before they can commit attacks. For example, the FBI was able to apprehend Zacharius Moussouai, the so-called "20th hijacker", before September 11. Imagine if they had been able to apprehend just a few more of the prospective hijackers? It would have prevented those hijackers from attacking, and most likely would have deterred the other hijackers from attempting an operation. American law enforcement needs to focus on counter-terrorism as a top priority. This means reorienting their capabilities and their culture, and improving coordination with the federal government and the new Department of Homeland Security. If they are successful, America will be better prepared to face the threats on the frontlines of its homeland.

Stop Terrorist Funding

To prevent future attacks we must also dry up the financial resources that allow terrorists to plan and execute attacks. Al Qaeda has thrived in large part because of its extensive financial resources. Its financial network is far-flung, complex and diversified. Al Qaeda has a broad array of funding sources; including donations, legitimate businesses, and criminal enterprises in drugs and weapons trading. The biggest source of terrorist fund-raising is Islamic charities, especially in Saudi Arabia, where money donated to fund Islamic schools and cultural initiatives ended up funding al Qaeda camps in Afghanistan and vitriolic anti-American and anti-Semitic madrassas in Pakistan.

While pursuing the terrorist money trail, we must recognize that we will never be able to completely dry up the money that goes to terrorism. Terrorists are very good at hiding their resources, and even if we shut down current funding sources, they will find new ones. For example, al Qaeda has recently shifted many of their assets into gold, and has shipped the gold out of Pakistan and into Sudan. The global financial system also makes it easy for terrorists to hide money. Consider that today there are 300,000 companies registered in the Virgin Islands, and $800 billion deposited in the Cayman islands.

Terrorists often rely on informal exchanges, smuggling, fraud, and the poor auditing and surveillance of certain countries. Tracking down terrorist assets will therefore demand the cooperation of all of our coalition partners, as well as banks and private individuals. So far we have had some success cooperating with banks in Europe and countries such as Saudi Arabia, where a more careful auditing of Islamic charities has led to progress in stopping the flow of money into terrorist coffers. There are also signs that we are making some progress in tracking the freewheeling financial system of the Gulf States so that we can detect and deter the movement of money by terrorists.

But some of our coalition partners, and even special interests in this country, are resisting this aspect of our antiterrorism campaign because they want to preserve the secrecy of their financial transactions. U.S.-European divisions have emerged and hindered the drive to block terrorist assets. I see no reason why account holders, including offshore account holders, should not disclose their identities when conducting financial transactions. We must remain resolute in following the money trail: seizing the resources that terrorists depend on is too important to preventing future attacks.

We must insist that banks pursue terrorist funds more actively, and give law enforcement authorities access to their books on suspect accounts. If we succeed in drying up most of the money that goes to terrorism, we will significantly hinder the terrorists' ability to carry out elaborate operations – particularly their pursuit of the world's most deadly weapons.

Protection

After prevention, the second element of a strategy for homeland security is protection. We must invest far more resources in protecting the crucial infrastructure of our economy, financial systems, energy supplies, and computer networks. We must also tighten the security on our borders, transportation hubs and cities.

The task is daunting. The U.S. shares a 5,525 mile border with Canada and a 1,989 mile border with Mexico. Our maritime border includes 95,000 miles of shoreline and navigable waterways, as well as a 3.4 million square mile exclusive economic zone. Each year more than 500 million people enter the country legally, and some 330 million of those are non-citizens. In addition, our infrastructure is vast and the terrorists have an endless list of targets to choose from.

Currently, there is insufficient monitoring of the nation's 220,000 miles of railroads, 25,000 miles of waterways, and 1,000 harbors and channels. Add to that our many nuclear plants, countless skyscrapers, national monuments, stadiums and arenas and you begin to sense the enormity of the task. The problem for policymakers in protecting the homeland is that there are so many targets to attack and so many weapons that the terrorists can attack with – nuclear, biological, chemical, or conventional.

So while trying to improve all of our defenses, we must focus on the potentially catastrophic methods of attack and the most vulnerable targets. Setting priorities is tough, but we must do so if we are going to best deploy our resources for protection.

Transportation

In the wake of 9/11, transportation became the focus of added security. Air travel has now been fundamentally changed in this country, with more intrusive security measures, tighter regulation, and a greater law-enforcement presence in airports and planes. More sensitive detection machines are also coming on-line. These are important steps in addressing the vulnerability of relatively open American air travel that the terrorists exploited on September 11.

Still, there are disturbing reports of security breaches at American airports. Securing our airports and planes must not be a short-term priority if we truly want to ensure that something like 9/11 never happens again. We must also be resolute in protecting our other systems of transport – trains, subways and buses. The freedom of movement is an important American right and a foundation of our economy. We must protect this crucial foundation against another catastrophic attack.

Borders

We must also increase protection on our borders. It was disturbing to many Americans that several of the September 11 hijackers were in America legally despite the fact that they had been monitored abroad by various intelligence agencies. Even more disturbing was the revelation that several of their visas were still being processed by the I.N.S. months after the attack. This is unacceptable.

The U.S. has a proud tradition of openness to foreign visitors, but for years efficiency has trumped security. We should not close our borders or put up excessive barriers to entry, but me must improve our monitoring of cross-border traffic and of foreigners in the U.S. We must screen visa applicants with greater scrutiny and pursue foreign nationals who have overstayed their visas. The Department of Homeland Security will assume responsibility for reforming the INS, separating the agency's enforcement and service functions. This should increase the agency's ability to respond in a timely manner to visa requests, while making it easier to identify and pursue those in the U.S. who are a security threat.

We must also increase our ability to screen and verify the security of goods crossing our borders. In the past, we have been alerted to explosive materials being smuggled across the Canadian border, and we are increasingly aware of the threat posed by goods that enter the U.S. in shipping containers – consider that 90% of the world's cargo moves by container, 6 million containers enter the U.S. every year, and very few of these are screened.

We must establish security measures to identify high-risk containers, and pre-screen these containers before they enter U.S. ports. If we ignore this vital point of entry to our shores, shipping containers could prove to be an easy way for terrorist to smuggle dangerous materials – or people – into the U.S. Foreign exporters and their governments must be held to strict requirements regarding the security of goods entering the U.S. – they should supply detailed, verifiable information about the contents of the containers.

We must push the front-line of defense away from U.S. shorelines and increase the advance warning of ships entering U.S. ports. We have to work to establish a chain of custody for all cargo – this chain would assure that the container was packed in a safe environment, and that it was sealed and not tampered with, and that there was a certifiable shipper. This will involve an expanded U.S. Customs, Coast guard, and maritime inspectors under the auspices of the Department of Homeland Security.

Monitoring the movement of all these people and goods crossing our borders is indeed a monumental challenge. It involves intelligence, advanced inspection technology, government-industry partnerships, a well-trained workforce, and sophisticated systems to exchange and analyze mountains of data. But if we succeed in implementing tighter protection on our borders – with increased monitoring of the people and goods that enter our nation – then we will take an important step towards protecting ourselves against future attacks.

Infrastructure

Within our borders, we must identify our critical infrastructure and key assets and protect them from attack.

In order to do so, we must set priorities. We know that terrorists exploit vulnerabilities: they will be the ones to choose the location and method of attack, so we must deploy our resources to the most valuable elements of our infrastructure to protect against the most likely and damaging attacks.

We can define our critical infrastructure as assets whose destruction would cause a catastrophic crisis – to our physical and economic security, public health, or emergency response systems. For example, after 9/11 it became clear that there was not adequate security at our nuclear power plants. A successful attack on any of our nuclear resources could have devastating consequences, in loss of life and energy, and in environmental fallout. Since 9/11, we have significantly tightened security around these critical elements of our infrastructure. We have also acted on information regarding other potential targets, including bridges and dams.

In protecting our infrastructure, we must consider non-conventional targets. The national strategy for homeland security has identified cyberspace as a crucial target that must be secured against attack. Consider that the cost to our economy from attacks on our information systems has grown by 400% in four years. Far too many individuals or companies know how devastating it can be when information systems are penetrated or manipulated by outsiders. We also know that a single act of sabotage can cause extensive damage and disruption to our information systems, and the perpetrator doesn't even have to enter the United States to strike. We are therefore taking steps to secure our information and telecommunications infrastructure.

This effort involves cooperation between the federal and local governments, as well as cooperation between the public and private sectors. We must act to secure this vital sector of our economy. A good part of our infrastructure is transnational, and requires cooperation with our neighbors and allies. We share much of our energy infrastructure with Canada and Mexico in a vast system of pipelines and power connections. Thus, it is possible that a terrorist could deal a significant blow to our energy supply without entering the United States by striking in one of these neighboring countries.

We must therefore heighten our cooperation with our neighbors on securing infrastructure as well as borders. We cannot protect everything at once. But if we identify our vulnerabilities and our most critical assets, we can effectively deploy our resources to guard against the most likely, and most devastating, potential attacks.

Response

The third component of our homeland security strategy is response. In the event that there is a terrorist attack, we must be certain that our emergency response services are ready and able to respond. Nobody will forget the courage demonstrated by rescue workers who aided their fellow Americans on September 11. We must honor their commitment by ensuring that our local and federal response teams are fully prepared for any kind of attack, with the right equipment and the ability to coordinate an effective response.

We must also be prepared for new methods of attack. Do you know if your local hospital or law-enforcement can adequately respond to a conventional terrorist attack? What about a biological or chemical attack? It is the new threat of attacks with the world's most horrifying weapons that demands a significant upgrade in our response capabilities. The anthrax attacks of last fall demonstrated that we were not prepared for the threat of biological terrorism – our response was often confused and unnerving.

Since last year we have made some important improvements, as vaccines are being stockpiled for diseases such as smallpox. The best defense against a chemical or biological attack is good surveillance and detection, and the deployment of a rapid-response team. We must be able to immediately identify the nature of the attack, and then deploy our resources to minimize the damage.

Just as firefighters and police saved thousands of lives by evacuating people from the World Trade Center, the deployment of antibiotics, vaccines, or decontaminates to the location of a biological or chemical attack could save thousands of lives. Our primary goal, of course, must be to prevent terrorist attacks, but we must be prepared in the event that we are struck again. The three basic elements of our homeland defense are prevention, protection and security. The better we perform each task, the safer we will be.

So are we safer today than we were last September 11? One year after September 11, Americans are safer than they were. We have denied al Qaeda its base in Afghanistan and we have not been struck by the worst-case scenario of another catastrophic attack.

We can point to tangible steps that we have taken to improve our security at home. We have:

- expanded the screening of passengers and baggage in airports, and the use of air marshals on planes;
- restructured the FBI and CIA to focus on counter-terrorism;
- cracked down on terrorist assets around the globe;
- begun the process of creating a Department of Homeland Security;
- secured parts of our vital infrastructure;
- acquired new equipment and begun new training for response units;
- better secured our nuclear materials;
- taken steps to tighten our boarder controls with respect to the flow of people and goods; and

– stockpiled vaccines and drugs to counter certain biological attacks.

But we are still vulnerable in so many ways and in so many places, and we have not achieved many of our goals. Osama bin Laden is not captured or confirmed dead, much of the al Qaeda leadership is still at large, and the network is certainly operational and dangerous. Vice-President Cheney, Secretary Rumsfeld and FBI Director Mueller have all warned that we should expect further attacks. Americans are still fearful.

Challenges - Abroad

Abroad, we must continue to be resolute in hunting down al Qaeda and destroying the terrorist network, and we must enhance our commitment to bringing peace and stability to Afghanistan. We must not permit a return to the chaos and instability that made Afghanistan such a successful base for al Qaeda operations in the past. We must also refuse to let ourselves be distracted from our other foreign policy goals.

Settling the world's most intractable conflicts, bringing economic growth and democracy to the developing world, and maintaining productive relations with our allies will help eliminate the root causes of terrorism. We must keep in mind that bombs and guns alone cannot defeat global terrorism. We must also fight with the tools of peace: diplomacy, the rule of law, cultural exchange, economic growth, and good governance. By working to export our fundamental values of democracy, security, prosperity and human rights abroad, we will make ourselves safer at home.

In securing the homeland, we also have much more work to do. The reorganization of government that is under way is a solid step in the right direction. Defending the homeland is indeed a daunting task – terrorists have countless methods and an endless list of targets to attack, and plans for the new Department of Homeland Security will take years to implement.

Thus we must continue to have clear priorities. We must continue to determine what kind of attacks are most likely and what targets are most vulnerable, so that our personnel and resources are focused on the areas of greatest risk. If we use risk-assessment and intelligence to produce a strategy that encompasses prevention, protection and response, we can adapt our means of defense to face the terrorist threat.

Hard choices must be made as we go forward. Our resources are limited and our obligation is to be cost-effective. But by effectively managing our homeland defense, we can improve our security while getting other benefits from our investments – for example, improved emergency response systems will also help us to manage natural disasters and industrial accidents, and much-needed improvements in our preparation for biological attacks will strengthen the public health system.

The most important resource that we have in combating terrorism is public awareness. Americans have responded to that terrible morning with courage, compassion, strength and resolve. Across America, customs agents are more vigilant, local emergency services are more prepared, scientists are searching for vaccines and decontaminants, banks are cracking down on terrorist assets, and citizens are more alert.

The apprehension of the shoe bomber is perhaps the best example of our new commitment to security. Before September 11, people might not have been so attentive to strange behaviour on an airplane. Indeed, who would have predicted that somebody would attempt to ignite explosives in his shoes? By keeping the American people informed of the terrorist threat, we can ensure that an informed public will continue to be our best safeguard against uncertain threats.

Rights and Liberties

But as we improve our awareness and law enforcement capabilities, we must be careful to safeguard the very rights and liberties that we are fighting to defend. In wartime, presidents and law enforcement agencies naturally increase their capabilities to crack down on threats to national security. But some of the actions that the administration has taken are troubling. We see:

- the establishment of military tribunals that allow the executive branch to try people in secret;
- the interrogation and detention of thousands of Middle Eastern men, and secret deportations;
- vast new powers of domestic surveillance for the FBI and the CIA;
- authorized eavesdropping on lawyer-client conversations; and
- detainment of American citizens as 'enemy combatants' without a right to trial or counsel.

There are compelling reasons for some of the government's actions, but I worry that some of these actions are unnecessarily rolling back the very rights that we are fighting to protect. Both the President and the Congress – indeed, all of us – must appreciate more fully the risks to American liberty and to innocent people when the government assumes such wide and unchecked power. Congress must also be more willing to use its power of oversight to ensure that the powers of the government and law enforcement are employed judiciously and with a respect for civil liberties and individual rights.

Our crucial task is to ensure that this new era is not an era of fear and hatred, but rather an era of greater security: an opportunity to combat terrorism and protect democracy. The goals of security and liberty need not be mutually exclusive. On the contrary, closely guarding our liberty enhances our security; just as closely guarding our security protects our liberty. A victory over terrorism will require a successful effort to build a more peaceful and secure world while preserving our cherished freedoms at home.

8

Theory of Counterterrorism

The Proteus Monograph Series

The Proteus Monograph Series Fellows Program (PMSFP) funds research by scholars who are not affiliated with the U.S. Government and military. These scholars can be located either in the United States or abroad. This program is designed to support the Proteus Management Group's charter to promote further discourse, study, and research focusing on the refinement, development, and application of new and emerging "futures" concepts, methods, processes, and scenarios. The overarching goal of this effort is to provide value-added and relevant commentary that will assist strategic and high-operational level decision makers, planners, and analysts with "outside the box" considerations and critical analysis of national, military and intelligence issues within the Joint, Interagency, Intergovernmental, and Multinational (JIIM) environment.

The views expressed in this monograph are those of the author and do not necessarily reflect the official policy or position of the Department of the Army, the Department of Defense, the Office of the Director of National Intelligence, or the U.S. Government. This report is cleared for public release; distribution is unlimited.

This is a mathematics monograph about a nonmathematical subject. As a mathematics paper, we will include theorems and proofs. It is not expected that the non-mathematically-inclined reader will wade through these proofs, or even the more symbol-laden definitions or statements of theorems. We do hope, however, that no reader will be dissuaded by the more technical portions of this paper, that he instead will choose to pass over them if the waters appear too rough; and we hope that all readers will at least be able to appreciate our main conclusions, the definitions of *poset*, *cutset*, and *tree*, and our elucidation of the structure of the "perfect" tree. At the same time, we hope more mathematical audiences will forgive the simplicity and verbosity of our exposition. When we write statements like "let *b*e"2," we mean, "Let *b* be a positive integer greater than or equal to 2." If a set *S* has *k* elements, we write "$|S|=k$."

When U.S. Secretary of Defense Donald Rumsfeld was making the above statement, the RAND journal *Studies in Conflict and Terrorism* was already attempting to address his concern. Wars are composed of battles, so presumably the war on terror is composed—at least in part—of battles against terrorist cells. But how can one tell if those battles have been won? One could ask for the annihilation of the opposing side, but surely that is too crude a measure; Paris's Troy may have been sacked, but not Petain's Paris.

One could declare a battle won if the terrorist cell has not conducted an attack, but of course it is the *potential* for attack that is the chief concern. How can we measure that? In the first part of this paper, we will review a mathematical model for answering questions like this. This model has many shortcomings, but also perhaps some uses; details and suggestions for possible improvements will be found below.

But if one accepts the formalism of the model, with a few additional—and, we trust, reasonable—assumptions, one can ask, "What is the structure of the 'perfect' terrorist cell, the most robust terrorist cell, the cell that is least likely to be disrupted if a certain number of its members have been captured or killed?" This becomes a precise mathematical question, which we address in the latter part of this paper. Finally we propose additional mathematics problems engendered by our research; we hope government investigators, academics, and students will pursue them.

The Pentagon's New Math

In March 2006, *The New York Times* Magazine published an article entitled, "Can Network Theory Thwart Terrorists?" When terrorist cells are depicted schematically, they are often shown as structures called *graphs*. These are not the graphs readers may have plotted in high school algebra, but collections of dots (called *nodes*), representing individuals, and lines (called *edges*) between nodes, representing any sort of relationship between the two corresponding individuals, such as a direct communications link. In Krebs 2002, one finds graphs of the alleged September 11 hijackers, and Rodríguez 2005 contains graphs of the alleged Madrid bombers.

Of course a graph can represent any sort of social network, not just terrorists; for instance, your network of friends or the leadership of the U.S. government. Of course, the physical location of a node in the real world or on the page or screen is less relevant than data about which node is connected to which.

The usual game is to identify what nodes to remove (corresponding to capturing or killing an enemy agent) in order to break up or disrupt a terrorist cell. The network is now *disconnected*: it has been broken up into several components that are not themselves joined by lines. The network has been disrupted. Or has it? Consider the organization chart of a terrorist cell. In this, the top-to-bottom hierarchy is important: agents *A*, *B*, and *C* at the top of the picture are the leaders of the cell; agents *I*, *J*, and

K at the bottom of the picture are the foot soldiers. Even if we remove agents *E, G,* and *K* one quarter of the network there is still a complete chain of command from *A* down to *I* (through *D* and *F*). Presumably terrorist cell leader *A* could transmit attack plans down to foot soldier *I,* so the cell remains a threat. Even though it has been disconnected, it has not been "disrupted."

The above example illustrates one reason why the graph-theoretic perspective is inadequate. (Others can be found in Farley 2006.) More structure is needed: the actual hierarchy of the cell. A *partially ordered set,* or *poset,* is such a structure, and lattice theory is the branch of mathematics that deals with such structures. Below we will delve into posets in more detail, but first we give a brief overview.

A poset in our setting is just a fancy name for an organization chart. The nodes at the top represent the people at the top of the organization; the nodes at the bottom represent the people at the bottom. All a graph tells you is who is connected with whom. It does not say whether the middle figure is the boss or the subordinate. Partially ordered sets are not wholly unfamiliar creatures. The set of all numbers is a poset; equivalently, we could be looking at four military officers, a general, a colonel, a major, and a captain. (We call such simply ordered posets *chains.*) In fact, as with numbers, the notation "*a*d"*b*" is used to indicate that *a* is either the same person as *b* (*a*=*b*), or else *a* is a subordinate of *b* (*a*<*b*), albeit not necessarily an immediate subordinate.

The advantage of this type of abstraction is that we do not need to be concerned (at least, at this level of analysis) with the precise mode by which two individuals communicate by cell phone, email, Morse code, smoke signals, or ads in *The Washington Times* we are only concerned with whether or not two individuals do or do not directly communicate. So the new model is that terrorist plans are formulated by the nodes at the top of the organization chart or poset (the leaders or *maximal* nodes); these plans are then transmitted down via the edges to the nodes at the bottom (the foot soldiers or *minimal* nodes), who presumably execute those plans. The message, we assume, only needs to reach one foot soldier for damage to result.

For example, suppose the poset represents a courier network. Only one messenger needs to succeed in parlaying the message; but the message must get through. We endeavor to block all routes from the maximal nodes (any one of those nodes) to the minimal nodes (any one of them) by capturing or killing some subset of the agents. Note that the agents we remove need not be maximal *or* minimal. Such a subset is called a *cutset*. The set of k-member cutsets in a poset P is denoted Cut (P, k).

Imagine that the poset represents a system of pipes, down which water (information) may flow. Each node is a faucet, which can be on (letting water flow through) or off. If water only enters the system through the top, and all the faucets are initially on, we wish to find a collection of faucets to shut off so that no water drips off the bottom of the diagram. This cutset "cuts off" the flow of water, or, in the terrorism context, it cuts off the leaders from the foot soldiers. If k is a number, and k terrorists are killed or captured at random, the probability we have found a cutset (and hence disrupted the cell, according to our newer model) is the number of cutsets of size k divided by the total number of subsets of size k.

In the war on terror, how can we tell if we have won a battle? Gordon Woo, a Catastrophe Consultant for the company Risk Management Solutions, has suggested modeling terrorist cells as *graphs* or *networks*—that is, as collections of points or nodes connected by lines. The nodes represent individual terrorists, and a line is drawn between two nodes if the two individuals have a direct communications link.

The task of law enforcement is to remove nodes from a graph representing a terrorist cell by capturing or killing members of that cell so that its organizational structure is disrupted. Woo suggests modeling this idea mathematically by asking the following question: How many nodes must you remove from the graph before it becomes disconnected (that is, before it separates into two or more pieces)? We might call this the Connectedness Criterion.

If terrorist *A* is captured, the six remaining nodes are still connected and remain a cohesive whole. If, on the other hand, terrorists *E* and *G* are captured, then the graph breaks up into two parts that can no longer communicate directly with one another. There is a growing literature on modeling terrorist networks as graphs, an outgrowth of the existing literature concerning other types of criminal networks. There is also literature on destabilizing networks, modeled as graphs, by seeing how connections do or do not dissipate when nodes are removed.

Our view is that modeling terrorist cells as graphs does not give us enough information to deal with the threat. Modeling terrorist cells as graphs ignores an important aspect of their structure, namely, their hierarchy, and the fact that they are composed of leaders and of followers. It is not enough simply to seek to disconnect terrorist networks. For while doing so may succeed in creating two clusters of terrorists incapable of communicating directly with each other, one of the clusters may yet contain a leader and enough followers to carry out a devastating attack.

If terrorists *B* and *E* were captured, the remaining cell would certainly be disconnected. Indeed, the cell would be broken into three components. Nonetheless, there would still be a chain of command from the leader *A* down to two foot soldiers (*J* and *K*) capable of carrying out attacks. The proper framework for our investigations is therefore that of *order theory*. We do not merely want to break up terrorist networks into disconnected (non-communicating) parts.

We want also to cut the leaders off from the followers. If we do that, then we can reasonably claim to have neutralized the network.

Why does this matter? It may not always be feasible to capture *every* member of a terrorist cell. It may not even be cost-effective to capture a majority of the members. The analysis we present below will enable intelligence agencies to estimate better the number of terrorist agents they must eliminate in order to cripple a cell. That way they may decide—based on quantitative information—how many millions of dollars they wish to devote towards targeting a particular cell, or whether they wish to spend their scarce resources in another theater of operations in the war on terror.

Refinements of our ideas should enable intelligence agencies to state, for example, that they are 85% certain that they have broken the terrorist cell they are investigating. Of course, our definition of what it means to have "broken" a terrorist cell is something one could debate, for even lone actors—from the Unabomber to the Shoe Bomber—can inflict serious damage. And we recognize the fact that, even if we are 85% sure that we have broken a terrorist cell, there is still a 15% chance that we have not—and hence there remains a chance that terrorists might commit another September 11. Nevertheless, law enforcement and intelligence agencies must allocate money and personnel, and our analysis would enable them to do so more rationally than at present.

Breaking the Chains of Command

A common way to represent visually a group of people and the relationships between them is by means of a *graph* or *network*. We have seen several examples already. The individuals are represented by dots or nodes, and if two individuals are related in some fashion (for instance, if they are friends), then a line is drawn between the corresponding nodes. In the case of a terrorist cell, one might draw a line if the two individuals can communicate directly with one another.

A graph inadequately represents a terrorist cell, however, because it fails to capture the fact that, in any cell, there will most likely be a hierarchy—leaders and followers—with orders passed down from leaders to followers. All three graphs represent three people, Mary, James, and Robin. Mary can communicate to both James and Robin; Robin and James can each communicate only to Mary. What the graphs fail to capture is the fact that Mary might be the boss with two employees reporting to her, as in the middle picture, or Mary might be a secretary shared by two professors, as in the final picture. The last two pictures represent the same relationship-graph but different *ordered sets*.

Note that lines only connect individuals who are *directly* related to one another. It is unlikely that a general would communicate directly with a lieutenant. Of course a given general would normally have more than one colonel reporting to him, with neither colonel subordinate to the other, so in general we would not have a *total* order but a *partial* order. Is it valid to use ordered sets to model terrorist cells? In his study of criminal networks, Klerks argues that we should not assume that criminal networks are organized hierarchically simply because law enforcement agencies are so organized.

If we were to follow Klerks, we would not be so quick to model criminal networks as ordered sets. But while Klerks' conclusions may be valid for ordinary criminal networks, it seems as if terrorist networks *are* in fact organized hierarchically, sometimes even along military lines. Now suppose operations are being conducted against a specific terrorist cell. Short of capturing all of its members, how can we ascertain whether or not we have successfully disabled the cell? One criterion might be to say that a terrorist cell has been broken if it is no longer able to pass orders down from the leaders to the foot soldiers—the men and women who, presumably, would carry out the attacks. This is by no means the only possible criterion, but it enables us to make more reasonable quantitative estimates of the possibility that our operations have successfully disabled a terrorist cell.

The leaders are represented by the topmost nodes in the diagram of the ordered set, and the foot soldiers are represented by the bottommost nodes. (In order theory, these are called *maximal* and *minimal* nodes, respectively.) A chain of command linking a leader with a foot soldier is called a *maximal chain* in the ordered set.

We could also more simply write *CEFJ*.

Below we list all of the maximal chains:

ADFI ADFJ ADGI ADGK

AEFI AEFJ AEHJ

BEFI BEFJ BEHJ

CEFI CEFJ CEHJ

CK

Each of these chains represents a chain of command through which terrorist leaders *A*, *B*, and *C* could pass instructions down to terrorist foot soldiers *I*, *J*, and *K*. In order to prevent such orders from being passed down and carried out, each of these 14 chains must be broken by means of the removal (death or capture) of at least one agent from each chain. A collection of nodes that intersects every maximal chain is called a *cutset*.

Quantifying the Effectiveness of an Operation against a Terrorist Cell

In what way can law enforcement *quantify* how effective it has been in disrupting a particular terrorist cell? As we have stated, one way to make this precise is to say that a terrorist cell has been disrupted *not* when all of its members have been captured or killed (which might be too costly in terms of money, agents, and agents' time), but when all chains of command have been broken. That is, the collection of nodes in the network corresponding to the terrorists who have been killed or captured should be a cutset.

This enables us to *calculate*—not merely guess—the probability that a terrorist cell has been disrupted. Let T be a terrorist cell with *n* members (*n*=19 in the case of the alleged September 11 hijackers). Denote by Pr (T, *k*) the probability that T has been disrupted once *k* members have been captured or killed, where *k* is some whole number. Let Cut (T, *k*) be the number of cutsets in the ordered set T with *k* members.

Shortcomings of, and Possible Improvements to, the "Break the Chains" Model.

There are many ways our model could be improved. First, we do not consider the situation where there are several terrorists in a particular cell who have the same rank. (For instance, suppose two or more terrorists share the same apartment in Hamburg. All of them are in direct communication with one another, but none of them outranks the others.) This can be handled by considering *preordered* or *quasiordered* sets.

Second, we could consider the fact that terrorist operations take time. Perhaps agent *A* passed down plans to *B* on Monday, and on Tuesday *B* passed those attack plans down to C. Then there might still be an attack even though the cell was broken. Counterterrorist operations also take time. For instance, after *B*'s capture, the cell will be broken. But if too much time passes, the cell may reorganize. For a general ordered set, the collection of cutsets will change after reorganization. But, assuming the changes are local (that is, if they only involve a node and its neighboring nodes), this situation, too, can be handled with only a slightly more detailed analysis.

Instead of assuming that the terrorists are removed simultaneously and that terrorist plans are transmitted instantaneously, queuing theory might give us a better model, or perhaps we could do experiments like McGough 2005. Third, we assumed in our model that all the terrorists had an equal chance of getting captured. In reality, it may be the case that foot soldiers have the highest chance of being captured, since they are less well protected. Or it may be the case that leaders and foot soldiers are more likely to be captured than middle-level captains, since law enforcement might place a greater emphasis on capturing prominent leaders than middle-level ones. Our overall analysis, however, remains the same even if we vary the probability distribution.

And although we assume that every terrorist has the same chance of being captured, whereas in reality some would be hard to catch and some not, from the terrorists' point of view, even if the United States were to target, say, the leaders or the foot soldiers more, obviously the terrorists cannot predict who will be arrested next (or else they would be able to evade capture). The safest way for them to model the situation (if they wanted to design the perfect cell) would be in fact to assume a "uniform probability distribution." Another idea that stems from this is an interesting metric of the importance of an individual *X* in a cell: given that we have captured a cutset, what is the probability we have captured *X*?

Our model has more shortcomings. For instance, we do not necessarily know the structure of the particular terrorist cell under investigation. A priori, it could be any ordered set. A naive way around this might be to try to calculate Pr (T, k) for every possible ordered set T. This option is not feasible; however, as there are 4,483,130, 665,195,087 possible ordered sets to which a 16-member cell (for instance) might correspond.

In fact, the situation is not as bleak as that. The order structure of a terrorist cell T is an empirical question. Presumably intelligence sources can tell us who the leaders are, who the captains are, and who the foot soldiers are. There are also tools available for piecing together the structure of a terrorist network.

It is likely that terrorist cells are organized as *trees*, a common type of organizational structure. Trees have exactly one maximal element corresponding to the fact that a terrorist cell, like a military unit, probably has just one leader and no portion of a tree resembles the "V" structure. This corresponds to the fact that it is unlikely that a terrorist would have direct contact with more than one superior: if he were captured, he could give away information about several other conspirators more valuable than himself. Another argument is that only in a tree can you avoid the situation of non-complementary commands being issued to an agent from two different leaders.

Of course, there are still possible "tree" structures to which a 16-member cell might correspond (Sloane). We can eliminate most trees, however, as it is unlikely that a terrorist cell would have more than 20 or 0 members, and the hierarchy would probably have no more than 5 levels. This, along with empirical data concerning the cell under investigation, greatly reduces the number of possible order structures the cell might have.

Our model has more serious problems, however, namely its two assumptions. First, we assume that terrorist attacks occur when orders are passed down from leaders to foot soldiers. It may be instead that some terrorists act on their own (for instance, the so-called "Shoe Bomber"). This does not invalidate our model, though, as in these cases the terrorists are not properly part of a larger cell at all, but instead effectively form their own one-man cell.

Second, critics might charge that being 90% sure that a

cell has been broken may be dangerously misleading. Even a 10% chance that another September 11 might occur gives the public little comfort. Nonetheless, decisions do have to be made about how to allocate scarce resources in the war against terror, and even when terrorist attacks do succeed, intelligence agencies will want quantitative data at their disposal to defend themselves from the ensuing public criticism (concerning why they did not devote the resources necessary to foil the attack). Our model enables law enforcement to plan its operations in less of an ad hoc fashion than they might be able to do otherwise.

One issue that deserves attention is the problem of redundancy. We know that it is good to safeguard a system by adding redundant components (although caution is urged by Perrow 1984). In most of our examples, if you remove a terrorist, no other terrorist has precisely the same connections as the removed individual. Where is the redundancy in our model? We have already said that redundancy could be incorporated by using quasiordered instead of partially ordered sets, but in fact redundancy already exists: the mere existence of multiple chains of command by which terrorist plans could be transmitted represents redundancy.

Laura Donohue has objected to this sort of model by asking how one distinguishes between the very different types of terrorist organizations, from the KKK and Al Qaeda to the IRA. It is true that there is much that "pure" models fail to take into account. (We do not, for instance, get into how the cell members communicate or cryptological matters.) It would be very interesting to see if data could be found relating to this issue. But our response is that we are not trying to precisely describe reality (although we believe our assumptions are not unduly unrealistic). That task is for experts in fields like cultural anthropology, psychology, criminology, and intelligence. We are merely trying to provide decision-making tools to people in law enforcement and intelligence, something better than guessing.

Of Terrorists and Trees

In this section we will begin to try to determine the structure of the perfect terrorist cell. There are two arguments in favor of trying to do this. The first is that, where we do have gaps in our knowledge of the structure of a cell, it is best to fill them in with the best possible structure it is better to assume that terrorists are smart rather than stupid. (They may also have discovered the ideal structure through evolutionary processes.) Perhaps this will help us see into the shadow when drawing the map of terrorist networks.

The second relates to the possibility that, by studying our work, terrorists could learn the most effective ways to organize. That, however, could be to our benefit because, if they do, it will decrease the possible number of organizational schemes from, say, 4 quadrillion (the number of ways a 16-member cell could organize) to something far more manageable and far easier to analyze. As with a jigsaw puzzle, the range of possibilities that law enforcement would need to consider would be reduced so that, when they capture someone, they might be able to deduce where he could fit in the organization. Given all the assumptions of the previous section, our task translates into the following mathematical question:

Question. What partially ordered set with n elements (members) has the fewest cutsets of size k?

The answer is trivial: an *antichain,* a poset with n members such that no two are connected by lines. This is so because each member is both a leader and a foot soldier, and so constitutes a maximal chain all by himself. Hence, to break all the chains of command, you have to capture all n members. Therefore, there are no cutsets of size k if $k<n$, and (exactly) one if $k=n$. (Every poset of size n has exactly one cutset of size n, namely the entire poset.)

As long as the poset has at least two members, however, the antichain is disconnected; there are at least two parts that are for all intents and purposes independent. It seems as if a terrorist cell ought to be a *connected* poset.

A simple way to avoid having a disconnected poset is to have the (almost) "flat" structure– one leader with n-1 (say, 18) followers: Unless you capture the leader, you must capture *all* the followers. But this may be unrealistic as well: it may be hard for one person to manage a large number of immediate subordinates. Moreover, it is reasonable to suppose that the more direct links you have with other terrorists (the greater the *degree* of the node, in graph theory parlance), the greater the likelihood of betrayal: any one of the 18 could be captured and give you away. Moreover, it may be the case that terrorists would not even want to take the small—but appreciable—risk that the whole cell could unravel with the capture of a single person.

So another reasonable assumption is that there should be a (small) bound b on the number of immediate subordinates each person can have.

Definition. Let *be*"1. A poset is *b-ary* if no member has more than b immediate subordinates. If b=2, we call such a poset *binary*.

Example. The poset is binary. Note we are not saying that every element must have exactly b immediate subordinates. The poset is ternary but not binary. Of course the poset is binary, but seems unrealistic because half the cell members are "leaders." So perhaps there should be a (small) bound on the number of leaders as well. We will not necessarily assume that a cell has a single leader, which brings us a surprise: Which of the posets is better? (The reader may wish to pause to consider this before continuing.)

Let us count the cutsets. It helps to have the following notation.

Notation. Let Cutsets (*a*1, *a*2, *a*3, *a*4, *a*5) denote the number of cutsets of size 1, 2, 4, 5, respectively.

To calculate cutsets, it often helps to know the *minimal* cutsets. These are subsets that are just barely cutsets: no smaller subset of a minimal cutset is a cutset.

Example. The poset (ii) has minimal cutsets: 2 of size 2 (*ab* and *ae*) and 1 of size 3(*cde*). The cutset *cde* is minimal because none of *cd, ce,* or *de* is a cutset. (For example, the maximal chain *ae* misses *cd*, showing that *cd* is not a cutset.)

We will use the vector notation just established for minimal cutsets as well. (For us a "vector" is just a sequence of numbers.) So for the poset, we write Min Cutsets (1, 0,0,1,0) to indicate that there is 1 minimal cutset of size 1 (the leader), and 1 of size 4 (capture all 4 of the followers).

In his essay "Lewis F. Richardson's Mathematical Theory of War," Anatol Rapoport observes, "A mathematical model is more characteristically a point of departure rather than a point of arrival in the construction of a theory," adding, "the builder of a mathematical social science must virtually pull assumptions out of his hat." Models can always be made more sophisticated, but the modeler should nonetheless endeavor to avoid the mistake of Lewis Carroll's mapmaker. There are also other aspects besides reliability that one might wish to optimize for, such as susceptibility to betrayals. With our assumptions, we have found that the *n*-member terrorist cell organized as a *b*-ary tree is least likely to be disrupted when it is structured like the special pure *b*-ary fishbone poset (of Corollary A0.1 or A0.2, when *b* equals 2).

It would now be interesting to see if examples could be found of terrorist or insurgent networks organizing in this way. It would also be interesting to see how much better the "perfect" or most efficient cell structure is than other common cell structures. Our ideas could be pushed further, to handle more general categories of cell structures, not just (binary) trees. And of course, if our assumptions are accepted, the same ideas could be applied to designing the "perfect" organizational structure for counterinsurgency teams. Wein suggests that perhaps government forces could do a game-theoretic analysis: given that the terrorists form the "perfect" cell, what are the optimal ways of combating it. Paté-Cornell adds that perhaps there should be multiple layers of links, representing different types of networks (communications, financial, etc.), and some sort of scale to indicate the intensity of the link (whatever that is).

Terrorism is not an academic subject. When academics suggest new tools for combating terrorism, we should be skeptical. This is especially true when it comes to an abstruse field such as mathematics and, in particular, order theory.

Yet it remains true that, in the war on terror, decisions have to be made quantitative decisions, concerning the allocation of resources, money, and manpower. Our methods should help law enforcement and intelligence agencies make these decisions or at least give them credible arguments with which to defend their decisions before the public and congressional oversight committees.

Our tools help answer the question, "Have we disabled a terrorist cell, or is it still capable of carrying out attacks?" While we cannot answer such a question with certainty, our methods help us determine the probability that we have disrupted a particular terrorist cell.

We treat the cell $\tilde{\mathbf{A}}$ as an *ordered set*, a network with a built-in hierarchy (leaders, foot soldiers, and so on). We say that a terrorist cell has been rendered incapable of carrying out attacks if we have *broken the chains of command*, that is, disrupted every possible line of communication between leaders and foot soldiers. We do this by capturing or killing terrorists who collectively form a *cutset* of the ordered set. By counting all of the cutsets with k members in T, we can compute the probability Pr (T, k) of disrupting T by capturing or killing k of its members.

In conclusion, while the model can be improved, we do not believe our assumptions do too much violence to the real world. We hope others can use our approach to help reduce violence in the real world.

Counting Cutsets in Complete Binary Trees

Let us consider the complete binary trees with n=2m-1 members. When m=3, we have n=7. The minimal cutsets are as follows:

Minimal 1-member cutset: *a*

Minimal 2-member cutset: *bc*

Minimal 3-member cutsets: *bfg cde*

Minimal 4-member cutset: *defg*

Let us see how to calculate the number of m-member cutsets. (Recall that m=3.) Remember that every cutset must contain one of the five minimal ones. We will try to list all the cutsets that contain *a*; then all the cutsets that contain *bc* but not *a*; then all the cutsets that contain *bfg* but not *a* or *bc*; then all the cutsets that contain *cde* but not *a*, *bc*, or *bfg*; then all the cutsets that contain *defg* but not *a*, *bc*, *bfg*, or *cde*. Note that any subset containing a cutset is also a cutset. *The 3-member cutsets containing* a. Any subset containing *a* is a cutset, so we can take *a* and any 2 of the remaining 6 members of the tree; so that are 6C2=15 such cutsets.

Of course the war on terror is not simply about battling terrorist cells, or even networks of cells, as one reader of this manuscript has noted: a more important goal is to stop the propagation of terrorist cells, or even to eliminate the causes of terrorism itself. It is not even an accurate measure. Algeria defeated France, even though the French lost 15,000 soldiers and the Algerians nearly one million.

Note that we are not talking about battling terrorist cells that have already received their orders and are completely prepared to execute them; in such cases there may no longer be a need for any further communication.

We are talking about terrorist cells that are in the process of hatching plots that still require communication within the cell in order for the plans to be carried out. Keefe (2006) in this monograph, the words "network" and "cell" have the same meaning. We represent both with the mathematical concepts of *graph* or *poset* (technical terms with distinct meanings, to be defined later). In the terrorism literature, the term "network" is often taken to mean (although often it is not spelled out) a loose, non-hierarchically-organized confederation of individuals, usually wide-ranging, as in the term "the global Al Qaeda network," or the phrase, "It takes a network to fight a network".

When we speak of cells or networks, by contrast we *will* mean a hierarchical structure close to the ground, like the nineteen alleged September 11 hijackers. Of course, one might try to handle the situation of multiple cells that might be coupled in some way. Technically a poset is a set with a binary relation that is reflexive, transitive, and antisymmetric. In this paper, all posets are finite (a statement known as Trotter's Axiom). Of course it goes without saying that law enforcement would be able to do much more if they did know the mode by which terrorists communicated and could intercept messages.

Alternatively, we could focus on the communications links between nodes and seek to sever (or redirect) these. It would be worthwhile to do the "link" analysis; the mathematics involved would be similar to what we do here. In fact, one ought to consider the result of removing both nodes and links together. Again, this only means the cell would be unable to carry out new plans, plans that still required communication from above. The cell could still perhaps carry out plans that had already been disseminated.

One could also ask for the number of *edges* that need to be removed in order for the graph to become disconnected, or the number of nodes and edges. A reader of a draft of this manuscript emphasizes that one could focus on edges. Removing edges would be tantamount to preventing terrorists from communicating—for instance, by blocking certain cell phones or crashing jihadist websites. Focusing on edges also enables one to track the nodes—the senders and receivers of messages—and possibly to "hijack" lines of communication so as to send confusing, false, or misleading information.

We choose to focus on nodes instead of edges since the mathematics involved is virtually the same, and hence what we do here could be easily mimicked for edges; but our intuition is that, from a practical standpoint, there are so many lines of communication available to terrorists that it might be impossible to block all the ways one terrorist could communicate with another without having a fix on the terrorists themselves. Indeed, according to the United States Defense Department's transcript of the video allegedly made by Osama bin Laden, in which he says, "Those who were trained to fly didn't know the others.

One group of people did not know the other group." One might infer, therefore, that at that low level in the network, the clusters of nodes corresponding to the hijackers were already disconnected. But they posed a danger because it was still possible for orders to filter down from above: According to the tape, "[T]hey were trained and we did not reveal the operation to them until...just before they boarded the planes." We make no claims about the authenticity of the video or the accuracy of the transcript.

Order theory does not preclude looking at edges; indeed, in a partially ordered set, the partial order relation—essentially, the set of edges—is at least as important as the set of nodes. See Conclusions for how to incorporate an analysis of edges—and our estimate of their strength and nature—in order to construct a better estimate of the likelihood that a cell has been disrupted. These are sets with a binary relation that is reflexive and transitive but not necessarily antisymmetric.

Of course, understanding how terrorist cells "heal"—that is, recruit new members, acquire new leaders when old ones are captured, with intermediate captains moving up in the hierarchy—requires looking at empirical data. For instance, how long does it take for a communications link to reform, or for nodes to be replaced? The author would like to thank an attendee of one of his talks for suggesting an idea close to this. Chin Peng believes Malayan communist Lee Meng was captured by the British because she was not "made to undertake only one specific task at a time. Either she should operate only as a courier under the direction of the Central Committee, or, she should be restricted to guerrilla activities under the state committee."

In the case of the alleged September 11 hijackers, for instance, it was not enough for the commands to get through to one person, since a team of four or five was needed to hijack an aircraft. In cases like this, a single minimal node (or a single equivalence class in a quasiorder) might correspond to four or five individuals. Also, as Earl Burress (personal communication 2006) has suggested, a terrorist cell might want to maximize the chance that paths to at least two minimal nodes remain unbroken.

The case of the jumbo jet that crashed in New York City in November 2001 was regarded as an accident and not an Al Qaeda attack because it was a solitary incident; three planes striking their targets on September 11, 2001, however, could not be so dismissed. On the other hand, US Federal Aviation Administration counterterrorism expert Bogdan Dzakovic states, "If I was a terrorist mastermind plotting another big attack...and I could muster up another 20 guys, I'd scatter them around to different airports around the country. I would give each one of them three bombs and three different sets of luggage. Some of those bombs will make it onto flights." This suggests that perhaps our model—where only one maximal chain need be left unblocked—is not so far off the mark.

We are perhaps being too neglectful of redundancy in *communications*—for instance, a website could be used as a backup in case there is a breakdown in cell phone communications—which could be represented by having multiple links between two nodes. This, as a reader points out, might be viewed as the key, since how cell members communicate relates directly to how vulnerable they are to message interception and surveillance.

We will not discuss the ideal size of a terrorist cell based on what functions the cell needs to perform (although, as one commentator has suggested, this could be incorporated into our model). We will try to determine the ideal structure of a terrorist cell *given* that it has a certain size. Also, the edges add another layer of complexity, as in reality there could be multiple edges, two-way edges, etc., which we do not consider here.

Academics will appreciate the difficulty of managing 18 graduate students simultaneously. To calculate the number of cutsets, you often need to know more than just the *number* of minimal cutsets. This leads us to consider how terrorist cells adapt once it is discovered that their structure is known and hence they cannot be as effective as they would desire. Ideas from reflexive control or game theory should also be utilized to see how a terrorist cell balances its goals of minimizing the number of cutsets and keeping its structure relatively unknown. Farley discusses the use of cellular automata and the mathematics of diffusion processes; in future work we hope to draw on mathematical models of tumor formation to see how we might describe the transformation of a terrorist cell as it is being attacked. We also hope to use tools from mathematical epidemiology in order to model the long-term spread of radical ideologies, viewed as a contagion infecting a population.

Guerrilla forces of the Malayan Communist Party, however, were jointly headed by two individuals. The poset is a tree according to *graph* theory, however. A *graph* is a tree if between any two nodes there is exactly one way to get from one to the other. See the directions for further research at the end of the monograph. We actually have not checked to see if complete binary trees do not have the most maximal chains, nor have we confirmed that there is a relationship between the number of cutsets and the number of maximal chains.

Note that there is no reason to believe—just a hope—that there is a "best" binary tree, or that there is a "best" tree for all sizes of cutsets. A priori, for trees with 15 members, there may be *several* trees that have the smallest possible number of 7-member cutsets, and another set of trees that have the smallest possible number of 8-member cutsets. (Whether or not this is true, we shall see later.)

John Stembridge's main contribution to the theory of ordered sets has been to develop Maple packages and a database of small posets. This could be used for Problem 1. Every finite poset with a single leader has a spanning tree that is also a tree as a poset: Let the *dual rank* of a member x of a finite poset be the size of the largest maximal chain in the subposet of elements bigger than x. For each element of dual rank k erase all connections to immediate superiors except for one that connects to an immediate superior of dual rank k-1. The resulting structure is a tree, even with the same dual rank function. One might naively believe that a four-crown tower with an additional leader added on would be a binary poset with fewer cutsets than its spanning trees, since it has so many maximal chains. This is false, however. The four-crown tower with 4 members has cutset vector (0, 2, 4, 1). The four-crown tower with 6 members has cutset vector: The cutsets consist of the cutsets of the four-crown tower with 4 members, and either none or one of the new leaders; or both of the leaders along with *any* subset of the remaining four members.

9

The Threat of Terrorism

In the fall of 2002, the Indonesian island of Bali, once known for its luscious beaches and vibrant Hindu culture, became synonymous with terror and radicalism. After a massive bombing in Bali's nightclub district killed more than 200 people, the world suddenly realized what many locals had known for years: Indonesia, the largest Muslim nation on Earth, faced a serious internal terror threat. Even before the Bali attack, Indonesia had suffered a wave of bombings in the winter of 2000, and earlier that year someone had bombed the Jakarta Stock Exchange. The Al Qaeda affiliate Jemaah Islamiah was actively recruiting across the archipelago, establishing radical schools to train a young generation of jihadis and planning attacks in Indonesia and throughout the region, including in the Philippines and Thailand.

But today, Indonesia has become a far different kind of example. Even as terrorism continues to grow more common in nations from Pakistan to Algeria, Indonesia is heading in the opposite direction, destroying its internal terrorist networks and winning the broader public battle against radicalism. And it has done so not only by cracking heads but by using a softer, innovative plan that employs former jihadis to wean radicals away from terror.

Indonesia's successes are striking. Once a threat capable of waging war across Southeast Asia, Jemaah Islamiah is in a shell today. Indonesian authorities have captured most of its top leaders, including the deputy commander who allegedly helped plan the Bali attacks. Indonesian police have overrun JI's operational bases, forcing most of its members to live on the run, making it harder for them to plan bombings. Indonesia has suffered no major terror attacks in two years, and JI's ability to raise money and find recruits has been shattered. "There is not much of JI left," Indonesia terrorism authority Kenneth Conboy told reporters.

To be sure, effective police work has made a difference. Backed by U.S. training and high-end surveillance equipment, Indonesia's elite counter-terrorism squad has established an effective internal intelligence network, relying on informants to point the way to terrorist hide-outs and arresting hundreds of JI members. But if they really hoped to reduce the pool of possible new recruits for groups like Jemaah Islamiah, Indonesian leaders realized they had to win public support for their battle. Otherwise, police could arrest or kill hundreds of militants, and new radicals would just take their place.

To win militants' hearts and minds, Indonesia instituted a program called deradicalization. Realizing that hard-core militants will not listen to prominent Muslim moderates, whom they view as soft, as irreligious or as tools of the government, the deradicalization initiative employs other militants — former terrorist fighters or trainers. These are men like Nasir Abas, once a Jemaah Islamiah leader, who have sworn off most types of violence. Former fighters who agree to help the deradicalization program often receive incentives, such as reduced sentences or assistance for their families.

The co-opted radicals are sent as advocates into Indonesian prisons, major breeding grounds of militants. In the jails and other sites, they work to convince would-be terrorists that attacking civilians are not acceptable in Islam, to show that terror actually alienates average people from their religion, to suggest that the police are not anti-Islam and to exploit internal antagonisms within terror networks to turn militants against each other.

These intense debates, which rely partly on Koranic scholarship, can last for months. Meanwhile, other former militants appear on Indonesian television to express remorse for having killed their countrymen and women. The deradicalization program already has delivered. According to a recent report by the independent, nonprofit International Crisis Group, the Indonesian plan has "persuaded about two dozen members of Jemaah Islamiah ... to cooperate with the police."

Deradicalization could work far beyond Southeast Asia. In 2004, Saudi Arabia launched its own version of deradicalization. Under the Saudi version, militants in jail who agree to undergo intense classroom sessions receive shorter sentences. The sessions, designed to convince extremists that Islam does not condone terror, come combined with psychological deprogramming. The deprogramming resembles techniques used on cult members, and it also allows psychologists to assess whether militants are joining the deradicalization program just to be released and return to extremism. Police then follow up with extremists who have completed the program and been released from jail to ensure that they do not return to their old ways.

Saudi officials say the program has been very successful. Major terrorist attacks in Saudi Arabia have plummeted compared with 2004. The Saudi plan also appears to have a broader regional impact. Gen. David Petraeus, commander of U.S. forces in Iraq, has said that the Saudi initiative may be one reason for the sharp decline in the number of foreign fighters coming into Iraq. Other countries have created variants on the program. Egypt has established a deradicalization initiative in which former jihadist thinkers argue that the Islamic concepts that militants use to justify violence are wrong. Singapore, Malaysia, Jordan and Yemen have enacted reeducation strategies, often focusing on prison populations. Drawing on Jakarta's experience, nations such as Pakistan have launched deradicalization cooperation with Indonesia.

Even Western nations facing radical threats seem to be learning. The Netherlands this summer announced it would spend the equivalent of $40 million to launch deradicalization programs, train imams and other religious leaders and promote intercultural dialogue. In perhaps the most sweeping Western initiative, Britain, stunned by a wave of terror attacks committed by British citizens, has attempted to build far deeper relationships with domestic Muslim groups, relying on them to help deradicalize potential young militants who could be transformed into suicide bombers.

"Our strategy of funding and engagement must shift significantly toward those organizations that are taking a proactive leadership role in tackling extremism," declared British Cabinet minister Ruth Kelly last year. In other words, Britain has finally learned what Indonesia already knew.

To fight terror groups with such lineage, creative capabilities, and adaptability with military power alone is to ignore the lessons of history and ignore the realities of today's world. The Iraq Study Group Report sought to bring our effort to realign our national interest in the Iraq conflict into a more integrated dimension in which all elements of national power are used to more effective ends. Extrapolated and expanded, the Report should be reworked to apply against the global war against terrorists and extremism. Increased multilateral diplomatic and economic initiatives, out-of-the-box analytical approaches, increased linguistic and cultural capabilities in government agencies are just a few of the subjects addressed by the recommendations included in the Report that are applicable to this war at large.

Indeed the type of effort represented by the Iraq Study Group project in which bipartisan public sector practitioners with collective experience in all domains of government participate should be a regular feature of our policy establishment as we move forward in the 21st century. The addition of public and private sector personalities with appropriate experience would be a valuable innovation to U.S. foreign policy formulation. There are some signs that this may slowly be taking place.

The fact that we have been so flat-footed in this war is a sad commentary on our current abilities to manage complexity in the modern world. The national power element of information is an instructive example. We are the nation that invented the Internet and developed the fundamental techniques of mass communications. Yet in spite of this, we now face an adversary that makes maximum use of the Internet to promote a militant ideology, command and control forces, raise funds, and attract recruits. In addition, they use it to bring the war to our desktops in the way that television brought the Vietnam War into our living rooms. In a way that seems to elude us, they have managed to bring Marshall McLuhan's vision of the global village to a new level.

Much of the militants' ideology gains traction by default simply because no one refutes it. Their most outrageous claims are believed because we have no systematic effort to put the lie to them. Despite years of a continuing problem in this regard, we still have no comprehensive interagency strategic communications strategy. The absorption of the U.S. Information Agency into the State Department in 1999 left the country without an effective capability to promote our messages just as the need became the greatest. Multiplying adversaries and new communications technologies made the case for a new approach to strategic communications more important than ever.

After 911, we paid a steep price for our inability to effectively communicate. Karen Hughes' valiant efforts notwithstanding, public diplomacy in the face of such a skilled adversary demanded more than ad agency skills as she has painfully learned. It also costs money. Hollywood productions routinely cost hundreds of millions of dollars to produce but the government is loath to spend on a similar scale to exploit new and old media to promote U.S. policy. There are glimmers of hope on the horizon. Public and private efforts are slowly taking up the challenge but not as fast as they should to counter our nimble adversaries.

The Center for the Study of the Presidency is now laying the groundwork for the creation of a proposed Foundation for International Understanding which would harness all forms of media to promote understanding, respect, and shared learning across borders and cultures, with a special focus on reaching young people across the world. To reach broad and diverse audiences, the FIU would support a wide range of media productions including television and radio programming and new media applications such as webcasts, podcasts, educational video games, content for cell phone and other mobile media devices, and international video-conferencing.

It would respond to new challenges in understanding and tolerance, and to innovations in today's technology-driven media and entertainment markets. The FIU would not produce or distribute programming itself but would promote and seed efforts globally through grant awards. It would become to public and private diplomacy efforts what the National Science Foundation is to scientific research. The Language Corps, an initiative announced in May 2007 by the Department of Defense, seeks to address the dire need for language and cultural capabilities throughout the government. In a three-year pilot program, DoD will take the lead in organizing a civilian volunteer program that will draw upon language skills of the general population.

The Corps will be composed of members who volunteer to serve for a predefined period in times of national emergency for all agencies of government. Drawing upon the linguistic diversity that is an integral part of American culture, the Language Corps aims to bridge the language preparedness gap throughout the government, give citizens an opportunity to contribute in times of national need, and reinforce the importance of language skills in the United States, especially in the educational system. This creative program leverages America's unique strengths and intellectual capital and is precisely the type of approach so sorely need in confronting our current unconventional adversary.

Other private NGO's, or non-governmental organizations, are undertaking similar creative approaches. Bill Drayton's Ashoka Foundation, which conceived of "social entrepreneurship" by applying the venture capital model to social innovation worldwide, is already a known quantity in the innovative development world. The Kroll Foundation's Social Edge online community of social entrepreneurs and supporters is exploiting technology to create global networks to share ideas and best practices to further promote social entrepreneurship. Greg Mortenson's Central Asia Foundation is forging partnerships with locals under the most demanding circumstances in Pakistan, Afghanistan, and other Central Asian locations to build girls' schools. Mortenson has been so successful that graduates of his first schools have now trained teachers for newer schools educating newer generations of female students.

This type of development activity is what democracy is made of. In their groundbreaking work on the impact of culture on political and social development, Ronald Inglehart of the University of Michigan and Christian Welzel of the International University Bremen have quantified the effects of economic development on social change and the evolution of democracy in traditional societies. One of their most significant findings is that survival level needs must be met on an individual level before the group dynamics of civil society can begin to manifest themselves as a prelude to the adoption of democratic systems. Inglehart, the Chairman of the World Values Survey Association, presides over a network of social scientists that have carried out surveys measuring social values and attitudes in over 80 countries since 1981.

It is this data on which their work is based. The implications of their work are staggering because it shows that our foreign policy obsession with elections as a prelude to democracy adoption puts the cart before the horse. It show that individuals must feel secure and be open to interpersonal trust before they can begin the civil society implementation that leads to open and reliable institutions that, in turn, lead to democratic elections. This is a reality our adversaries know all too well. By providing the social services lacking in many parts of the world, militant Islamists and others create a feeling of individual security that they then manipulate for political ends.

In Iraq and Afghanistan, we have managed to do the opposite. We have violated almost every element of the survival imperative and then forced elections which paved the way for election victories by Islamic radicals and warlords who are enforcing the peace locally, as harsh as their methods may be. Our traditional method of elite-to-elite diplomacy is clearly not up to the task of countering our adversaries in the post-cold war world. Conducting this traditional type of private diplomacy from embassy and consulate fortresses far from the public eye, many embassy staffs appear remote and distant from the citizens of the countries in which they serve.

One of Condoleeza Rice's first actions as Secretary of State was to issue a directive assigning more State Department personnel further out from the capitals of their countries' missions. This was a good start but more needs to be done to match the comprehensive social and cultural depth of our adversaries. While we dispense more foreign assistance than any other nation on earth, we often hand it over to host country governments or organizations like the UN who dispense it while the U.S. government remains invisible. There must be more direct involvement by U.S. representatives at all levels to demonstrate that American foreign policy involves more than writing checks and, as our adversaries claim, bullying innocent populations with military force.

One enduring institution that accomplishes this objective is the Peace Corps. Since 1961, it has sent Americans to the developing world where they serve at those levels of society in which traditional diplomatic efforts were absent. Originally conceived to win hearts and minds during the cold war, over 187,000 Americans have passed through its ranks and served as volunteers often under the most trying circumstances. As a public diplomacy asset, the Peace Corps is probably the most cost effective tool in the U.S. soft power tool kit. And as a Brooking Institution brief noted in 2003, "its cost is miniscule."

Today there are 7,749 volunteers serving in 73 countries, with an annual budget of $318.8 million. That works out to a net cost of $41,140 per volunteer – a bargain compared to other government programs. Despite the Bush administration's proposal in 2003 to double the size of the Peace Corps to 14,000, it has remained static since then. Its effectiveness is constrained by this limited scope despite the fact that it is an established "brand" in the limited U.S. repertoire of people-to-people public diplomacy. The Peace Corps yields other benefits that are perhaps its strongest suite. The third objective of the Peace Corps states that returned Peace Corps volunteers share their experiences and knowledge of their countries of service with their fellow citizens once they return home – and this is a lifelong commitment.

In this era of globalization, citizens with intimate knowledge of foreign cultures and languages are crucial to an informed electorate in our own democracy. Kevin Quigley, the President of the National Peace Corps Association, which is the national association of Peace Corps veterans, hopes to use the power of modern communications technologies to put this collective experience to greater use. He proposes to establish online communities to facilitate communications between current and former Peace Corps volunteers and people in their countries of service in a dramatic digital people-to-people initiative. This type of public diplomacy is exactly the type of creative effort needed to put the lie to the type of anti-American misinformation that is so central to our adversaries' propaganda.

If people in their target audiences could immediately verify the veracity, or lack thereof, of the numerous canards that are promoted daily by adversarial information conduits, it would foster a wholesale exchange of ideas that could greatly benefit forces of moderation and diminish extremists' arguments. Asked recently about the disjointed governmental activities in the war on terror, Center for the Study of the Presidency President David Abshire – a man with over 50 years of experience in the military and foreign policy establishments – responded by pointing to a passage from Abraham Lincoln's second annual address to Congress in 1862: "The dogmas of the quiet past are inadequate to the stormy present. The occasion is piled high with difficulty, and we must rise with the occasion.

As our case is new, so we must think anew, and act anew." Indeed, an integrated approach marshalling all instruments of national power and the creativity of the nation is required if we are to prevail. Hard military power, necessary to this effort and carried out by the brave few, needs to be matched by soft power efforts from all corners of government. Former Australian Army colonel and current US advisor David Kilcullen recently wrote an incisive analysis of our current security challenge in an article entitled New Paradigms for 21st Century Conflict. In it, he argues that our current adversary challenges almost every paradigm upon which our foreign policies and security policies are predicated.

He concludes that "finding new, breakthrough ideas to understand and defeat these threats may prove to be the most important challenge we face." More importantly, these breakthroughs need to be managed and synchronized with a coherency that matches the task so that our ideas and policies are effective through attraction rather than coercion. Almost six years after the September 11 attacks, seven years after the USS Cole attack, nine years after the bombings of US embassies in Kenya and Tanzania, 14 years after the first World Trade Center attack, 24 years after the Beirut embassy and Marine barracks bombings, and 28 years after the Iranian revolution, we are still groping to come to terms with a set of adversaries that grows increasingly lethal with every passing year.

Like Gulliver, we find ourselves held hostage by what policy makers thought were weaker, inferior adversaries. Despite our strength, we have been unable to marshal all the elements of national power – diplomatic, economic, information, and military - effectively, preferring to rely on military strength to defeat seemingly weaker enemies. If using all the instruments of U.S. national power is like conducting an orchestra, we are trying to play a symphony with only the percussion section in executing the war against extremists and terrorists. Judged in light of achieving strategic and tactical objectives, our primary reliance on hard military power has been a failure by most measurements.

Iraq is bringing chaos to the region, Afghanistan is lawless without an effective government, Al-Qaida's leadership is still out there, and a violent, religious-based ideology is gaining more adherents by the day throughout the world, including in Western countries. This is certainly not to question the significant role and successes of the military in the greater war against the terrorists and extremists we now face. But we are obviously witnessing the limits of military power as we know it. These limitations were exemplified by the fanfare with which the "shock and awe" doctrine was promoted as the basis of our strategy in the run up to the Iraq war. The term "shock and awe" has become synonymous with the use of overwhelming force, especially massive bombardment, since it was trumpeted as an innovative military strategy at the beginning of the Iraq war.

Coming on the heels of an impressive projection of military power in Afghanistan in 2001, it held forth high hopes that the Iraq war could be won quickly and with a minimum of troops on the ground. Harland Ullman, the former naval officer and professor at National Defense University who is a coauthor of the concept along with James Wade, now says that the term was misunderstood and erroneously described by the press at the time. He says that the strategy actually involves doing anything to undermine the enemy's will and achieve rapid domination and victory. Almost any tactic can be employed, from psychological operations to the rapid seizure of key military, social, communications and commercial targets.

In addition to impressive uses of force, the "aim is to convince the majority that resistance is futile by targeting and harming the few." But even given that clarified definition, this assumes expertise that goes far beyond the military's core competencies and puts it in a stressful position operationally. Ironically, Ullman and Wade's book by the same name that first portrayed the shock and awe concept also explained its weaknesses. In one particularly prophetic passage, the authors described one of its weak points as "its major dependence on intelligence. One must be certain that the will and perceptions of the adversary can be manipulated.

The classic backfire is the adversary who is not impressed and, instead, is further provoked to action by the unintended actions of the aggressor." This brings us to our current impasse in our approach to a war against terrorists and extremists, with its over-reliance on a single instrument of power. We should make no mistake about the nature of our adversary. Militant radical Islam, foremost amongst the adversaries we now face, is a mass movement of the first order and, as mass movements go, it makes communism look like a parlor game. Communism at least had to meet a set of logic tests that it ultimately failed.

While it celebrated the masses and offered a powerful narrative and social critique, it ultimately foundered on delivering real world solutions to survival level needs. Militant radical Islam is revolution ordained by God and carried out for religious and political gain. As such, it glosses over any lapses of logic by declaring divine mandate. And benefits need not be delivered in this world. By invoking an afterlife with infinite rewards, failure to deliver in this world is easily explained away. By playing to the same survival level needs, militant radical Islam avoids the real world pitfalls of communism and affects a powerful resonance by exploiting the most basic wants and beliefs of its target audiences.

Doing so allows it to achieve comprehensive social and cultural depth at all strata of society to advance its political agenda, making it a powerful faith-based mass movement. By manipulating and appealing to religious identity, it transcends the nation-state framework in which we are bound. It involves mainstream believers who otherwise would not share the militants' aims and promotes resistance identities under the cloak of religion. Once this appeal gains traction, it is only a small step to making the case that a war against Islam is being waged by any number of coalitions.

of unbelievers led by the West, especially, but not limited to, the United States, as governments in Europe, Africa, and Asia have discovered.

There are those who argue that this adversary presents no real danger as it cannot field enough force to do us real harm, compared with our former Soviet foes. These arguments are usually made by those with a cold war frame of reference who are accustomed to thinking in terms of nuclear mega tonnage and orders of battle that can be used to calculate how many Soviet tanks would thunder through the Fulda Gap. They have not fully assimilated the nature of this adversary and what enables the powerful asymmetry it represents.

Their former Soviet counterparts probably labour under no similar illusion, having twice been humbled by this "inferior" adversary – once in Afghanistan and again in Chechnya. We have not yet come to a clear calculation of the new orders of battle in this new type of war. Our adversaries are clearly ahead of us in this regard for they know us better than we know them. This is evidenced by public pronouncements by Osama bin Laden and his fellow executives of Al-Qaida, Inc. and subsequent results on the ground.

They have taken the measure of the United States and other Western powers, and they know the greatest weaknesses that they can use, like jujitsu masters, to make us defeat ourselves. In 1996, in an interview with Abdel Bari Atwan, the managing editor of the London-based pan-Arab daily Al-Qods Al-Arabi, bin Laden made a telling remark. "We want to bring the Americans to fight us on Muslim lands," he said. "If we can fight them on our own territory we will beat them, because the battle will be on our own terms in a land they neither know nor understand."

In another example, articulated more recently in his pronouncement released before the presidential elections in November, 2004, bin Laden speaks of the "bleed until bankruptcy" strategy. "And even more dangerous and bitter for America is that the mujahidin recently forced Bush to resort to emergency funds to continue the fight in Afghanistan and Iraq, which is evidence of the success of the bleed-until-bankruptcy plan..." This part of the adversary's strategy seems to be working as the total costs of the war now approaches $1 trillion. But this approach involves more than defense expenditures.

The most serious challenge to our wellbeing is Al-Qaida's repeated threat to use "the oil weapon" against the West by attacking oil facilities. In a statement issued on February 8 of this year in an on-line publication by Al-Qaida in the Arabian peninsula, the threat was expanded from attacking oil facilities in Saudi Arabia to attacking facilities internationally, including in the western hemisphere. This, coupled with the Ahmedinajad government's stated intent to attack oil shipping going through the Straits of Hormuz in the event of war, and the ongoing instability in Nigeria, now makes national energy policy inseparable from national security policy.

A wholesale and sustained disruption of oil supplies would change life as we know it. And Sunni militant radical Islamic groups, their Iranian fellow travelers, Nigerian nationalists, and grandstanders such as Hugo Chavez know this. It is at this intersection and others that these disparate groups of adversaries find common cause. Yet we have lived under this same sword of Damocles since the 1970's. After the fall of the Shah, shipping disruptions in the Straits of Hormuz were also a danger, and earlier oil embargoes hobbled the U.S. and Europe. We have done little about it in the intervening years so it is no wonder bin Laden and company target our energy addiction as part of their grand strategy.

Their return on investment would be phenomenal. Some of the same social and economic issues that drove communism are now more effective grist for our current adversaries' mill. There has been considerable debate during the past decade, for example, about the relationship between poverty and terror. A number of researchers and social scientists have been quick to point out that the 911 hijackers and other high-profile terrorists came from middle class families and had been raised among the best social classes in their societies.

Many held advanced degrees and had benefited from Western educations. Mohammad Atta, for example, studied urban planning in Germany, and Aymin Al-Zawahiri, Al-Qaida's second in command, was a successful middle class pediatrician in his native Egypt. This argument ignores other terrorists, such as the Moroccan suicide bombers who struck in May 2003 and again in March 2007, all of whom came from Sidi Moumen, the largest shantytown in the country. Similarly, many Moroccan militants involved in the Madrid bombings and numerous suicide bombings in Iraq came from a ten-block area of the poor Jamia Mezouak quarter in the northern Moroccan town of Tetouan.

One of the most cynical examples of this type of equal opportunity terrorist exploitation of the poor also occurred in Morocco in 2003 when police arrested two 13 year-old twin girls, Sanaa and Imane Laghrissi, who were planning to undertake suicide bombings in Rabat. One sister planned to blow herself up in the liquor department of a large supermarket and the other aimed to kill King Mohammed VI as he entered parliament to give that year's opening day's address. Recruited for these operations in the slum where they lived in desperate poverty, they went to an imam of a local mosque to get his blessing.

Though no shrinking violet himself as he was reported to have recruited volunteers to fight the Soviets in Afghanistan, he saw the excess in this case and called the police. The twins were tried and sentenced to five years in prison. In 2005, they received a royal pardon from the king, who saw no wisdom in further punishing two obvious victims of circumstance. Four suicide bombings in the center of Algiers in April and December 2007 that targeted the Algerian prime minister's office, the country's highest court, other governmental and UN offices, were also carried out by operatives who emerged from the underclass in that country.

In the most recent December attacks, one of the suicide bombers was 64 years old, showing Al-Qaida's multigenerational appeal and its ability to adapt and evolve, thus working around security profiles. Indeed, the pan-Arab news daily Asharq Alawsat ran a news item earlier that prophetically described a fatal flaw in Algeria's amnesty program for Islamic militants that was part of a larger national reconciliation effort undertaken by that country's government to stem the violence.

The militants who accepted the offer and others who were earlier imprisoned and released as part of the initiative, sat idly unemployed as jobs programs for them failed to materialize. Some of these experienced militants are now heeding Al-Qaida's siren song as it franchises in North Africa under a new umbrella organization, Al-Qaida in the Islamic Maghreb – the organization that claimed responsibilities for the April suicide attacks. Abu Musab Zarqawi, who became our chief al-Qaida nemesis in Iraq, was another prominent exception to the "poverty doesn't cause terrorism" hypothesis.

Although his father was a minor civil servant, the circumstances of Zarqawi's upbringing could hardly be called well-to-do. His youth was spent as a juvenile delinquent who led a life more akin to an L.A. gang member than a militant political extremist. There are other examples as well but we tend to focus on a small group of terror leaders whose background information we have ready access to. There is little doubt that poverty, political repression, and lack of opportunity form the soil in which violent extremist movements thrive.

With swelling urban populations - which now equal rural populations globally for the first time in history according to the UN – and under-25 youth bulges, countries in the Islamic world have well educated young people with little to do. These young people populate Al-Qaida's waiting room - the fewer the opportunities, the greater their risk. Once ideologies like this take root in these settings, they will be almost impossible to drive out. The leadership of militant Islamic groups, like other past and contemporary terrorist groups, does draw heavily from the more prosperous segments of society but to characterize these groups and all their supporters as all coming from such backgrounds speaks more to our thought processes than it does to the reality.

Even those well-to-do leaders come from societies mired in poverty linked to extreme inequitable distribution of wealth. Susceptible to feelings of "vicarious poverty" (a term suggested by Marc Sageman who has conducted exhaustive research into Islamic terrorists' backgrounds), they want to do something to improve their own societies, but are checked by the corrupt control exerted by brutal dictatorships and absolute monarchies that hold sway in almost every country in the Islamic world. Many who spend time in Western countries, often as students, are constantly reminded of the inequities in their home regions.

In unfamiliar surroundings, disoriented by what they see around them, they gravitate to familiar settings of mosques and Islamic organizations where promoters of radicalism, cloaked as altruists and faith-based activists, look for "cognitive openings," or chinks in one's psychological armor, that can be exploited for the recruitment process. Immigrant children in Diasporas are similarly vulnerable, as researcher Quintan Wiktorowicz documented in seminal work Radical Islam Rising: Muslim Extremism in the West. Mohammed Atta and many of the 911 hijackers started on this path in Hamburg, Germany and followed it to New

York, Washington, and Shanksville. This primary adversary we face has a long and cherished tradition of systematic organization, agitprop, and activism at all levels.

For example, many prominent Islamic militants and their organizations had their origins in the Muslim Brotherhood. Founded by Egyptian schoolteacher Hassan Al-Banna in 1928 in reaction to the decline of Egyptian society under colonial rule, it began as a social activist movement designed to adapt Islam to the modern world as well as provide social services and personal development for its members and their communities. As an answer to secular Western ideologies gaining ground at the time, Al-Banna carefully crafted a system for organizing, setting objectives, and accomplishing goals all in keeping with the tenets of fundamentalist Islamic belief. He devised the organization to be self-funding and emphasized use of the latest in communications technology and organizational theory.

The Brotherhood organized at all levels of society by ministering to the poor and organizing professional and trade groups including teachers, doctors, lawyers, and engineers. By doing so, it achieved unprecedented social and cultural depth to advance political goals. The Brotherhood was later used to check atheistic communist influence by governments who believed they could manipulate the religious approach to their own ends. The Brotherhood organization later grew a militant wing and gradually spawned offshoots and ideologically different splinter groups throughout the Islamic world.

The late University of Michigan professor and researcher Richard Mitchell wrote the definitive history of the early Brotherhood in the 1960's and reading it explains how modern Islamic terror groups can be at once anchored in 7th century fundamentalist interpretations of Islam while using modern technology and organizational skills to utmost advantage in the modern world. It is therefore not surprising that Abdullah Azzam, Osama bin Laden, Aymin Al-Zawahiri, Abu Qatada, Omar Bakri and many other luminaries of modern militant radical Sunni Islam started out in its ranks. They are using a proven system brought to a militant extreme.

And it has an added benefit – it has grown and adapted to operating under the most repressive regimes in the world, learning to fly beneath the radar of ruthless security services that have tried unsuccessfully to eliminate it for the past 60 years. Indeed, Al-Banna himself was assassinated by Egyptian secret police. The Syrian Muslim Brotherhood was hammered by Hafez Al-Assad's forces in the town of Hama in February 1982 as part of an operation to destroy it that resulted in over 20,000 casualties.

The subsequent flight of surviving militants throughout the Islamic world and to Europe was a major factor in the increase and spread of militant radical Islam globally. One of the most fervent advocates of the use of extreme violence in the cause of Islamic resistance and global jihad – Abu Musab al-Suri, the author of the Call to Global Islamic Resistance — a voluminous body of work on violent global jihad — is one such refugee of the Hama crackdown who sought safety in Spain and then went on to Al-Qaida's camps in Afghanistan. The group lives on in both Egypt and Syria - a testament to its ability to adapt and survive.

Improving Transatlantic Counterterrorism Ties

With U.S. government assistance, three "homegrown" terrorist suspects were arrested in Germany several weeks ago. Despite this success story, transatlantic counterterrorism ties have been seriously tested over the past three months: prosecutors in Munich called for the extradition of CIA agents allegedly involved in abducting a German citizen; an Italian trial began against twenty-six CIA employees charged in absentia with kidnapping an imam in Milan; and Britain released a report accusing the United States of ignoring its concerns regarding terrorist "renditions."

These latest developments have undoubtedly reinforced perceptions on both sides of the Atlantic that U.S. and European counterterrorism efforts have been at odds since the September 11 attacks. Unfortunately, significant commonalities have been lost amid the heated rhetoric, both in terms of approach and problems encountered. Shifting these perceptions is critical for future counterterrorism efforts and should be a priority for U.S. and European policymakers.

Similar Threats, Similar Approaches

The United States and Europe are now facing similar terrorist threats. Before September 11, al-Qaeda focused exclusively on the United States, which Osama bin Laden considered "the head of the snake." Although American targets remain a high priority for al-Qaeda, the 2004 Madrid attacks, the 2005 London attacks, and the recently thwarted plots in Germany, England, and Scotland have demonstrated that America is no longer alone on the list.

In many areas, the United States and Europe have used similar counterterrorism approaches. For example, several European countries have followed the U.S. lead in transforming the roles of prosecutors and law enforcement agencies to deal primarily with terrorism prevention instead of post-attack investigation. This preventive strategy has revolved around an increasingly aggressive law enforcement approach. In 2006 alone, for example, European authorities arrested a total of 260 terrorist suspects.

Most of these individuals were charged not with plotting attacks, but with a variety of other terrorism-related offenses such as financing, recruiting, and facilitation. The scale of the September 11 attacks and the potential lethality of future attacks have influenced this change in strategy. For example, in early 2003, Nicolas Sarkozy, then France's interior minister, explained law enforcement's early intervention in a case involving a possible chemical attack by stating, "When you are dealing with suspects like this, it is better to arrest them before, not after."

A German prosecutor put it more bluntly during her closing arguments in an early 2005 terrorism trial: "We cannot wait until attacks have been carried out and the dead are lying on the street." Post-September 11 legal changes have facilitated law enforcement's proactive posture. Just as the United States passed the USA PATRIOT Act soon after the attacks, a number of European countries have passed their own comprehensive counterterrorism legislation. For example, Britain adopted the Anti-terrorism, Crime, and Security Act in 2001, the Prevention of Terrorism Act in 2005, and the Terrorism Act in 2006. Germany, Italy, France, and the Netherlands have also made major legislative changes, increasing the counterterrorism authority of prosecutors and law enforcement agencies.

Difficulties in Prosecuting Suspected Terrorists

The United States and Europe are also facing similar problems. In terms of prosecuting suspected terrorists, for example, acquittals, overturned convictions, and dropped charges have overshadowed the successes. Prosecutions are hindered by the same factors on both sides of the Atlantic: the difficulties associated with using intelligence information, the pressure to disrupt plots at early stages, and the need for extensive international cooperation.

Moreover, rhetoric has damaged transatlantic relations and affected collaboration on critical counterterrorism matters. As Michael Scheuer, former chief of the CIA unit tasked with hunting bin Laden, noted, "Friction between Europe and [the] United States is something that certainly benefits Osama bin Laden." Al-Qaeda can exploit fractured ties between the United States and Europe because of their interdependent security interests. Recent events demonstrate that terrorists based in Europe remain interested in attacking both U.S. and European targets.

For example, according to a recent European Union report, the suspects involved in the foiled August 2006 plot to bomb flights from the United Kingdom to the United States were allegedly intending to "strike a target that would hit both the UK and the United States at the same time." Indeed, the September 11 attacks are an enduring reminder that terrorists living and operating freely in Europe — like the so-called "Hamburg cell" members — can pose a serious threat to the United States.

Build Stronger Ties

Despite transatlantic friction, Washington and its European allies must overcome the perception that their counterterrorism efforts are at odds. With new leadership in Britain, Germany, and France, there is an opportunity to set a different tone — one emphasizing shared counterterrorism approaches and mutual difficulties.

Focusing on the commonalities might show American and European audiences that the two sides are not as far apart as is publicly portrayed. Americans would be reassured to know that various European countries have made major counterterrorism improvements. Europeans might also be surprised to learn about the full extent of the nonmilitary aspects of U.S. counterterrorism efforts.

To demonstrate their commitment to strategic collaboration, the United States and Europe should establish a joint commission to review their counterterrorism successes and failures, beginning with the law enforcement arena. They should review individual cases as well as overarching strategies and legal standards. Although a "one size fits all" solution is not possible, the commission could focus on finding areas where common solutions can be developed. The more similar strategies the United States and Europe adopt, the more effectively they will work together — both on individual cases and more broadly. Whatever form it takes, an increased focus on commonalities will make it far easier for officials in Washington and abroad to collaborate on the most important and sensitive counterterrorism issue: protecting those on both sides of the Atlantic.

Prosecuting Terrorism beyond 'Material Support'

On January 11, 2008, a Boston federal court convicted Emadeddin Muntasser, Samir Almonla, and Muhammad Mubayid of conspiring to defraud and conceal information from the U.S. government. Prosecutors proved the defendants fraudulently used the charity they ran — Care International — "to solicit and obtain tax deductible donations for the purpose of supporting and promoting the mujahedin (Muslim holy warriors) and jihad (violent armed conflict)."

The defendants concealed from U.S. authorities the fact that Care was an outgrowth of and successor to the al-Kifah Refugee Center, and engaged in non-charitable activities such as the solicitation and expenditure of funds to support violent jihad. Coming on the heels of partial convictions and hung juries in other recent "material support" cases, this recent case highlights the strategic utility of charging terrorists and their supporters for ordinary criminal activities that the government can easily prosecute. Such legal strategy, however, should not cloud the fact that this was a terrorism case at heart.

Part of the Afghan Services Bureau

The 9/11 Commission Report noted that al-Kifah was an "outpost" of Mektab al-Khidmat (MAK), the Afghan Services Bureau established by Sheikh Abdullah Azzam and Osama Bin Laden to support jihad in Afghanistan and around the world. According to the commission, "al-Kifah recruited American Muslims to fight in Afghanistan; some of them would participate in terrorist actions in the United States in the early 1990s and in al-Qaeda operations elsewhere, including the 1998 attacks on U.S. embassies in East Africa." A flyer distributed by al-Kifah corroborates this description: "al-Kifah Refugee Center is an organization founded by Sheikh Abdullah Azzam to serve the cause of jihad."

Shared leadership and activities helped demonstrate that Care was an outgrowth of al-Kifah. Even Suheil Laher, a past president of Care, conceded to the FBI that the officers of al-Kifah Boston carried over and became officers of Care. Indeed, Muntasser not only founded and incorporated Care in Massachusetts, but according to an al-Kifah flyer, he also served as director of the Boston branch of al-Kifah Refugee Center. In the early 1990s, al-Kifah's bi-monthly newsletter, al-Hussam (The Sword), announced it was a "newsletter of the al-Kifah Refugee Center-USA" in English with an Arabic subtitle reading "Maktab al-Kidmat," or MAK. As early as June 1993, however, Care assumed publication of al-Hussam, with a nearly identical header that read "al-Hussam; Newsletter published by Maktab al-Kidmat, Boston USA; Care International."

The timing of the name change is particularly significant as it came on the heels of press reports linking al-Kifah to the 1993 World Trade Center bombing. Two days after the second of these articles appeared, on April 13, 1993, Muntasser incorporated the new organization under the name Care International, Inc. Care filed its articles of incorporation using the same Boston address used by al-Kifah in earlier editions of al-Hussam. Just a month prior to its incorporation under its new name, al-Kifah ran an article in its March 5, 1993 issue of al-Hussam encouraging readers to engage in jihad and become martyrs. That issue included another article entitled "Boston Offers More

Martyrs," which proudly announced the death of an individual from Boston who fought in Afghanistan.

Economic Jihad

Like other radical Islamist organizations, Care took advantage of the otherwise laudable Islamic tradition of charity and good works not only to teach its particular version of Islam but also to actively support terrorist operations. The organization couched its solicitations in the context of the Muslim obligation to donate alms (zakat), instructing donors that they were under religious obligation to make sure at least some of the alms gone to finance jihad. In response, the organization received checks from donors with directions to support various jihad causes, including comments on the memo line of checks such as "Bosnia mujahedin," "for jihad only," and "Chechen Muslim Fighters."

Indeed, while terrorist fundraisers frequently frame their fundraising pitch in terms of their groups' humanitarian activities, Care specifically called for funding violent jihad. Employing the concept of "economic jihad" (jihad bil-mal), a tool that features prominently in the fundraising techniques of radical Islamist groups, Care successfully raised approximately $1.7 million from 1993 to 2003. The concept is simple in practice: radical leaders tell their followers they have a religious duty to engage in jihad, either by physically fighting or by supporting those who do. Proponents of this logic ground their position in the Quran, surah 9 (al-Tawbah) Verse 41: "Fight with your possessions and your souls in the way of Allah."

Highlighting the concept of economic jihad, a speaker on one of Care's audiotapes explicitly calls on his listeners "to commit jihad with their wealth as well as their souls." The lecturer went on to state that "weapons training is open to all and that all should take advantage of this opportunity to receive training." In its other literature, Care argued that supporting jihadists was insufficient and could not supplant the obligation to personally fight in jihad.

An al-Hussam article argued "jihad with money, without jihad of the soul, is not beneficial to the person even if they spend all the money on earth. It is useless if they do not take part in wars." Al-Hussam quoted Azzam calling on readers to join jihad, noting "the individual obligatory nature of jihad remains in effect until the lands are purified from the pollution of the disbelievers."

Support for the Global Jihadist Movement

A clear sign of Care's relationship to global jihadist groups is found in the group's edition of Azzam's publication, "Join the Caravan." The publication encourages readers to participate in the Afghan jihad and provides telephone numbers in Afghanistan to facilitate such travel. Care financial statements also reveal that from August 1993 to June 1995, Muntasser wired close to $167,000 in the name of Care or al-Kifah to the Human Service Office (another name for MAK) in Bosnia.

Care publications and websites regularly provided updates on the fighting in various parts of the world where al-Qaeda movements operate, such as Chechnya, Afghanistan, Bosnia, and Algeria. News updates included glowing references to prominent terrorists and their attacks, including Chechnya's Shamel Basiev and Ibn Al-Khattab, and Gulbuddin Hekmatyar, the Libyan Islamic Fighting Group, among others. Despite all of the above evidence tying Care to terrorism, the organization — like Al Capone — was ultimately held accountable for mundane charges on which the government could secure criminal convictions.

In fact, the judge barred the word "terrorism" throughout the trial in an effort to keep the jury focused on the specific charges at hand. But the ultimate effect of the tax law conviction was to expose and hold accountable a fundraising network that raised significant amounts of money for al-Qaeda and its affiliated groups. Detractors may say the lack of a specific terrorism charge proves this was not a terrorism case, but the evidence belies such claims. Sometimes the best strategy for a terrorism prosecution is to focus on the underlying and mundane criminal activity.

9

G8 Recommendations on Counterterrorism

Preamble

The G8 attaches the highest importance to preventing and combating terrorism. To assist in the effort, the G8 have defined a series of principles which provide guidance to strengthen capacities to combat terrorism. The following recommendations are the result of a revision of the Counter-Terrorism Experts Group 25 Measures, adopted in Paris in 1996. The revision was initiated by the United States, conducted by the G8 Counter-Terrorism Experts Group (Roma Group), and coordinated by the Canadian Presidency.

The recommendations update the Counter-Terrorism Experts Group 25 Measures to address new terrorist threats as well as to complement the 40 Recommendations of the G8 crime group, known as the Lyon Group (1996). The Lyon Recommendations have also been modified in order to address more effectively the challenge of transnational crime threats. The revised Lyon Group Recommendations, now entitled the *G8 Recommendations on Transnational Crime,* were endorsed by G8 Ministers of Justice and the Interior (Mont-Tremblant, May 13-14, 2002).

These recommendations are intended to complement the work of experts in other regional organizations and international forum. This includes other experts groups of the G8 such as the Non-Proliferation Experts' Groups which has developed Principles to prevent terrorists, or those that harbour them, from gaining access to weapons of mass destruction, radiological weapons and missiles.

The following revised *G8 Recommendations on Counter-Terrorism* comprise standards, principles, best practices, actions and relationships that the G8 views as providing improvements to the mechanisms, procedures and networks that exist to protect our societies from terrorist threats. They are intended as commitments by the G8, which we commend as guiding principles to all States. States should ensure that their strategies for combating terrorism are dynamic and sufficiently flexible and innovative to respond to the constantly changing challenges. We urge all States to join the G8 in the implementation of the following measures.

Section 1: Rapid Implementation of Existing Counter-Terrorism Instruments

We commit ourselves and urge all other States to:

1. Take actions to ensure, as rapidly as possible, full adherence to the following instruments relating to the prevention and suppression of terrorism:
    a. the twelve United Nations conventions and protocols addressing counter-terrorism issues listed in the annex;
    b. all relevant United Nations Security Council Resolutions, in particular, United Nations Security Council Resolution 1373 (2001); and,
2. Become a party, if entitled, to the Council of Europe's Convention on Cybercrime (2001), ensuring full and rapid implementation of its terms, or, ensure the availability of a legal framework approximating the measures called for in the Convention, as it provides

useful measures to combat attacks by terrorists and other criminals on computer systems, as well as to gather electronic evidence of terrorism and other crimes.

Section 2: Support for Additional Multilateral Counter-Terrorism Initiatives and Instruments

We commit ourselves and urge all other States to:

1. Work within the United Nations system to complete the draft UN Comprehensive Convention on International Terrorism, and coordinate our efforts in this regard.
2. Promote appropriate action in multilateral organizations of which we are members, including at the regional level, in order to usefully supplement counter-terrorism measures already taken or under development at the global level.

Section 3: Chemical, Biological, Radiological, Nuclear Weapons

We commit ourselves and urge all other States to:

1.
    a. With respect to ensuring effective action against the use of biological weapons by terrorists, make crimes the offences established in the Biological and Toxin Weapons Convention (1972), prosecute such crimes or, where appropriate, extradite individuals, in accordance with national law and bilateral extradition agreements, and work cooperatively to develop best practices to deter and detect such offences.
    b. Take measures to work cooperatively to develop effective mechanisms to track and curb the illicit possession and transfer of selected biological agents both domestically and internationally, and to explore additional measures to prevent biological

agents from being used to commit terrorist attacks.

2. Work within the United Nations system to complete work on the draft International Convention for the Suppression of Acts of Nuclear Terrorism and strengthen our cooperative efforts to this end.
3. Support ongoing negotiations to strengthen the 1980 Convention on the Physical Protection of Nuclear Material and explore together potential additional international measures to advance its ends and investigate enhanced measures aimed at the problem of nuclear smuggling.
4. Work cooperatively to develop, in appropriate international forum, best practices to ensure the protection of chemical, biological, radiological, nuclear and related infrastructures against terrorist actions, and explore means to prevent sensitive information pertaining to these infrastructures from being used by terrorists for targeting purposes.
5. Coordinate efforts and encourage support in other forum where concerted CBRN prevention programs are underway, such as at the International Atomic Energy Agency (IAEA).
6. Develop best practice guidelines for contingency planning at national levels and strengthen existing arrangements for crisis response.

Section 4: Explosives and Firearms

We commit ourselves and urge all other States to:

1. Accelerate research and development of methods of detection of explosives and weapons and other harmful substances that cause death or injury, and undertake consultations on the development of standards for marking explosives in order to identify their origin in post-blast investigations, and to promote cooperation, where appropriate.

2. Adopt effective domestic laws and regulations including export controls to govern manufacture, trading, transport, and export of firearms, explosives, or any device designed to cause violent injury, damage, or destruction, in order to prevent their use for terrorists' acts.

Section 5: Financing Of Terrorism

We commit ourselves and urge all other States to:

1. As rapidly as possible, ensure full implementation of the United Nations Security Council Resolution 1373, the International Convention for the Suppression of the Financing of Terrorism and the Financial Action Task Force's (FATF) Special Recommendations on Terrorist Financing (2001), and participate in the fulfillment of the FATF global action plans.
2. Adopt the steps to remove obstacles to effective common action to combat terrorist financing contained in the Report of the G8 Meeting on Legal Measures to Combat Terrorist Financing (2002), endorsed by G8 Justice and Interior Ministers (2002), and move beyond freezing to also forfeit terrorist assets in order to permanently deprive terrorists of their funds.
3. Implement the recommendations on "Money Laundering, Related Terrorist Financing and Asset Forfeiture" contained in the G8 Recommendations on Transnational Crime (2002).
4. Facilitate, through appropriate domestic measures, the traceability of terrorist funds and ensure that mutual legal assistance is not refused on the grounds of bank secrecy or that the request involves a fiscal offence.

Section 6: Transportation Security

We commit ourselves and urge all other States to:

1. Maintain strong financial support through voluntary contributions for the International Civil Aviation

Organization (ICAO) aviation security activities to fulfill its standards and recommended practices with a view to deterring and detecting terrorism.

2. Cooperate in conducting an expeditious review of aviation security conventions, international standards and recommended practices in the ICAO, with a view to updating such standards in order to deter and detect terrorism, including by applying mechanisms referred to the G8 Recommendations on Transnational Crime.
3. Work as expeditiously as possible towards implementation of a common global standard for the collection and transmission of advance passenger information (API).
4. Enhance their abilities to share timely information internationally with law enforcement and other appropriate counterparts, in accordance with applicable laws, with respect to passengers concerning whom there are specific and serious reasons to consider they may engage in a terrorist act.
5. Work closely with each other and the International Maritime Organization (IMO) in order to improve the capability of governments to deter and prosecute terrorist attacks on maritime vessels or the use of such vessels to further terrorist activities.
6. Cooperate in conducting an expeditious review of maritime safety conventions, international standards and recommended practices in the IMO, with a view to updating such standards in order to deter and detect terrorism.
7. Work with relevant international organizations to develop and implement an improved global container security regime to identify and examine high-risk containers, their in-transit integrity, implement the global common standards for electronic customs reporting, and work within the World Customs Organization (WCO) on advance information

pertaining to containers as early as possible in the trade chain.

8. Urgently intensify consultations among transport security and other relevant officials to improve the capability of governments to prevent, investigate, and respond to terrorist attacks on modes of mass ground transportation, such as railway, underground and bus transport systems, and to cooperate with other governments in this regard.

Section 7: Internal Coordination against Terrorism

We commit ourselves and urge all other States to:

Strengthen internal cooperation between various national agencies and services which may deal with different aspects of counter-terrorism.

Section 8: International Cooperation

We commit ourselves and urge all other States to:

1. Take all possible measures to deny safe havens to those who finance, plan, support, or commit terrorist acts, or provide safe havens.
2. Ensure, in conformity with international law and, in particular, the 1951 Convention Relating to the Status of Refugees and its 1967 Protocol, that refugee status is not abused by the perpetrators, organizers or facilitators of terrorist acts.
3. Identify and eliminate obstacles to extradition to the greatest extent possible, including those referred to in "Part II: Enhancing International Cooperation" of the G8 Recommendations on Transnational Crime (2002).
4. Take strong measures, including relevant legislative measures if necessary, in cooperation with other countries, to prevent terrorist acts and the international movement of terrorists by strengthening, *inter alia*, border, immigration, and travel document control and information sharing.

Attach special priority to mutual legal assistance and law enforcement cooperation with respect to terrorism offences in order to ensure a quick and effective response, including those referred to in the recommendations on "Mutual Legal Assistance and Law Enforcement Channels" of the G8 Recommendations on Transnational Crime (2002).

5. Develop effective measures for obtaining the rapid freezing, seizing and confiscation of assets related to terrorist activities.
6. Ensure that claims of political motivation are not recognized as grounds for refusing requests for the extradition of alleged terrorists and, exclude or reduce to the greatest possible extent any application of the political offence exception in responding to a request for mutual legal assistance concerning terrorist offences.

Links between Terrorism and Transnational Crime

We commit ourselves and urge all other States to:

1.
   a. Ensure that an effective framework is in place to fight against transnational crimes that can support or facilitate terrorist activity, such as that provided by the G8 Recommendations on Transnational Crime (2002).
   b. Examine and exchange information to determine the nature of links between terrorism and transnational crime, in particular, of the manner in which terrorist organizations can support their activities through the commission of other crimes, and develop strategies, as required, to enable concerted effort to disrupt and disable such activities.
2. Support the efforts of the United Nations International Drug Control Programme (UNDCP) and its donors to coordinate counter-narcotics assistance in combating the

drug trade in and emanating from Afghanistan, to strengthen the "security belts" around it and to maximize the effectiveness of UNDCP programmes in the region.

Outreach to Non-G8 States

We commit ourselves and urge all other States to:

1. Conduct outreach, including technical assistance, to other countries, in coordination with each other and with other parts of the G8 structure as well as regional organizations, with a view to building capacity to implement UNSCR 1373, the twelve United Nations counter-terrorism conventions and protocols listed in the annex, the Roma Group counter-terrorism recommendations, and the G8 Recommendations on Transnational Crime (2002), for the purpose of combating terrorism-related activities.
2. As appropriate, develop best practices to facilitate such outreach and cooperate closely on capacity building and outreach with the United Nations Security Council's Counter-Terrorism Committee (UNSC CTC).
3. Develop additional measures, in cooperation with international organizations and civil society, to increase the awareness of all individuals that any act or threat of terrorism represents a serious crime with appropriate penalties.

Annex

United Nations Conventions and Protocols addressing Counter-Terrorism:

1. Convention on Offences and Certain Other Acts Committed on Board Aircraft, done at Tokyo, on 14 September 1963;
2. Convention for the Suppression of Unlawful Seizure of Aircraft, done at The Hague on 16 December 1970.

3. Convention for the Suppression of Unlawful Acts against the Safety of Civil Aviation, done at Montreal on 23 September 1971.
4. Convention on the Prevention and Punishment of Crimes against Internationally Protected Persons, including Diplomatic Agents, adopted by the General Assembly of the United Nations on 14 December 1973.
5. International Convention against the Taking of Hostages, adopted by the General Assembly of the United Nations on 17 December 1979.
6. Convention on the Physical Protection of Nuclear Material, adopted at Vienna on 3 March 1980.
7. Protocol for the Suppression of Unlawful Acts of Violence at Airports Serving International Civil Aviation, supplementary to the Convention for the Suppression of Unlawful Acts against the Safety of Civil Aviation, done at Montreal on 24 February 1988.
8. Convention for the Suppression of Unlawful Acts against the Safety of Maritime Navigation, done at Rome on 10 March1988.
9. Protocol for the Suppression of Unlawful Acts against the Safety of Fixed Platform located on the Continental Shelf, done at Rome on 10 March 1988.
10. Convention on the Marking of Plastic Explosives for the Purpose of Detection, done at Montreal on 1 March 1991.
11. International Convention for the Suppression of Terrorist Bombings, adopted by the General Assembly of the United Nations on 15 December 1997.
12. International Convention for the Suppression of the Financing of Terrorism, adopted by the General Assembly of the United Nations on 9 December 1999.

10

ASEAN Efforts to Counterterrorism

Introduction

ASEAN Leaders, at their 7th Summit on 5 November 2001 in Brunei Darussalam, adopted the 2001 ASEAN Declaration on Joint Action to Counter Terrorism. The ASEAN Leaders viewed terrorism as a profound threat to international peace and security and "a direct challenge to the attainment of peace, progress and prosperity of ASEAN and the realization of ASEAN Vision 2020". They expressed commitment to combat terrorism in accordance with the Charter of the United Nations, other international laws and relevant UN resolutions. They also underlined that "cooperative efforts in this regard should consider joint practical counter-terrorism measures in line with specific circumstances in the region and in each member country".

They also identified specific measures for ASEAN to implement the Declaration, namely:

- Review and strengthen national mechanisms to combat terrorism;
- Call for the early signing/ratification of or accession to all relevant anti-terrorist conventions including the International Convention for the Suppression of the

Financing of Terrorism;

- Deepen cooperation among ASEAN's front-line law enforcement agencies in combating terrorism and sharing "best practices";
- Study relevant international conventions on terrorism with the view to integrating them with ASEAN mechanisms on combating international terrorism;
- Enhance information/intelligence exchange to facilitate the flow of information, in particular, on terrorists and terrorist organisations, their movement and funding, and any other information needed to protect lives, property and the security of all modes of travel;
- Strengthen existing cooperation and coordination between the ASEAN Ministerial Meeting on Transnational Crime (AMMTC) and other relevant ASEAN bodies in countering, preventing and suppressing all forms of terrorist acts. Particular attention would be paid to finding ways to combat terrorist organisations, support infrastructure and funding and bringing the perpetrators to justice;
- Develop regional capacity building programmes to enhance existing capabilities of ASEAN member countries to investigate, detect, monitor and report on terrorist acts;
- Discuss and explore practical ideas and initiatives to increase ASEAN's role in and involvement with the international community including extra-regional partners within existing frameworks such as the ASEAN + 3, the ASEAN Dialogue Partners and the ASEAN Regional Forum (ARF), to make the fight against terrorism a truly regional and global endeavour;
- Strengthen cooperation at the bilateral, regional and international levels in combating terrorism in a comprehensive manner and affirm that at the

international level the United Nations should play a major role in this regard.

- The specific measures outlined in the Declaration have been incorporated in the Terrorism component of the Work Programme to Implement the ASEAN Plan of Action to Combat Transnational Crime adopted in May 2002. The Work Programme is based along 6 strategic thrust namely:
    - information exchange;
    - cooperation in legal matters;
    - cooperation in law enforcement matters;
    - institutional capacity building;
    - training; and
    - extra-regional cooperation.

ASEAN is also carrying out training programmes and projects in counter terrorism in 2003, including on psychological operation/psychological warfare courses for law enforcement authorities and on intelligence procuring. Courses on bomb/explosive detection, post-blast investigation, airport security and passport/document security and inspection are also planned. In addition, ASEAN focal points on counter-terrorism have also been established.

Stage A:

Several ASEAN Member Countries have already become the party to some of the 12 international conventions and protocols relating to terrorism. In the Work Programme, ASEAN Member Countries are also urged towards an early signing or ratification of or accession to all relevant anti-terrorist conventions including the International Convention for the Suppression of the Financing of Terrorism.

As part of the Terrorism Component of the ASEAN

Work Programme, ASEAN Member Countries are now working toward the establishment of a regional database for disseminating information on respective national laws, regulations, bilateral and multilateral treaties or agreements of respective countries.

The Terrorism Component, in addressing the issue of prevention and suppression of terrorist financing, calls for the enhancement of information or intelligence exchange to facilitate the flow of information, in particular, on terrorists and terrorist organizations, their movement and funding, and any other information needed to protect lives, property and the security of all modes of travel.

Stage B:

The Annual Conference of ASEAN Chiefs of Police (ASEANAPOL) held in May 2002, called for a joint cooperation among the ASEANAPOL members in fighting terrorism. ASEAN Chief of Police are committed to developing capacity-building initiatives to ensure that each ASEANAPOL member has the capacity to effectively monitor, share information on and combat all forms of terrorist activities. They also agreed to enhance cooperation among law enforcement agencies through the sharing of experiences on counter-terrorism and the exchange of information on suspected terrorists, organizations and their modus operandi.

In addition, ASEAN immigration authorities have committed to assist and to coordinate with the other ASEAN law enforcement authorities to prevent the movement of terrorists or cross-border terrorism by working toward the establishment of intelligence units in their respective agencies on the issues of trafficking in persons, human smuggling and terrorism. They have also set up an ASEAN focal point directory for ASEAN immigration authorities to exchange information.

Stage C:

In May 2002, Indonesia, Malaysia and the Philippines signed the Agreement on Information Exchange and Establishment of Communication Procedures to cooperate among them to combat transnational crime, including terrorism. Thailand and Cambodia have also acceded to the Agreement.

ASEAN senior officials are also looking at the possibility of a regional convention to combat terrorism. In addition, several Member Countries within ASEAN are looking at a regional Mutual Legal Assistance Agreement.

In terms of information exchange, the Work Programme has put in place a comprehensive information exchange mechanism to facilitate sharing of information and analysis of critical intelligence information such as "modus operandi" and offences involving terrorist activities. ASEAN is taking a comprehensive and coordinated approach in tackling the various areas of transnational crimes that have links to terrorism as the Work Programme also has components on trafficking in small arms, illegal drug trafficking and money laundering.

In January 2003, ASEAN police and law enforcement officials agreed that each ASEAN Member Country shall establish an anti-terrorism task force to strengthen cooperation on counter-terrorism and to collaborate with the affected ASEAN member country following a terrorist attack. Such assistance requested can be in the form of, but not limited to identifying, pursuing and apprehending suspects, examination of witness (es), searching and seizing evidence, evacuating and treating of victims, forensic and crime laboratory.

In terms of cooperation at the international and regional levels, ASEAN and China, in November 2002, issued a Joint Declaration of ASEAN and China on Cooperation in the Field of Non-Traditional Security Issues where counterterrorism has been included as one of the priorities for ASEAN-China cooperation.

ASEAN is cooperating with China, Japan and the Republic of Korea under the ASEAN+3 process of East Asia cooperation to address the threats of terrorism and transnational crimes. The ASEAN Ministers on Transnational Crime will start holding joint consultations with their counterparts from China, Japan and the Republic of Korea (the AMMTC+3) in Thailand this year.

At the 9th ministerial meeting of the ASEAN Regional Forum (ARF) in Bandar Seri Begawan on 30 July 2002, the ARF Statement on Measures against Terrorist Financing was adopted. The ARF participating states and organization (the EU) agreed on concrete steps that included: freezing terrorist assets, implementation of international standards, cooperation on exchange of information and outreach, and technical assistance.

The 9th ARF also agreed to establish the inter-sessional meeting on counter-terrorism and transnational crimes (ISM-CT/TC), which will be co-chaired in the 2002-2003 year by Malaysia and the U.S.A. Malaysia plans to convene the first meeting of the ISM-CT/TC in Sabah in March 2003.

ASEAN and the U.S.A. signed the Joint Declaration for Cooperation to Combat International Terrorism during the 35th AMM/PMC in Bandar Seri Begawan on 1 August 2002. One of the objectives of the cooperation is to prevent, disrupt and combat international terrorism through the exchange and flow of information, intelligence and capacity-building assistance.

ASEAN and the E.U. issued the Joint Declaration on Cooperation to Combat Terrorism at the end of the 14th ASEAN-EU Ministerial Meeting in Brussels on 28 January 2003. The Joint Declaration reiterated the commitment of the two sides to work together and contribute to the global efforts to stamp out terrorism

In addition, some ASEAN member countries have entered into bilateral cooperation arrangements with other countries outside the ASEAN region to enhance their capability in counter-terrorism. Malaysia and the U.S.A., for example, have established the Regional Counter-terrorism Center in November 2002 in Kuala Lumpur. Indonesia and Australia have formed the joint task force to investigate the Bali terrorist bomb blasts.

11

Implications for Strategy

Terrorism is, among other things, a weapon used by the weak against the strong. The United States will move into the 21st century as a preeminent, global power in a period of tremendous flux within societies, among nations, and across states and regions. Terrorism will accompany changes at each of these levels, as it has in other periods of flux in the international environment. This analysis deliberately avoids any detailed discussion of the definition of terrorism, in part because such discussions tend to be inconclusive but also because the rapidly changing nature of the phenomenon renders many traditional definitions misleading. The fashionable and often politically charged debate about terrorism makes the definition of terrorism a highly subjective, even ethno-centric exercise.

The old adage about "one person's terrorist being another's freedom fighter" summarizes the problem. In RAND's continuing research on this subject, terrorism has generally been defined by the nature of the act, not the identity of the terrorists or the nature of the cause: "terrorism is violence or the threat of violence calculated to create an atmosphere of fear or alarm," generally in support of political or systemic objectives. To the extent that the United States continues to be engaged as a global power, terrorism will have the potential to affect American interests directly and indirectly, from attacks on U.S. territory—including low-probability but high-consequence "superterrorism" with weapons of mass destruction— to attacks affecting our diplomatic and economic ties abroad, or our ability to maintain a forward military presence or project power in times of crisis.

The United States will also have a unique, systemic interest in terrorism as a global problem—including acts of "domestic" terrorism confined within state borders that make up the bulk of terrorism worldwide—even where the United States is not directly or even indirectly targeted. In one way or another, terrorism can affect our freedom of action, not just with regard to national security strategy narrowly defined, but across a range of compelling issues, from drugs and money laundering to information and energy policy. Many of our high-priority national objectives have been shaken by the recent experience of terrorism. The Oklahoma and World Trade Center bombings struck at our sense of security within our borders. Attacks against U.S. forces in Saudi Arabia raise questions about our strategy for presence and stability in an area of critical importance for world energy supply.

The U.S. embassy bombings in Kenya and Tanzania raise questions about the exposure that comes with active engagement in world affairs, and point to the risks of privately sponsored terrorism. The assassination of Prime Minister Rabin and the campaign of suicide bombings in Israel have put the Middle East peace process in serious jeopardy, threatening a critical and longstanding U.S. diplomatic objective. Elsewhere, terrorism has destabilized allies (in Egypt and Turkey), and has rendered counternarcotics relationships difficult (in Colombia and Mexico). Where societies and regions are fundamentally unstable, and where political outcomes are delicately poised, terrorism will have a particular ability to affect strategic futures.

Understanding and Countering the "New" Terrorism

This chapter explores the problem of terrorism in the broader national and international security context. It takes as its point of departure completed analyses of terrorism trends and prospects, as well as specialized assessments of weapons of mass destruction (WMD) and information-related risks. These analysis points to the steady augmentation of the traditional patterns of terrorism by new forms of the phenomenon, both as stand-alone threats and in the context of more conventional conflict (i.e., as an asymmetric strategy). This new terrorism is increasingly networked; more diverse in terms of motivations, sponsorship, and security consequences; more global in reach; and more lethal.

As a result, much existing counterterrorism experience may be losing its relevance as network forms of organization replace the canonical terrorist hierarchies, or as state sponsorship becomes more subtle and difficult to expose. Similarly, many of the leading concepts of air power in relation to counterterrorism strategy may need to be revised. There will be a continuing need for preemption, deterrence, and retaliation in relation to state sponsors. But the key tasks for air and space power in the future may have as much or more to do with the surveillance, exposure, and targeting of nonstate actors, and even individuals. The transforming contribution of air and space power to national counterterrorism strategy will be making terrorism—an inherently amorphous phenomenon—more transparent for policymakers and the international community.

This chapter focuses to a great extent on "international terrorism" and terrorism in the international arena. The problem of domestic terrorism in the United States is addressed only in passing, a consequence of the need to limit the scope and focus of the study rather than a judgment about the significance of the problem. Indeed, the problem of domestic terrorism is growing and the threat of domestic and "insider" terrorism against U.S. military facilities and personnel would be a fertile area for further analysis.

It is also worth noting that terrorism experts are increasingly uncomfortable with the traditional distinction between domestic and international terror in an age of global communications and networked terrorism. Many of the most serious terrorist risks to U.S. national security—above all, those of mass destruction and mass disruption in periods of crisis or conflict—can have a transnational dimension. The following discussion places terrorism in strategic context by exploring terrorist threats to U.S. interests and future sources of risk, examines past U.S. and allied experience, offers a framework for counterterrorism strategy, and provides overall findings and implications for the U.S. military.

Terrorism in Strategic Context

Four Dimensions

Terrorism provokes alarm and repugnance, but how meaningful is it as a threat to U.S. national security? Where does terrorism rank in relation to other security challenges? To gauge the extent of terrorism's challenge in strategic terms, it is useful to explore the terrorist threat to U.S. interests in four key dimensions: direct, indirect, systemic, and asymmetric. At the same time, perceptions and policies in relation to terrorism are being shaped by changing definitions of security and the evolving place of terrorism on the spectrum of domestic and international conflict.

Direct Threats

The most dramatic and proximate source of risk arises from direct terrorist attacks against U.S. citizens and property, overseas or on U.S. territory (or against U.S. forces in peacetime). The United States has been a leading target of international terrorists, a trend that shows few signs of abating. Until recent years, however, few of these attacks took place within the United States, partly because traditional terrorist groups found the prospect of operations in the United States too difficult, politically counterproductive, or simply unnecessary. Most observers now believe the threshold for significant international terrorism in the United States has been crossed, especially in the wake of the World Trade Center bombing and the 1997 apprehension of terrorist bombers in New York. The prospect of further direct attacks within U.S. territory, coupled with the increasing lethality of international terrorism, has begun to inspire new concerns about "homeland defense," above all defense against terrorist use of nuclear, biological, or chemical weapons against urban targets.

Regardless of changes in the size of the U.S. military presence abroad, there will always be more than enough U.S. citizens and interests engaged around the world (as businessmen, diplomats, students, and tourists) to provide ready targets for terrorists looking to strike at the United States. But the changing motivations and agendas of terrorists may raise the symbolic value of more-direct attacks against targets on U.S. territory. State sponsors, bent on revenge (e.g., Iraq or Libya), might see special merit in supporting operations within the United States. Similarly, movements with transcendental objectives, whether religious or political, may place greater emphasis on acts that shake the confidence and security of U.S. citizens at home.

At the same time, the rise of terrorist networks blurs the distinction between domestic and international terrorism, and could facilitate the use of amateur proxies, including self-appointed proxies, for attacks within our borders. Terrorist groups have already found the United

States to be a fertile environment for fundraising and associated political activities. Some of this infrastructure could also be used to support more violent activities. Terrorist motives for the direct attack of U.S. targets may be practical, systemic, or symbolic. In practical terms, terrorists may seek to alter U.S. policy or to influence public opinion with a specific objective (e.g., non-intervention in a regional conflict).

In such cases, the use of force is likely to be limited and tailored to achieve a political end without an unintended backlash. Palestinian terrorism in the 1970s and 1980s fit this pattern, as did the attacks by Puerto Rican separatists in New York and at Muniz Air Base in 1981. Unlike Western Europe, the United States has not suffered from pervasive "systemic" terrorism, aimed at provoking fundamental social or political change. But the bombing in Oklahoma City as well as the militia movements suggest the existence of a reservoir of potential terrorism along these lines. Symbolic attacks, such as the bombing of Pan Am 107 or the World Trade Center bombing, imply fewer constraints on lethality and potentially much more destructive attacks. Without dismissing the potentially significant harm in terms of loss of life, economic disruption, and erosion of public confidence from direct attacks motivated by practical and systemic agendas, the strategic effect of such attacks is likely to be limited.

Leading terrorism analysts tend to agree on the general ineffectiveness of terrorism as a weapon against well-established democracies, although some exceptions should be noted. Certainly, there is little to indicate that terrorism or the threat of terrorism has been successful in changing U.S. policy on issues such as support for key allies or the use of force, much less questions of territorial integrity or domestic public policy. Similarly, the United States has not been a particularly fertile ground for ideological extremism of any stripe. The Khobar Towers attack appears to have embraced both practical and symbolic motives—encouraging the departure of U.S. forces from Saudi Arabia, a blow to the Saudi regime, and, not least, a strike at U.S. power and prestige.

To the extent that the United States remains engaged as a strategic actor around the globe—or at least in key regions—the terrorist instrument is likely to remain as an attractive means of striking at far-flung manifestations of American power and influence, as well as host regimes (the symbolic component). It may also be an attractive tactic or strategy (if part of a campaign) to compel a U.S. withdrawal from specific regions or to severely limit the prospects for access, over flight, and security cooperation. The scale and value—in lives, money, and strategic utility—of the U.S. military overseas presence makes it an attractive target for terrorists motivated by practical and symbolic agendas. Symbolic terrorism of sufficient scale presents a different type of challenge.

Certainly, terrorist use of weapons of mass destruction on U.S. soil, or against U.S. civilian or military targets abroad, would be a watershed event, especially if highly destructive. Concerns about the potential use of nuclear or other unconventional devices on U.S. soil—arguably higher now than during the nuclear targeting of the Cold War years—have become a significant feature of the national security debate. Wider availability of WMD materials and expertise, coupled with the increasingly transcendental agendas of terrorist groups, are at the heart of this concern. To the extent that terrorist use of WMD for symbolic purposes succeeds in significantly altering strategic thinking and perceptions of risk—as it almost certainly would—it might have a strategic effect by definition. Certain types of terrorist campaigns aimed at the U.S. economy and information infrastructure could also impose significant costs.

The potential for information-based attacks on the banking, telecommunications, and electric-power systems is now widely debated. RAND analysis certainly suggests that terrorist networks are steadily acquiring the expertise to engage in such attacks, although their motivation to do so remains largely untested. Terrorists may well be more interested in "keeping the Net up" to use for their own intelligence and disinformation purposes. Similarly, with the exception of hackers who acquire political agendas, terrorists are unlikely to engage in information warfare as an alternative to more destructive attacks. They are more likely to employ IW as a force multiplier—in combination with more conventional tactics—to avoid detection or to complicate efforts at mitigation and response. The progression from military and political targets to economic infrastructure—and potentially to information systems—has already been noted in relation to the evolution of IRA terrorism.

Indirect Attacks Affecting U.S. Interests

Terrorist campaigns need not directly threaten U.S. lives and territory to affect American interests. Many U.S. allies, as well as key regional states, confront serious challenges arising from terrorism. Terrorism in Israel and the Palestinian territories is a potent spoiler in relation to the Middle East peace process—a key U.S. diplomatic interest—as well as threatening the stability of the West Bank and Gaza. PKK (Kurdistan Workers Party), Islamist, and leftist terrorism in Turkey affects the stability of a key NATO ally. Islamist violence in Egypt and elsewhere in the Middle East threatens the security of pro- U.S. regimes. The need to contain internal violence distorts the behaviour of key actors, limiting their ability to play a positive regional role. Similar effects can be seen as a result of political and drug related terrorism in Mexico, Colombia, and elsewhere in Latin America and the Caribbean.

Terrorism on America's southern periphery impedes political reform and, in many cases, prevents the development of bilateral cooperation on trade and investment. It can also be an important engine of uncontrolled migration and refugee movements affecting the United States. Terrorism aimed at allied states can also have a more direct effect on U.S. citizens and interests, as witnessed through the 1970s and early 1980s in Western Europe and Japan. Acts carried out by groups such as the Red Brigades, the Bader-Meinhoff gang, Action Direct, November 17, and the Japanese Red Army Faction, aimed primarily at their own societies, occasionally spilled over into violence against American civilians and military personnel. Not only are terrorist risks becoming transnational, but with the growth of multinational businesses and nongovernmental organizations, the potential victims of terrorists are becoming less national and more global in character. Indeed, this has long been the case with international air travel; carriers may be national airlines, but the passengers are likely to be of varied nationality.

Systemic Consequences

A third perspective focuses on the overall consequences of terrorism, worldwide and domestic, for the international security environment and U.S. global engagement. The body of "international terrorist incidents," as defined by the leading terrorism databases, captures only a small fraction of global terrorism. Terrorist acts associated with international causes and Western targets claim the lion's share of media attention and policymakers' concern, but the vast bulk of terrorism worldwide is contained within state borders and is local in character. Factional terrorism in Algeria has probably claimed over 80,000 lives since 1992, and multiple incidents with as many as 100 deaths each continue to occur on a weekly basis. In Northern Ireland alone, deaths from domestic terrorism in some years have been four times the number of deaths from international terrorism in Europe as a whole. If one includes the ethnic terrorism in sub-Saharan Africa, the Balkans, and the Caucasus, it becomes clear that terrorism's global toll in lives, property, and stability is larger indeed.

As a global power with global interests, the United States will be affected by instances of large-scale ethnic terrorism, even if the effects of this chaos—the breakdown of social and political order described by Robert Kaplan in terms of "the coming anarchy"—are distant and long term. Mass terrorism in central Africa may be held at arm's length in Western perceptions. But even smaller-scale instances of ethnic terror in the Balkans, the Caucasus, or elsewhere in the former Soviet Union or China could significantly affect the strategic evolution of these regions. Third World and newly independent states are not only the major settings for terrorism, they are also the least well equipped in terms of resources and expertise to counter terrorist.

Terrorism in the War Paradigm

Fourth, terrorism can take the form of an "asymmetric" strategy employed by adversaries in conflict with the United States or its allies, as a substitute for more conventional attacks, as a waypoint to more direct aggression, or as an adjunct to conventional warfare. This notion of terrorism in the "war paradigm" is most likely to arise from the perception that the United States and the West (including Israel) more generally, have developed an unassailable capacity for conventional warfare. As a result, regional competitors wishing to change the political or territorial order must contend with a perceived revolution in military affairs that has conferred disproportionate advantages on the most developed military powers. The experience of the Gulf War offers a key lesson in this regard.

The Gulf War and subsequent operations in the Gulf, Bosnia, and elsewhere may also be seen as confirming the political will of the United States and its allies to use force in support of regional order. A potential aggressor reviewing this experience may well draw the conclusion that terrorism (as well as other unconventional instruments such as the use of weapons of mass destruction) might be employed as a means of subverting regional competitors without necessarily triggering a U.S. response. Terrorism might provide a means of throwing deployed forces off balance, gaining time for the aggressor to consolidate a cross-border operation against a U.S. ally. Finally, it may also represent an attractive means of striking at the United States directly, for symbolism or revenge, and as a means of influencing U.S. public opinion when the costs and benefits of intervention are in debate. Some of these objectives might be achieved simply through the *threat* of terrorist attacks.

The threat to use terrorists as a low-tech delivery system for chemical, biological, or nuclear weapons adds a troubling dimension. That said, the systematic use of terrorism as a strategy by regional powers confronting the United States can face substantial obstacles, as the Iraqi experience during the Gulf War suggests. During the run-up to war in the Gulf, it was widely and reasonably predicted that Saddam Hussein would mobilize sympathetic terrorist organizations to engage in attacks on Western targets, both civilian and military. In the event, terrorism was a negligible feature of the crisis, and Iraqi-sponsored terrorism certainly did not constitute anything like the potent "fifth column" some had envisioned. A range of explanations has been offered for the failure of Saddam Hussein's announced terrorism campaign, including pressure by other state sponsors (e.g., Syria), lack of planning and effective communications (exacerbated by the bombing campaign against Baghdad), and effective Western antiterrorism measures.

The prospect for terrorist attacks against harder military targets in the Gulf was probably doubly limited by the short notice and the general unpreparedness of terrorist groups, especially those with close ties to Baghdad such as the Palestinian Liberation Front and the Fatah Revolutionary Council, for attacks on deployed forces. With better preparation, both political and material, the outcome might have been quite different. Moreover, as discussed below, it may be too soon to gauge the longer-term effects of the Gulf War on Iraqi-sponsored terrorism. A variation on this theme of terrorism as an asymmetric strategy goes further to suggest that unconventional modes of conflict will stem not just from the desire to outflank the United States but from a shift in the nature of conflict itself. In this paradigm, unconventional terrorist attacks on the sinews of modern, information-intensive societies will become the norm, largely replacing conventional conflicts over the control of territory or people.

Carried to its logical conclusion, this is a future in which terrorism of all sorts, and especially information- related terrorism, becomes a more pervasive phenomenon, or even the dominant mode of war. It may, by definition; Terrorism in various forms may be used deliberately by an adversary to deter certain types of attacks in war or during periods of tension in which U.S. intervention is likely. The use of air power, in particular, may face constraints imposed by mass hostage taking, including the dispersal of hostages to likely target sites. This tactic has been employed by Bosnian Serbs as a deterrent to NATO attacks, as well as by Saddam Hussein during the Gulf War and by Chechen separatists in their conflict with Moscow. This constraint can also be a factor in the more general problem of the discriminate use of air power in urban settings.

Changing Definitions of Security

A principal characteristic of terrorism, distinguishing it from many other forms of violence, is its ability to strike directly at perceptions of personal security. The potential for nuclear war or cross-border aggression by states may inspire a sense of fear among individuals, but the sense of vulnerability is collective and abstract. Individuals will certainly be the victims of conflict between states, but leaderships and military establishments are most often seen as the real targets. By contrast, terrorism may be indiscriminate or precisely targeted, but in either instance the victims are individuals within society. This characteristic of terrorism is arguably gaining visibility from the point of view of perpetrators and sponsors as well as publics and governments as post–Cold War definitions of security evolve.

In addition to a greater emphasis on "economic security," "environmental security," and other issues that were of distinctly secondary importance during the Cold War, security perceptions are now increasingly driven by concerns about personal security and what may be termed "security of identity." The terrorist instrument has particular leverage in both contexts. For example, the victory of Benjamin Netanyahu in the most recent Israeli elections was less the result of a referendum on the peace process than a referendum on personal security in the wake of multiple terrorist attacks. In many places around the world—including the United States—debates about security are to a great degree about personal security rather than the security of the state. This is certainly true in much of the Third World, and increasingly true in the former Soviet Union, where terrorism and crime are now rampant.

One indicator of this phenomenon has been the rapid growth in private security services worldwide. This privatization of security may have some negative consequences for counterterrorism to the extent that more material and know-how finds it way into terrorist hands. Security of identity has emerged as an important issue in many settings. It is not necessary to accept arguments about a global clash of civilizations to acknowledge that perceptions of cultural identity are shaping relations between societies and regions in the post–Cold War era. Violent reactions can arise when identities are under siege, sometimes in the form of terrorism.

Current examples include the Uighur region in western China, Sri Lanka, Kashmir, and the Kurdish region of southeastern Turkey. Reactions to cultural assimilation can also take the form of global fears of cultural imperialism—a criticism most often aimed at the United States with its overwhelming role as purveyor of international tastes and information. The net result of this trend may be to increase the exposure of institutions engaged in integrative activities of all sorts (U.S. entertainment and communications firms, the European Union (EU) bureaucracies, regional organizations, etc.) to terrorist action.

Terrorism and the Conflict Spectrum

The canonical terrorist campaign in support of national liberation, religion, or ideology represents only a small portion of the ends to which terrorism is harnessed—and perhaps not even the most pervasive. Terrorism occupies an increasingly broad place on the conflict spectrum, from activity barely distinguishable from crime or vendetta, through conventional terrorism in support of political and transcendental objectives, to potential "superterrorism," perhaps as a means of proxy war. The common denominator throughout is the use of terrorism as a tactic, an aspect in which terrorism is becoming more diverse. Indeed, the vocabulary of terrorism analysis reflects this diversity, with increasing reference to narco-terrorism, environmental terrorism, economic terrorism, info-terrorism, and other threats traditionally outside mainstream security concerns.

Nor are these new dimensions of terror discrete points on the conflict spectrum. Rather, they may be difficult to differentiate at the margins and may reinforce one another. For example, the immense proceeds of drug trafficking can encourage narco-terrorism as a means of holding governments and rival cartels at bay, but may also increase the resources at the disposal of overtly political terrorist movements. Similarly, there is growing suspicion that maritime piracy, an increasingly serious problem in many places around the world, is being carried out in some instances with state sponsorship.

Terrorist movements are well placed to participate in such activities. To the extent that terrorist movements move toward network forms of organization and behaviour, their ability to shift focus from one application of terrorism to another, or to pursue multiple applications simultaneously, will increase (as in the confluence of drug related and political terror). Movements with political or religious agendas, but adept at applying similar tactics in other settings, may be recruited as proxies by state or nonstate sponsors looking to strike indirectly at U.S. or regional regimes. Terrorism's increasingly amorphous and diffuse nature has implications beyond the question of tactics and specific targets.

Its diffusion is changing the nature of terrorism as a strategic problem. One consequence of the growing pervasiveness of terrorism as a tactic across the conflict spectrum is that counterterrorism may be less and less accurately portrayed as a stand-alone activity. Counterterrorism strategies are becoming a prominent feature of a range of public policies and national strategy objectives, from urban emergency preparedness and drug policy to regional security assistance and power projection.

Future Terrorism Geopolitics

Terrorism and counterterrorism have most often been seen through a regional lens, with a natural focus on key regions such as the Middle East where terrorism has been pervasive and capable of reshaping political and strategic futures. Domestic terrorism, especially in the Third World, has been relatively neglected despite the enormous volume of incidents. Most recently, it has become fashionable to look beyond domestic and regional terrorism to consider transnational or global challenges. As other parts of this analysis suggest, there is good reason to take various transnational risks more seriously given the increasingly free movement of people and information, and the rise of networks based on these trends.

Despite these factors, it is arguable that the bulk of terrorism of whatever sort, worldwide, will have national or regional sources, even if terrorist activity crosses state and regional divides. True network terrorism may arise, where grievances and activists exist without reference to geography but are based solely on shared, functional agendas. Single-issue ideological or religious movements already exhibit some of these qualities. Yet much terrorism touching on U.S. interests will have an identifiable source, whether functional or geographic, with implications for counterterrorism strategy and planning.

Ethnic Separatism and Frustrated Nationalism

The post-1945 decolonization struggles brought a wave of terrorist campaigns affecting North and sub-Saharan Africa, South and Southeast Asia, and the Middle East, as well as the territories of the colonial powers themselves. In some cases, such as Algeria, the scale of terrorist violence associated with this period has left an enduring legacy. The post- Soviet, post–Cold War environment has encouraged a new wave of ethno-nationalist violence and much outright terrorism. In recent years, terrorism has been an instrument of large-scale "ethnic cleansing" in the Balkans, the Caucasus, and central Africa.

The impetus to create new states out of nations, and at a minimum, to carve out greater autonomy for ethnic groups, seems likely to persist as a key feature of the post–Cold War world. As in the 1940s, 1950s, and 1960s, terrorism is likely to be an accompanying feature of ethnic and national assertiveness. In particular, terrorism is likely to be most prominent as a catalyst in the early stages of ethnic conflict, "as a violent prelude to state formation," and in later stages as an expression of frustration or revenge in ethnic and nationalist endgames. Where insurgent movements have adopted terrorist tactics, this use of terrorism could increase as movements are defeated or contained. For every separatist movement that succeeds, many are likely to be unsuccessful, and the resulting frustration and perhaps desire for revenge against central authorities and intervening powers may be strong.

The increasing incidence of terrorist attacks against SFOR (the UN Stabilization Force) in Bosnia and the persistence of Chechen attacks against Russian targets even in the wake of a settlement provide useful examples. This phenomenon may also be present in the Middle East, where few would now disagree that a Palestinian state is inevitable. Yet the contours of the Palestinian- Israeli end-game are being defined by terrorism, despite the apparent success of the decades-long Palestinian drive for self-determination. In other cases—the Basque Homeland and Freedom movement, known by its Basque initials as ETA, in Spain and the Provisional IRA in Northern Ireland are exemplars—the political situation may evolve sufficiently to make the original terrorist cause an anachronism. But the tradition and infrastructure of terror remain and pose a continuing residual threat to security. Looking ahead, the successor states of the former Soviet Union represent a reservoir of ethno-nationalist terrorism. Unlike other such reservoirs in sub-Saharan Africa and Latin America, political violence emanating from these countries has a higher potential to affect U.S. interests given the region's energy reserves, the presence of nuclear weapons, and the general significance of Russian futures for international security.

Religious Extremism and "Postmodern" Terrorism

The rise of religious terrorist movements over the

past two decades is significant in several respects. First, it represents a significant shift away from the measured political agendas associated with ideological and national liberation groups active in the 1960s and 1970s. Second, and partly as a result of its transcendental or "total" character, it has been responsible for much of the increase in terrorism's lethality over the past decade. Third, religious terrorism is in no sense limited to Islamic extremists. Terrorism has been a favored tactic for violent confrontations across religious faultiness within and between states, whether in Kashmir, the former Yugoslavia, Egypt, or Sudan. Among Palestinians, Bosnians, Chechens, Sikhs, and others, politicized religious movements have played a key role in the evolution of political violence and have emerged as a geopolitical force.

There is little evidence that terrorism is losing its salience in this setting. The approach of the millennium has significance for a variety of religious and transcendental groups. The result could be an even more potent tendency toward nihilist and transcendental violence which has accompanied the end of previous centuries. Extremist millenarians and other groups on the pattern of the Aum Shinrikyo (Supreme Truth) cult in Japan may well wish to "give history a shove" through acts of superterrorism with weapons of mass destruction, and U.S. and other Western societies generally may offer especially symbolic targets. Such groups may also be among the most likely to envision transnational acts of destruction and disruption. In this context, it is notable that by 1995 the Aum cult responsible for the lethal sarin gas attack on the Tokyo subway had more members in Russia than in Japan. Groups motivated by apocalyptic impulses, together with the maturing of more traditional politically oriented terrorist movements, suggest the rise of what Walter Laqueur has described as "postmodern terrorism."

Low-Intensity Product of Regional Rivalries

The post–Cold War world abounds in active state-to-state rivalries, largely along south- south rather than north-south lines. Some rivalries will result in conventional threats to borders and direct confrontations between regimes. In other cases, the costs of direct confrontation may be too high or outcomes too uncertain. Those states may wish to exert pressure through other means, including terrorism, most likely carried out through proxies.

Current examples include North Korean sponsorship of terrorism against South Korea; Syrian and Iranian support for PKK terrorism in Turkey; Sudanese and Iranian support for Islamist terrorism in Egypt and other Middle Eastern states; and Pakistani sponsorship of Kashmiri terrorism in India. A revived Iraq with regional ambitions might well turn to the terrorism instrument as a lever in dealing with neighboring regimes. In Europe, the potential for Western intervention in Balkan rivalries may fuel less direct attempts at pressure and subversion through terrorism. Alleged Greek support for the PKK could, if relations deteriorate in the Aegean, lead to an escalating tit-for-tat campaign of state sponsored terrorism.

New Ideological Clashes

In the wake of the collapse of the Soviet Union, the notion of ideological struggle disappeared from the strategic scene. Those regimes still professing a socialist or communist agenda—Cuba, North Korea, China (in a formal sense) — appeared as quaint anachronisms. In the realm of terrorism, few vigorous movements remain on the extreme left. Some, such as the Shining Path and Tupac Amaru movements in Peru have suffered striking defeats in recent years. In Italy, Germany, France, and elsewhere in Europe, leftist and anarchist terror has been effectively contained since the early 1980s. Has this apparent triumph of liberal capitalism entirely undercut the ideological bases for 20th-century terror?

The outlook in terms of political violence is not as clear as speculations about the "end of history" might suggest. Indeed, it is possible that the apparent victory of liberal democracy in the Cold War also contains the seeds of a reaction, perhaps of violence. Economic transformation and reform across the former communist bloc is producing uneven results and is engendering resentment in many quarters. Even in the West, the dismantling of the welfare state, especially in Europe, is having a divisive effect on societies with high rates of unemployment. Elsewhere, economic reform and higher rates of economic growth are producing marked disparities in income and a mounting perception of inequality. In countries such as Mexico, Turkey, Egypt, and Indonesia, the divide between "haves" and "have nots" is making issues of class and economic opportunity central to political change. Given past experience in societies as diverse as 19th century Russia and 20th century Iran, it would be surprising if some portion of frustration with economic conditions did not find expression in acts of terrorism.

Anarchism and communitarianism may yet reemerge as sources of terrorist violence in the 21st century. However, the connection among economic deprivation, political frustration, and terrorism is not clear or direct. Contemporary research has not been able to demonstrate any clear-cut relationship "between poverty, scarcity, inflation, or any other socioeconomic indicator and terrorism. Indeed, countries experiencing the highest levels of terrorism are often among the economically and socially most advanced nations in their region, and often the least authoritarian."

As with other forms of political turmoil and violence, relative rather than absolute deprivation may be a more significant influence on the rise of terrorism. Extreme right-wing terrorism existed alongside the more prominent leftist groups of the 1970s and early 1980s, and was responsible for highly lethal attacks, especially in Italy and Turkey. In the 1990s, right-wing extremism emerged as a violent force in Germany, Austria, and elsewhere in Europe. Attacks against immigrants and "foreigners" have been at the heart of these movements, but given their nationalist character, it is not inconceivable that U.S. military forces and civilians in Europe could emerge as targets. In the United States, right-wing militia and survivalist movements are a prominent source of terrorist risk, and are increasingly networked with likeminded groups worldwide. In short, ideologically motivated terrorism in the developed world is now as likely to emerge from the right as from the left.

Another potential source of terrorism might arise from the evolution of international relations along the conflictual, "civilizational" lines suggested by Samuel Huntington. At their most ragged, these civilizational frictions could have terrorism as a central feature, both within societies (especially the "torn" societies in Huntington's model) and among states—or like-minded groupings of states, particularly where conventional military confrontations are deterred or impractical. Among current terrorist movements, the extremist transnational Islamic groups (e.g., the Arab Afghans) come closest to this model.

Taking the Huntingtonian approach to extremes, one might speculate about the possibility of terrorist groups acting against the United States with Chinese sponsorship sometime in the 21st century, against the background of a U.S.–China cold war. A revived and antagonistic Russia could also emerge as the sponsor of terrorist proxies acting against U.S. interests and impelled by nationalist rather than leftist ideology. More likely, official and intellectual criticism in Asia and elsewhere of Western cultural dominance could encourage extremists, perhaps beyond the control of governments, to carry this critique into the terrorist realm.

Crime, Drugs, and the Privatization of Security—and Terror

Transnational crime, much of it related to drug trafficking, has emerged as a leading source of violence within both developed and developing societies. The weight of this criminal activity in many economies encourages the spillover of criminal violence into the political realm. States in Latin America and elsewhere are becoming destabilized through narco-terrorism. In Italy, the war between organized crime (the Mafia, Ndraghetta, and Camora) and the state has at times spilled over into acts of outright terrorism. In Turkey, proceeds from the drug trade have been used to support PKK terrorism as well as the counterterrorist activities of right-wing nationalist groups. Colombia provides the most striking contemporary example of this problem and its bearing on U.S. interests. There, private paramilitary armies exist alongside the Colombian military, violent drug cartels, and left-wing insurgents.

Terrorist tactics have become the norm in relations among these groups, and Colombia now faces the dismal prospect of deterioration into a narco-state or outright disintegration. Colombian terrorism is also beginning to undermine regional stability, with particular effect on the border with Venezuela. One consequence of this situation has been Colombia's emergence as a leading source of international and specifically anti- U.S. terrorism—Colombia led the global tally of anti-U.S. incidents with 56 in 1995 and 53 in 1996. As the United States becomes more heavily involved in counternarcotics cooperation with Mexico, Peru, Panama, Venezuela, Ecuador, and Brazil—and possibly, Colombia—the potential for narco-terrorism against U.S. targets, civilian and military, will likely increase.

Any proposals for expanded assistance, including air interdiction, will raise new force protection problems for U.S. forces deployed to the region. In an era of transnational terrorist networks (and drug cartels have been at the forefront of such networking), it is possible for narco-terrorists to strike for practical or symbolic reasons at U.S. targets far from the area of operations in Latin America and the Caribbean. The spread of transnational violence associated with international criminal activity is also one of the elements fueling rapid growth in the private security field worldwide. Multinational corporations, nongovernmental aid organizations, and others exposed to criminal and politically motivated terrorism are increasingly reliant on the services of security firms, which now must be considered antiterrorism actors in their own right, alongside states and international organizations.

This trend is particularly pronounced in Latin America, Africa, and the former Soviet Union, where crime and terrorism— often the two are difficult to distinguish—have become leading challenges for foreign businesses and investors. Yet this privatization of security also raises the prospect of growing security information and expertise on the international market and thus potentially at the service of terrorist networks. The interaction between transnational criminal organizations and political terrorism raises special concerns. This interaction is in no sense new, and terrorist organizations as diverse as Shining Path in Peru and the PKK in Turkey derive substantial revenue from drug related commerce. But the enormous sums of money involved, as well as numerous points of contact between leading mafias and legitimate institutions, can facilitate acts that would be difficult for politically motivated terrorist groups to undertake—and pay for—on their own.

This is a particular risk in relation to nuclear terrorism. Although details remain murky, Russian mafias are already reported to be involved in obtaining and smuggling nuclear materials, and in the most extreme case, perhaps even small nuclear weapons. Further turmoil in Russia could worsen the outlook for control of nuclear materials and technology. As the conflict between transnational mafias and concerned states becomes more direct, it raises the possibility that mafias themselves will threaten nuclear or other forms of unconventional terrorism. As the experience with Osama bin Laden, a rogue Saudi businessman with extreme Islamist and anti-American views, suggests, the future environment may see more international terrorism financed by private means.

Private sponsors of terrorist movements, not necessarily limited to Islamic radicalism and with full access to information technologies and techniques, may find it convenient to operate against regimes, rival movements, or the United States from far-flung bases. And as the bin Laden experience shows; targets will include the relatively "hard" U.S. overseas military presence as well as softer diplomatic and civilian targets. Bin Laden established himself in Afghanistan, along with other Arab Afghans, and Sudan offers another congenial environment. In the future, bases for privately sponsored terrorism might as easily be found in unstable regions elsewhere— in the Balkans or the Caucasus, or where wealthy elites exist against a background of strong anti-Western resentment, such as Malaysia. Arguably, the decline in overt state sponsorship may stimulate the rise of privately sponsored terrorism— the dark side of global philanthropy.

Losers in Confrontations with the United States and the West

Losers in confrontations with the United States may turn to terrorism as a means of expressing their frustration or carrying on their armed struggle. Such attacks may be launched against targets within the United States, or aimed at U.S. citizens or interests abroad. They may be carried out by aggrieved states, or conducted by networks of sympathetic individuals, including Diaspora groups, with or without the knowledge and backing of state actors. In the wake of the Gulf War, Baghdad apparently sanctioned a failed attempt to assassinate former President Bush, and some analysts have alleged an Iraqi hand in both the World Trade Center bombing and the 1995–1996 bombing against U.S. military targets in Saudi Arabia.

Given the scale of the military defeat and subsequent economic devastation inflicted on Iraq, it would be surprising if the United States did not continue to confront a risk of Iraqi-supported terrorism motivated largely by revenge and the desire to burnish Iraq's image in radical circles. Similarly, Iranian support for terrorism against U.S. targets in the Gulf and elsewhere may be aimed, in part, at keeping the United States off balance. A good deal of the impetus, however, may come from a less rational desire for revenge against the U.S. policy of isolation and containment.

There will be other, future candidates for sponsorship of revenge based terrorist campaigns against the United States and its allies, including radical Serb nationalists angered at NATO's role in Bosnia or Mexican drug lords enraged by aggressive U.S. antidrug efforts. Moreover, terrorist campaigns based in deep-rooted anger over defeat or abuses, real or perceived, can be very long-lived, as the almost hundred-year history of Armenian revenge attacks on Turkish officials demonstrates. It is worth asking why this form of terrorism looms as a serious risk in today's environment, when it did not follow the defeat of major powers in two world wars. The difference may lie in the fact that the Gulf War, the U.S. engagement in Bosnia, and the cold war with Iran all involve disproportionate power relationships. In addition, the propensity for terrorism on the part of the defeated or "contained" may be influenced by the extent of their isolation from the international community.

Under certain conditions, as in the case of Iraq, there may be strategic reasons for maintaining a policy of post-defeat containment, even if the risk of revenge-based terrorism is increased. Another possible explanation is that the rules of the game have changed; with states now more willing to engage in terrorism as an expression of frustration in their relations with stronger powers (would a defeated France have engaged in state-sponsored terrorism against Germany in the wake of the Franco-Prussian War?). Yet another useful distinction may be made between status quo and revolutionary states, with the former generally reluctant to use terrorism as an instrument of revenge, even in defeat or political frustration.

Anarchy and Rage

Western views of terrorism have been shaped by the period of nationalist and ideological terrorism, and more recently by the challenge of religious and "postmodern" terrorism. As a result, analysts and policymakers are attuned to the question of terrorist agendas, whether political or transcendental. Yet a considerable amount of global terrorism defies this sort of explanation. The horrific violence in Algeria springs from a political crisis, but is increasingly divorced from any coherent political explanation. What began as a struggle between the military government and extremists bent on the establishment of an Islamic state has deteriorated into a shadowy war of all against all, in which personal and clan vendettas, factional struggles, and criminal infighting probably account for much of the "terrorist" violence.

Despite the government's claims to have contained the terrorism, the country hovers on the verge of anarchy. The most clearly discernible impetus behind the violence is the profound alienation—rage is perhaps the more accurate term— of younger Algerians with no economic or social prospects. Terrorism in Algeria is a striking case of a phenomenon also seen elsewhere. Arguably, Rwanda, Haiti, and Somalia provide other examples where political crises have given way to terrorist behaviour and popular rage, often divorced from any clear political agenda. The net result is dissolution of society and normal constraints on violence. In the worst case, this is the future foreseen by some observers for the 21st century's failed states.

Populations are terrorized, and this terror may spill over to affect adjacent or involved states (as in the case of Algeria and France), but much of the original motivation for terrorism and counterterrorism has evaporated. Levels of underdevelopment and social stress in Africa, Latin America, and parts of Asia suggest that there is a reservoir of terrorism flowing from anarchy and rage. Much of this violence may not resemble terrorism in the classical sense, but the challenges it poses for Western policymakers and security establishments may be very similar, especially where foreigners emerge as favored targets.

Implications for the Future

Our discussion of future sources of terrorism contains implications for counterterrorism strategy and planning, most notably:

- The United States will need to look beyond traditional agendas and traditional regions in anticipating terrorist risks. Over the next decade, the Balkans, the Caucasus, and other centers of ethnic conflict could well emerge as leading producers and exporters of terrorism affecting U.S. interests.
- To a far greater extent than in the past, both terrorists and their victims may have little to do with states and much more to do with nonstate—even private or criminal—concerns.
- The revolution in military affairs may drive less-capable powers (i.e., most of the actors in the international

system) toward asymmetric strategies when in conflict with the United States and its allies, and these strategies may well include conventional and unconventional terrorism.

- New ideological struggles may emerge to fuel terrorism aimed at the security of individuals, states, and the international system itself.
- Successful U.S. engagement in the management or shaping of the security environment in key regions may produce residual risks in the form of terrorism carried out by the defeated or contained. Implications for Strategy 111
- Finally, there may be a growing tendency toward terrorism divorced from any coherent political agenda, motivated instead by transcendental or nihilist objectives, or simply rage at the failure of some societies and the success of others.

To the extent that most terrorism, worldwide, will remain within the borders of affected societies and will not have the United States as an explicit target, the phenomenon will have highly variable consequences for U.S. security. We must recognize that U.S. exposure goes beyond the direct vulnerability of citizens, property, and territory. Terrorism also has the potential to affect U.S. interests indirectly but significantly—through attacks on allies, corrosive effects on the stability of key states and regions, as well as broader, systemic consequences for the international security environment.

The Lessons and Relevance of Counterterrorism Experience

The U.S. counterterrorism experience yields ambiguous lessons for analysts, policymakers, and military planners. Unlike many of our allies, we have not until recently faced a real domestic terrorist threat. Over the past decades, the United States has been a prominent target internationally while enjoying virtual sanctuary within its borders. U.S. security interests have been threatened by terrorism, both directly and indirectly, but the stability and survival of the U.S. as a society has never been seriously threatened by terrorism—and is unlikely to be. In these respects, the U.S. experience is sharply differentiated from that of other key states where international terrorism has been a prominent, even existential concern. A full survey of the evolution of U.S. counterterrorism policy is beyond the scope of this discussion, but it is worth touching on some of the key, enduring facets.

The most visible and controversial elements of U.S. counterterrorism policy have involved the use of force, including air power in various forms—a pattern already evident in the global debate over the U.S. cruise missile strikes against terrorism-related targets in Afghanistan and Sudan. Indeed, there is a long experience along these lines. Apart from the ordeal of the U.S. embassy hostage crisis in Tehran and the failed attempt at intervention, the leading image of U.S. counterterrorism policy is the 1986 Operation El Dorado Canyon against Libya, ordered in response to Libyan involvement in the bombing of a Berlin disco frequented by U.S. military personnel. The air strike and its effects have been heavily debated. With the exception of Britain, allied support for the operation was poor, and many observers interpreted the operation as an unsuccessful effort to assassinate Colonel Qaddafi.

Arguably, the operation was designed to send a broad political signal, reduce Libyan enthusiasm for the sponsorship of international terrorism, and demonstrate a U.S. willingness to act. The last motivation, while vaguer in intent, should not be underestimated. Indeed, the desire for strategic catharsis is arguably an important component of counterterrorism policy generally. The Libyan case yields ambiguous lessons. On the one hand, the widespread perception that Operation El Dorado Canyon dissuaded the

Libyan regime from further acts of terror does not withstand close scrutiny. After a brief respite, Libya appears to have resumed, even increased, its involvement in international terrorism. At least 15 incidents in 1987 and eight in 1988 have been linked to Libya.

The 1988 bombing of Pan Am 103 in which 278 died is the most dramatic example of terrorism with a Libyan connection in the wake of the 1986 confrontation. Libyan-sponsored terrorism aimed at Britain (including new support for the IRA) also gathered pace after 1986. On the other hand, it is difficult to measure the deterrent effect on Libyan behaviour in net terms. Even more ambitious terrorist campaigns may have been planned and interrupted. The need for more covert sponsorship may well have reduced the scope of support and the scale of incidents in the years following Operation El Dorado Canyon. The deterrent effect of the air strike on other state sponsors of terrorism is similarly difficult to measure. Overall, the narrow measures of the utility of military responses to international terrorism (How many incidents prior? How many incidents after?) May not be the most appropriate for a global power with systemic interests in the containment of terrorism and the maintenance of credibility in security terms.

Having established Libyan culpability, especially against the background of a broader U.S.-Libyan confrontation, some direct response was inevitable and required. Before the events of August 1998, less attention had been devoted to U.S. operations aimed at individuals implicated in terrorist acts against U.S. citizens. Examples include the 1987 capture of Fawaz Younis, a Lebanese terrorist aboard a yacht near Cyprus and his subsequent trial and imprisonment in the United States; the interception of an Egyptian aircraft carrying terrorists involved in the *Achille Lauro* hijacking and their seizure at Sigonella; and the capture in Pakistan of Mir Aimal Kansi, responsible for the

1993 shooting outside the CIA headquarters in Virginia. The strikes against the bin Laden infrastructure in Afghanistan provide a more recent example.

Indeed, these more personalized applications of surveillance and the use of limited force may become prominent features of future policy to counter the new terrorism. The thrust of U.S. counterterrorism policy has been the application of economic sanctions against state sponsors, multilaterally where possible, and domestic legislation. The Omnibus Terrorism Act of 1986 made terrorist attacks on U.S. citizens abroad a federal crime and authorized extraterritorial arrest and trial in U.S. courts. Counterterrorism legislation developed under the Clinton Administration reflects the changing nature of terrorism and focuses on transnational threats, weapons of mass destruction, and terrorist funding sources. Like many of its allies, the United States has been committed in principle to the policy of "no negotiations" with terrorists, but this policy has been overwhelmed on numerous occasions by the pressure for resolution. Negotiations were integral to the release of the hostages in Teheran, and the United States has negotiated officially and unofficially for the release of hostages in Lebanon, including the notorious arms-for-hostages deal with Iran.

In the post–Cold War period, there has been a refocus of intelligence collection and analysis on terrorist risks, among other unconventional security challenges. Finally, there is a tradition of hardening in response to terrorist risks. The first wave of hardening came as a response to the hijackings of international airliners in 1970s and 1980s, often with loss of American lives. The current worldwide system of airport security has its origins in this era, and the United States remains a strong advocate for further hardening of air travel. Most analysts would judge efforts in this area to have been quite successful in reducing the incidence of hijackings and attacks on commercial aircraft.

A second period of hardening is now under way as a result of the Khobar Towers bombing, the embassy bombings in Tanzania and Kenya, and the perception of a growing terrorist threat to the U.S. military and civilian presence overseas. Just as terrorism is becoming an overtly transnational problem, the international dimension of counterterrorism policy is acquiring greater importance, both in terms of cooperative efforts and of comparative lessons to be learned. With this in mind, it is useful to explore perceptions and lessons from the experience of three key allies—Britain, France, and Israel. Although each has faced quite different terrorism risks, and the exposure of all three differs in important respects from that of the United States, aspects of their experience and counterterrorism strategies are relevant to the U.S. debate. In particular, these countries have their own understanding of national vulnerability, force protection problems, and the changing nature of terrorism. They also have distinct views about American exposure and policy with regard to international terrorism.

The United Kingdom Experience

Terrorism has historically been more of an internal problem for Britain than an international one. But internal in this context exceeds simply *domestic,* since much of Britain's experience of terrorism and counterterrorism has involved the struggle against nationalist revolutionaries in the heyday of the British Empire as well as in the intense period of decolonization after 1945. Only with the revival of political violence in Northern Ireland after 1969 Britain has faced a serious domestic terrorist challenge. Another related aspect of the British experience has been the primacy of internal over military instruments in the fight against terrorism.

Elements such as the Special Air Service (SAS) have taken part in counterterrorism operations, but the lead organizations have been and remain internal— Scotland Yard (especially the Special Branch and Specialist Operations Division), the Royal Ulster Constabulary, and above all the Security Service (MI-5). Contemporary British thinking on counterterrorism tends to reflect the internal dimension that is most relevant to the United Kingdom (UK). Not surprisingly, British military thinking also focuses on internal risks, especially in the context of Northern Ireland and the spillover of Provisional IRA violence in Britain and against UK forces in Germany. A secondary, residual influence on British military doctrine flows from the colonial and postcolonial counterinsurgency experience.

In general, there is a strong preference at all levels to give the police forces the central role in countering terrorism (this was true even in relation to counterinsurgency campaigns). With respect to counterterrorism, the military is always seen—in the British military vernacular—to be "acting in support of the civil authority." It is noteworthy that Royal Air Force (RAF) basic doctrine makes no mention whatsoever of counterterrorism as a role for air power. British Army doctrine does refer to it, but almost exclusively in the context of counterinsurgency operations (i.e., countering terrorism as a tactic employed by insurgents). This is in marked contrast to the doctrinal approach within the U.S. military, which tends to identify terrorism as a separate and specific type of low-intensity conflict.

Where Britain has employed military power for counterterrorist, or more broadly counterinsurgency, purposes, the consistent keynote has been the use of "minimum force" and close integration of intelligence and operations with civil authorities. This approach has been assessed by some observers as making a virtue of necessity, given the increasingly serious constraints on British defense manpower and resources in the postwar period. The close integration and use of local resources has been another key feature of the British approach in various counterterrorism settings. British forces, including the RAF, have had to address serious force protection risks arising from the Provisional IRA's campaign of attacks on military facilities in the UK and Germany. The Ministry of Defense and the services have invested heavily in countering IRA bombing tactics. The principal lesson of this experience has been that it is very difficult, even for sophisticated and highly motivated security establishments, to keep ahead of incremental evolutions in terrorist tactics and technology.

In the European context, Britain has been relatively well-disposed toward multilateral action against international terrorism, and on numerous occasions has severed relations with state sponsors, including Libya, Syria, and Iran. London has also been broadly supportive of U.S.-led diplomatic, economic, and military initiatives in the counterterrorism arena, most notably in providing logistic support for the 1986 Operation El Dorado Canyon. The UK has not, with a few specialized exceptions, deployed its military forces in direct counterterrorist missions. Elite units such as the SAS have reportedly advised local forces on hostage rescue operations, notably in Mogadishu (1977) and in Lima (1996–1997).

To date, neither IRA terrorism nor spillovers of Middle Eastern terrorism on British territory have posed an existential threat to British security. Britain's counterterrorism efforts may be judged as successful if the containment of casualties and economic disruption are taken as measures of success. The latter objective has come under pressure in recent years as IRA attacks on the mainland have come to focus on economic targets, including the disruption of rail, road, and air transport, bomb attacks in the City of London, and plans to sabotage electric power facilities. The attractiveness of London as a target for economic terrorism, even for far-flung groups with agendas unrelated to British policy, may be a defining feature of future terrorist risks facing Britain.

The French Experience

Like Britain, France has long dealt with terrorism in both its internal and international dimensions as a consequence of colonialism and a stressful process of decolonization. France has had to address terrorist risks emanating from the Algerian revolution (both Algerian nationalists and French "ultras"), as well as more generalized spillovers of political violence from Middle Eastern conflicts. In the 1970s, France, in common with other West European states, faced a low-key threat from leftist terrorist groups such as Action Direct. More recently, France has felt the spillover effects of a new wave of Islamist violence, reaction, and anarchy in Algeria. Less prominent, but of considerable importance in relation to force protection for the French military, has been the ongoing campaign of terrorism by Corsican separatists.

French counterterrorism strategy has been guided by two basic principles. First, domestic terrorism is treated as subversion, with a heavy emphasis on judicial investigation. Arguably, the leading actors in French counterterrorism efforts are not politicians or generals but magistrates. Intelligence for counterterrorism has received high priority and much attention is paid to the social roots of extremism and political violence, attention encouraged by the large pool of disaffected North Africans in French suburbs and their potential radicalization. In general, these fears have not materialized, although young North Africans have been implicated in terrorist attacks linked to the Algerian crisis. The focus on roots of terrorism has helped shape French attitudes toward international initiatives, including the U.S.-organized March 1996 terrorism summit in Sharm al-Shayk, which French officials felt paid too little attention to underlying stresses in the region.

Second, and more significantly, France has pursued a "sanctuary doctrine" aimed at isolating the country from international terrorism through neutrality and promotion of the idea that terrorists have "nothing to achieve and nothing to fear" in France. This doctrine, applied with considerable vigor and with some success through the 1970s, has been difficult to sustain since the 1980s. On the one hand, the movement toward deeper European cooperation in the fight against terrorism has compelled France to adopt a multilateral approach, through the Trevi Group and other forum, in which France's exposure to terrorism is more difficult to control. On the other hand, the doctrine of sanctuary cannot function when France is the target of choice. The latest experience of Algerian-related terrorism is a clear example.

Activists connected with Algeria's GIA (Armed Islamic Group) have engaged in a bombing campaign in the Paris Metro and elsewhere not out of convenience, but out of well-calculated symbolism and a desire to affect French perceptions. French observers stress the manpower-intensive nature of counterterrorist operations, in terms of both surveillance and presence, and tend to be skeptical of technology as a solution. French policy, especially in the wake of terrorist bombings in Paris, places considerable emphasis on public reassurance, which has led to a large-scale presence of police, gendarmerie, and regular military forces on French streets. This last dimension has touched off an active debate within the country on the implications for civil-military relations.

The memory of a near coup organized by right-wing officers angered at the perceived abandonment of Algeria under de Gaulle still haunts the intellectual debate on this issue in France. In some respects, France comes closest to the United States in its exposure and concern about force protection. France has a long experience in countering terrorist threats to its military forces abroad, from its colonial days to losses in Lebanon and elsewhere. French NGOs such as Medecins Sans Frontieres have also confronted this problem directly in Somalia and other crisis zones, and this experience has been examined with interest by military planners. French force protection efforts have developed alongside a doctrine of expeditionary warfare, with similarities to the way in which American strategy is evolving.

Within France, the principal force protection challenge arises from the activity of Corsican separatists. This has been a special concern for the French Air Force at Solenzara air base (built by the United States in 1944). Both the base and the local electric power infrastructure have been targeted by terrorists. The Algerian bombings in Paris, while not aimed at the military, have also compelled the armed forces to take the force protection mission seriously. French analysts see Algerian extremists, in Algeria, in France, and elsewhere in Europe, as exemplars of the "new" terrorism. The extremists are characterized by loose networks rather than hierarchical structures, with many acts seemingly the work of freelance individuals or small units—although often tied to the resources and expertise of more professional activists, with many cut-outs.

Although the bulk of Algerian-inspired terrorism on both sides of the Mediterranean has been carried out through conventional, even primitive means, at least one incident involved radiological material in Paris. To the extent that France has historically been able to manage, if not really to insulate itself from, terrorist risks to its territory and its forces abroad, its counterterrorism policy has been largely successful. Terrorism has not posed an existential threat to French society since the Algerian conflict in the 1950s and early 1960s. Nonetheless, France faces difficult adjustments to its policy, arising from a continuing decline in the viability of the "sanctuary" doctrine and growing exposure to spillovers of political violence emanating from across the Mediterranean and, potentially, from France's own immigrant population. French strategists are also increasingly concerned about the potential for "superterrorism" involving WMD.

Here too, France's proximity to North Africa and its history of political involvement in the region raises the specter of terrorism being used as a WMD delivery system against the background of confrontation with a rogue regime. With regard to force protection, France's willingness to employ limited force for political management on a global basis suggests an exposure not unlike that of the United States. Indeed, the presence of French and U.S. forces in regions of shared interest (e.g., the Balkans and the Gulf), with increasingly similar expeditionary strategies, suggests considerable potential for future cooperation.

The Israeli Experience

For Israel, terrorism is an extension of war, and counterterrorism is often and naturally discussed as part of a "war paradigm." Israel's exposure to terrorism is long-standing and intensive, and perhaps as a result various myths have arisen with regard to Israeli counterterrorism policy. These myths include the notion of "no negotiation" and the doctrine of preemption and prompt retaliation. Both doctrines have frayed to the point of being unrecognizable. Israel has, in fact, negotiated in detail with a variety of Palestinian and Shi'ite groups over prisoner exchanges and other matters. More broadly, Israel is engaged in a more or less continuous process of signaling and bargaining in the cycle of terrorism and response.

Not all terrorist attacks on Israel provoke a response, and much of Israel's counterterrorism activity is aimed at preemption, prevention, and disruption rather than simple retaliation. It has been suggested that the essential difference between Israeli and American approaches to counterterrorism is that the former is definably "offensive" while the latter has had the luxury of being "defensive" or reactive in character. Developments over the past decade suggest that this distinction has lost much of its validity (if indeed it was ever valid), as Israeli policy becomes more complex and U.S. policy becomes more aggressive. Israeli observers stress that because of the compact size of the society and the classification of terrorism as a first-order threat to the security of the state, the Israeli public, even more than Americans or Europeans, see any successful terrorist incident by definition as a failure of counterterrorism policy.

At the same time, the ongoing nature of terrorism compels Israeli policymakers to spend enormous energy on reassurance and the management of terrorism as a public relations problem as well as a physical threat. According to senior Israeli officials, current counterterrorism priorities are (in this order): intelligence, operational capabilities for counterterrorism, and protection. There is a strong intelligence emphasis on humint over technical means. Operational capabilities include, above all, the capacity for preventive action, both covert and military. Protection implies measures for close-in defense and the mitigation of damage and casualties. Like their French counterparts, Israeli officials and analysts stress the manpower-intensive nature of the counterterrorism mission, although Israel has devoted considerable energy to the application of sensor technology to surveillance and interdiction.

Israeli officials and analysts are among the most sensitive to the potential for unconventional terrorism (the term is understood in Israel to include suicide bombings), including the use of WMD. Factors such as Israeli geography, the intermixture of Arab and Israeli populations, and the capacity of regional terrorist networks and their supporters lead Israeli experts to worry, foremost, about chemical agents, and only secondarily about biological and nuclear terrorism. It is widely assumed that regional adversaries bent on developing a nuclear capability will wish to hold this card as a component of national power, rather than covertly transfer it to a terrorist organization. That said, it might be possible for adversaries to use terrorists as a primitive delivery system for nuclear weapons, in which case there would be the potential for WMD terrorism to trigger a state-to state exchange.

The notion of a "new" terrorism, characterized by diffuse networks and unclear sponsorship, is actively debated in Israel. However, Israeli strategy, like that of other Western states—but perhaps particularly the United States—faces a difficult adjustment in this context. Like the United States, Israel has traditionally viewed the application of sanctions and, ultimately, the use of force against state sponsors and terrorist leaderships as a central component of counterterrorism strategy. This made sense in relation to the bureaucratic and hierarchical terrorist organizations Israel has confronted in previous decades. The Israeli air attack on the PLO headquarters at Hamman-Lif near Tunis in October 1985 was aimed at disrupting the routine workings of an organization with payrolls, file cabinets, and conference rooms—as well as sending a strong signal of resolve. Few if any of the terrorist networks Israel confronts today present such targets.

The Tunis raid, and the 1982 intervention in Lebanon, was exemplars of an increasingly anachronistic strategy aimed at forms of terrorist organization and behaviour that have largely disappeared. With the exception of the situation in southern Lebanon (which has less to do with terrorism and more to do with an insurgency), Israel's counterterrorism strategy is increasingly a struggle against individuals and networks. Despite the images derived from the Tunis attack, Israeli air power has rarely been employed in a true counterterrorism mode. The Israeli military speaks of operations in southern Lebanon as "counterterrorism," but again, the environment is shaped by an insurgency against well-armed and organized irregular forces, with political constraints on the use of force. As in many other cases of low intensity conflict, terrorist tactics make an appearance alongside other conventional and unconventional modes of war.

It also appears that Hizbullah has responded to Israel's air superiority, and military superiority in general, with a horizontal terror strategy, retaliating for Israeli air strikes through terrorist attacks against Israeli and Jewish targets elsewhere, often far afield. The devastating 1994 bombing of the Jewish center in Buenos Aires, for example, is seen by some analysts as a horizontal response to a previous series of Israeli strikes against Hizbullah targets. Some also view it as successful in deterring more extensive Israeli strikes against the Hizbullah leadership. Has Israeli counterterrorism policy been successful in strategic terms? Not surprisingly, Israeli observers are divided on this question. Terrorism has not eliminated the state of Israel, so the most extreme terrorist objective has clearly been thwarted. But most terrorism aimed at Israel has had more limited goals. It is true that Israel has outlasted most of the terrorist groups with which it has been engaged over the last decades, but terrorist groups have their own life cycles and the systemic threat remains.

It is noteworthy that even in this setting; Israel has found it difficult to capitalize on its dominance of the air. The introduction of Stinger-type munitions has complicated the picture. Israel has made extensive use of unmanned aerial vehicles (UAVs) in conjunction with air and artillery operations in southern Lebanon, with mixed success. There is a perception that UAVs have performed well but cannot offset many of the fundamental constraints on air power in the south Lebanon environment, where guerrilla attacks are often launched from populated areas. Realistic strategists have characterized the true Israeli objective as living with terrorism, not eliminating it.

By this measure, Israeli success is mixed. Existential threats to the state have been avoided, but the future of the society and the overall quality of Israeli security are still driven to a great extent by the effects of terrorism in Israel and its surrounding region. Even by the narrow measure of "maintaining political freedom of action," the judgment is increasingly gloomy. The death of Prime Minister Rabin through terrorism and the ongoing campaign of suicide bombings have had profound consequences for the peace process and have set the limits on political change. Arguably, Israeli counterterrorism policy is now driven more by tactical considerations of personal security than by strategic objectives.

Allied Perspectives on Terrorist Challenges

The U.S. position *vis-à-vis* terrorism and force protection risks is followed closely and widely discussed in Britain, France, and Israel. Several perspectives stand out. First, experts and officials in all three countries believe that the terrorist threat to U.S. forces and other targets in the Gulf region is bound to deepen. For the most part, the United States is seen as a secondary but symbolic target of regime opponents. In some cases, as with bin Laden, the expulsion of Western forces from the Gulf region, and especially Saudi Arabia, has emerged as an objective in its own right. For Iraq and Iran, any large-scale presence of U.S. forces will present a lucrative target for terrorism, aimed at keeping Washington off balance and perhaps satisfying less-rational needs for revenge. Under these conditions, a reduction in presence and movement toward an expeditionary model for rapid deployment in crises is seen as appropriate. For both British and French observers, the U.S. experience in the Gulf suggests parallels with their own past as security managers in the Middle East (e.g., the Mahdist attacks on British forces in Sudan at the turn of the century).

Notably, Israeli officials and observers do not speak in terms of "force protection" as a distinctive problem or mission. Israel's small size and pervasive military reserve system encourage a seamless view of the Israeli Defense

Forces and civilian society as potential terrorist targets. Again, south Lebanon is perhaps an exception, but here the problem is in the nature of an insurgency. The terrorist risk facing U.S. forces deployed overseas has no real parallel in Israeli experience. Second, there is a widespread perception that U.S. technology and organizational innovation are driving the "revolution in military affairs," with an ever-increasing gap between the U.S. military and all other defense establishments in the capacity for conventional war fighting. British, French, and Israeli militaries also exhibit characteristics of this revolution, but the United States is likely to remain the exemplar.

As the United States (and the West generally) become more capable than their regional adversaries, terrorism and other forms of unconventional warfare as an asymmetric strategy will become more attractive. Because of the logistical and coalition dimensions of U.S. power projection activities; there is some concern that terrorism in the "war paradigm" aimed at the United States will inevitably affect U.S. allies in Europe and the Middle East. Closer cooperation on counterterrorism strategies may be a key feature of coalition strategy in this environment and may indeed be necessary to prevent terrorist risks from complicating arrangements for access and over flight in crises.

Few European or Israeli analysts view Saddam Hussein's failure to mobilize a terrorist front in the Gulf War with complacency, and the continued prospect of Iraqi involvement in terrorist activities is cited as a key question for the future. A third theme in British, French, and Israeli perception is a degree of skepticism about the ability of technology to counter terrorist threats. Without dismissing the utility of technical means for intelligence gathering, surveillance, and preventive action, analysts in all three countries emphasize the inherently manpower-intensive nature of the antiterrorist mission, especially in civilian settings. Even in force protection, where technology can contribute substantially to the defense of fixed installations, Israeli interlocutors especially insist that "beyond the perimeter" approaches are critical. One high ranking Israeli policymaker expressed the view that the best force protection investment for the United States in the Gulf (or elsewhere) would be the assiduous cultivation of influential elites at the local level, building a constituency with a stake in a continued and secure U.S. presence.

Lessons of the Allied Experience

Despite many differences of exposure and perspective, we can identify a few key lessons of the allied experience that are relevant to U.S. and USAF strategy and planning:

- Terrorist risks cannot be eliminated, only contained and managed.
- Effective counterterrorism strategies must address the problem of networks and individuals, not just state sponsors.
- Terrorists tend to innovate in an evolutionary rather than a revolutionary manner in their attacks on military forces and other targets, staying just ahead of countermeasures.
- There is an imperative of close coordination among intelligence, civilian, and military agencies.
- More expeditionary approaches to force protection are needed to accompany expeditionary approaches to power projection.

Conceptualizing National Counterterrorism Strategy

Discussions about counterterrorism and its strategies are generally conducted in isolation. Perhaps because terrorism is often treated in emotive terms and tends to strike directly at society's sense of security, the struggle against terrorism is frequently seen as an objective in its own right, divorced from broader national security concerns. A more comprehensive approach would place terrorist risks in the context of other risks to national security and would place counterterrorism in the context of other international security—or even "grand strategic"—aims. In short, we should approach U.S. counterterrorism strategy with an eye on the broader security environment, as well as the full range of instruments—diplomatic, economic, military, and covert—at the disposal of policymakers.

Above all, counterterrorism strategy must address the challenges posed by the "new" terrorism—more lethal; increasingly networked; more diverse in terms of motivations, sponsorship, and security consequences; and more global in reach. One suitable framework, developed at RAND for conceptualizing national counterterrorism strategy, treats the problem in three dimensions: "core" strategy, or furthering the most critical objectives over the longer term; "environment shaping," or fostering the conditions for day-to-day counterterrorism success; and "hedging" or reducing exposure and mitigating the consequences in anticipation of counterterrorism failures. In some areas, air and space power can make a significant contribution to a national counterterrorism strategy. In other areas, its contribution will be limited. As the nature of terrorism has changed, the utility of air and space power is also changing in ways that may render some of the stock images of deterrence and compulsion increasingly anachronistic.

Core Strategy

National counterterrorism strategy should include four core elements: reducing the systemic causes, deterring terrorists and their sponsors, reducing the risk of "superterrorism," and retaliating where deterrence fails. These elements address the longer-term terrorist risk to broader U.S. security interests (e.g., regional stability and freedom of action) as well as special, sharper threats to national security (e.g., terrorist use of WMD).

- *First, political violence, including terrorism, has systemic origins that can be ameliorated.* Social and economic pressures, frustrated political aspirations, and in a more proximate sense, the personal experiences of terrorists and their relations, all contribute to the terrorist reservoir. As one strategist has noted, "terrorism is not ubiquitous and neither is it uncontainable, but the potential for its occurrence is virtually as widespread as is the manifestation of bitter political antagonisms ... reduce the latter and you will reduce, though not eliminate, the former." That said, policies aimed at reducing the systemic causes for terrorism are by their very nature longer-term instruments.

The failure of regimes to provide for peaceful political change and the phenomenon of economies unable to keep pace with population growth and demands for more evenly distributed benefits can provide fertile ground for extremism and political violence affecting U.S. interests. For this reason, the United States has a stake in promoting political and economic reform as a means of reducing the potential for terrorism, some of which, as in Latin America, the Middle East, and the Gulf, may be directed at us. Similarly, unresolved ethnic and nationalist conflicts have traditionally been a leading source of terrorism. Diplomacy and the use of force can contribute both to the containment and the eventual resolution of such conflicts, whether in the context of the Palestinian issue, nationalist confrontations in the Balkans or the Caucasus, or ethnic frictions in Africa.

Left unresolved, these confrontations will persist as flashpoints for local and international terrorism. Incorporating policies aimed at reducing the body of grievances behind terrorism does not imply any reduction in the taboo against terrorism as a tactic or sympathy for terrorists. It simply treats terrorism as we would other sources of conflict and threats to security, by giving first priority to prevention. It is unlikely that air and space power can contribute significantly to national strategy in this area, which is largely the province of diplomacy and economic policy, and has more to do with the reform of societies than threat or use of force. Indirectly, however, air power can bolster the security of societies against external threats (as with our Gulf allies or Israel) and permit greater attention to domestic problems—if governments choose to do so intelligently. Where strategies for forestalling domestic and regional conflict fail, as in "pre-Dayton" Bosnia, air power can support peacekeeping, peacemaking, and humanitarian assistance and perhaps reduce the longer-term scope for terrorism and political violence.

- *A second core objective of counterterrorism strategy should be to strengthen and deepen deterrence.* This is a less and less straightforward challenge as terrorists and their sponsors become more diverse and diffuse. Against state sponsors, where these still exist in the traditional sense and can be identified, the most effective approach may be to find targets of value to the regime in the most direct sense, the loss of which would threaten the leadership's hold on power. More generalized diplomatic, economic, or military initiatives aimed at isolation or inflicting pain and embarrassment face many obstacles when the sponsor is a totalitarian or rogue regime. With the most extreme rogues, such as Libya or Iraq, there is the deeper question of whether their behaviour, including the sponsorship of terrorism, can be deterred at all—a dilemma that takes on greater significance if we consider terrorism with weapons of mass destruction.

Many analyses have addressed the difficulty of applying rational and ethnocentric strategic concepts to "crazy" states. In this setting, deterrence probably cannot be subtle. To be effective, the threat posed may need to be massive and "personal" to the leadership. Qaddafi's Libya is perhaps the best example of this. As noted earlier, the El Dorado Canyon raid may not have deterred Qaddafi from further involvement in international terrorism, but it probably did deter him from the open activity characteristic before 1986. In contrast, Syrian and Iranian support for terrorism does not follow the "crazy" state model. In both cases, and most clearly for Syria, sponsorship of terrorism continues to serve national and regime interests. Damascus views its ties to terrorist groups as a means of leverage in relations with Israel, Turkey, other Arab states, and the West.

It is a card to be kept, used, or traded away as circumstances dictate. As with Iraq, the propensity to become involved with terrorist movements may also flow from the oppressive security culture within the country or the natural link between "state terrorism" and the use of terrorism as an instrument beyond the state's borders. For Iran, international terrorism involvement might best be seen as a product of a "violent and unstable political history" (true of many states in the region) and the dictates of internal politics in the wake of the revolution—"an instrument of neither first nor last resort." Support for terrorism in this case has rational, if unacceptable, underpinnings, so a more diverse range of tactics can be useful to deter it, including embarrassment, isolation, and denial of key political and economic goals. Indeed, it is arguable that Iraqi, Iranian, and Syrian support for terrorism is a product of perceived strategic weakness and relative weakness in conventional military terms vis-à-vis the United States, Israel, and the West—a sort of ongoing asymmetric strategy.

To the extent that Iraq, Iran, and Syria develop stronger conventional and unconventional military capabilities, they may actually find the terrorist instrument less attractive—and turn to different, perhaps more serious challenges for the United States. In some cases, as in Afghanistan and Sudan, state behaviour may constitute a gray area, with tolerance for terrorist activity short of outright sponsorship. Such a regime may not be a U.S. target for preemption or retaliation, but it cannot expect to enjoy immunity from counterterrorist attacks or other sanctions. Air power has been and will likely continue to be a preferred instrument for striking state sponsors where U.S. interests are directly threatened. This capacity for preemption and retaliation, as demonstrated in Libya and Iraq, supports deterrence vis-à-vis state sponsors, especially where the calculus is more rational than "crazy." Looking beyond state sponsors, the task of deterrence becomes more difficult but also more imperative given trends in the nature of terrorism. Most observers agree that traditional state sponsorship, while still a factor in key instances, is waning.

The "new" terrorism is characterized by more diffuse groups with hazier links to sponsors, many of whom may be nonstate actors in their own right. As a result, the central problem for deterrence is likely to be dealing with individuals and networks rather than states and hierarchical terrorist organizations—as illustrated dramatically by the events of August 1998. shorthand for this challenge might be "personalized" deterrence. Our counterterrorism policy already shows an inclination in this direction; air power will very likely support this dimension in the future, with consequent requirements for technological leverage in dealing with small actors, even individuals, often in urban settings. Tasks in this setting would include the extraterritorial apprehension of terrorist suspects (as in the forcing down of Achille Lauro hijacking suspects over the Mediterranean at Sigonella), or the return of terrorists caught in far-flung places, with or without the cooperation of host countries.

The recent capture in Pakistan of the alleged perpetrator in the lethal shooting outside CIA headquarters provides another example along these lines. More generally, things of value to terrorists and their sponsors as individuals can be identified and held at risk, through the use of force or, equally, through administrative or information means. The targets might be bank accounts, safe-houses, or the individuals themselves. Personalizing our counterterrorism strategy suggests many possible tactics other than outright assassination, which is an unattractive and legally constrained policy and is, on balance, incompatible with U.S. interests. In seeking to end state sponsorship and to tailor deterrence to the growing role of individuals and networks in international terrorism, we should also be aware of potential and unintended consequences of success. State-sponsored terrorism has historically been among the most conservative in its tactics, and state sponsors may sometimes constrain the behaviour of violent groups.

If extremist groups shift from state sponsorship to the patronage of wealthy sympathizers or nonstate actors with criminal connections, the net result may be less restraint and greater lethality. That said, this trend is already well under way and has little to do with increased pressure on state sponsors. Similarly, in targeting network nodes and key individuals—personalizing deterrence—we may confront some undesirable consequences of such "decapitation." The experience of left-wing terrorism in Europe in the 1970s suggests that splintered and compartmentalized groups may be more violent, in part to demonstrate that they have not lost their ability to act.

Certainly, the current fragmented terrorism in Algeria exceeds in its violence anything committed by more coherent terrorist organizations in recent years. Yet it can be argued that the new, networked model of terrorist organization has arisen for reasons of its own and is by definition less affected by the loss of individuals. Such organizations cannot be decapitated in the traditional sense, but their effectiveness can be reduced by interfering with key nodes (people) in the infrastructure and removing key operatives from circulation.

- *A third and increasingly important "core" objective will be to reduce the risk of "superterrorism" involving weapons of mass destruction.* This is, above all, a problem of homeland defense for the United States, and perhaps the most serious homeland defense challenge in the post–Cold War environment. Indeed, the United States as a global power has a stake in containing this risk worldwide, not just on U.S. territory, since a devastating terrorist use of WMD— especially a nuclear device—would transform security perceptions and strategic reality everywhere. The potential for WMD terrorism has emerged as a driving force behind the public debate on terrorism and counterterrorism policy, as well as recent U.S. government initiatives on the same issues.

Nuclear, biological, chemical, or radiological attacks by terrorists, acting alone or as part of a sponsored strike against the United States, could cause mass casualties as well as immense economic and social disruption in urban areas. Military facilities, including air bases, will be vulnerable, although WMD attacks are unlikely to prove effective unless they are near or on the base. The global control and surveillance of WMD-related materials (and expertise) is an important objective. If state adversaries are manufacturing agents of mass destruction that could be delivered by terrorist means, preemptive action could be required, with consequent demands on air power for the attack of hardened targets. Specialized intelligence activities, in cooperation with allied states, are essential for warning, control, and intervention in this inherently global problem area.

- *Fourth, the United States must have the capacity and willingness to retaliate against terrorists and their sponsors when deterrence and preventive measures fail.* With the increasing lethality of international terrorism, the question of retaliation can be expected to loom even larger in the perceptions of policymakers and the public. A demonstrated willingness to retaliate makes an obvious contribution to deterrence, especially in relation to state sponsors with much to lose, but also serves less-tangible purposes. Retaliation, including the use of air power as in Operation El Dorado Canyon, as in Afghanistan and Sudan, can serve an important cathartic purpose, and reassures the public and international opinion that terrorism against U.S. interests does not fall below the threshold of U.S. action.

As in the consideration of deterrence, the principal challenge for the future is likely to be the adaptation of our retaliatory policies and techniques to deal with individuals, nonstate actors, and terrorist networks. Again, in many cases the appropriate response may not be the physical destruction of targets, but rather strikes against information and resources. It is worth noting here that terrorism itself can be a constraint on the use of force, including air power, by the United States in regional contingencies. Terrorist action against facilities, personnel, and equipment, either deployed or en route, is one problem. Another problem is posed by the demonstrated tendency of adversaries under threat of U.S. air strikes to take hostages as a means of deterring attacks. Saddam Hussein resorted to this tactic during Desert Shield, and Bosnian Serb commanders held UN peacekeepers for similar purposes. The likelihood that adversaries, especially weak adversaries, will employ such tactics in the future reinforces the need for accurate intelligence and surveillance, highly discrete targeting, and nonlethal technologies.

Environment Shaping

The core dimensions of counterterrorism strategy will need to be supported by a range of policies aimed at containing near-term risks and fostering the conditions for ongoing success. Several of these policies have implications for air and space power.

- *Make international terrorism more transparent.* Air and space power can contribute to the embarrassment and isolation of traditional state sponsors by making their support for terrorism more transparent to U.S. policymakers and world opinion. Examples are the use of space-based surveillance, reconnaissance aircraft, and unmanned aerial vehicles to expose terrorist camps or other forms of state or nonstate assistance. Overhead imagery helped explain the U.S. action against terrorist targets in Afghanistan. This is likely to be a key, high-leverage role for air and space power, and can have a synergistic effect with other counterterrorism instruments. Similarly, the actions of terrorist organizations and networks of individuals can be monitored from space and the information used by the United States or shared, where appropriate, to forestall terrorist attacks or to identify critical nodes in the terrorist infrastructure.

While it may be argued that this is largely the province of humint, the growing reliance of terrorist networks on modern information flows introduces new possibilities for surveillance and intelligence gathering by technical means short of space-based reconnaissance. The ability to make terrorism more transparent can help to build the case for coordinated, international responses to terrorist networks or to state sponsors, where otherwise evidence is often murky and insufficient to mobilize allied policymakers (as has been the case vis-à-vis Iran).87 Air and space power can also serve force protection in increasingly risk-prone environments such as the Gulf and Central America.

- *Shrink zones of chaos and terrorist sanctuary.* Just as reducing the root causes of terrorism is a core objective, so should we change the conditions in areas that have offered terrorists safe havens and bases for transnational operations. Afghanistan, Sudan, Northern Iraq, and Syrian-controlled areas of Lebanon are leading examples. In another setting, conditions in Colombia offer similar refuge. We must prevent the emergence of new zones of chaos and sanctuary. As noted earlier, there is significant potential for this in parts of the Balkans, the Caucasus, and Central Asia. Where domestic terrorism is rife, as in Algeria, there will also be a risk of cross-border activity. At the diplomatic level, we should be keenly aware of the risks inherent in allowing political vacuums to exist, with no clear-cut exercise of sovereignty. Such areas will be the natural operating environment for violent nonstate actors and terrorist networks. To the extent that notions of spreading anarchy on the periphery of the developed world prove correct, the problem of terrorist-friendly zones may become more widespread.

Governments presiding over sanctuaries, whether within their own territory (as in Sudan) or across their borders (as with Syria's role in Lebanon) must understand that closing down terrorist bases and expelling known activists are essential preconditions for any form of positive relations with the United States, and that continued tolerance of terrorist activity implies a high and continuing cost. With regard to the forcible apprehension of terrorist suspects, zones of chaos and sanctuary should be fair game for the United States and the international community. Large rewards for information on suspect individuals and groups in such areas may be effective.

- *Make counterterrorism an integral part of alliance strategies.* Alliance relationships in Europe and Asia are changing to reflect post–Cold War requirements. In parallel with the geographic enlargement of NATO, the Alliance is beginning to take up new missions, including peacekeeping and crisis management. Defense relationships with Japan, Israel, and even Russia are being driven in the direction of cooperation on security challenges rather than the defense of borders. Cooperation in the realm of counterterrorism should be high on the agenda for these evolving security relationships. In the case of NATO, this may require giving the Alliance a specific mandate to work in this area, since terrorism is still treated as a national responsibility. A coordinated approach to terrorism should be part of the broader dialogue on "third pillar" issues (crime, narcotics, migration, etc.) between Washington and the EU. If U.S. counterterrorism strategy concentrates on homeland defense against WMD terrorism and features more active efforts to apprehend suspects and preemptive action abroad, multilateral coordination will become essential if our policy is to avoid political frictions with allies.

- *Limit U.S. exposure worldwide, consistent with grand strategic objectives and operational requirements.* As a global power with pervasive economic and political interests, the United States will remain exposed to international terrorism. Although facilities can be hardened and tourists, businessmen, and diplomats can adjust their behaviour to present less-attractive targets, the very scale and importance of the U.S. engagement overseas suggests this must be an "accepted vulnerability." With regard to the U.S. military presence, more explicit choices are possible. The movement toward an expeditionary model for presence and power projection has many sources, but must include the desire to limit terrorist risks as a constraint on U.S. freedom of action. In some instances, as in Korea, requirements for immediate forward defense make reliance on a purely expeditionary model for power projection difficult. In Europe, and perhaps elsewhere, political imperatives will drive the balance between permanent presence and power projection. In the Gulf, where terrorist risks are high and probably growing, the expeditionary model has considerable advantages.

The resentments and frictions associated with a highly visible permanent presence may be reduced, limiting the incentives for terrorism directed at U.S. forces. At the same time, a more flexible and unpredictable approach to basing complicates the planning problem for terrorists bent on attacking U.S. facilities and personnel. The Air Expeditionary Force concept enjoys these and other advantages in relation to terrorist risks but also imposes new challenges for force protection, which must also become more expeditionary, adaptable, and conversant with conditions in advance of deployments to far-flung destinations. USAF force protection efforts are part of the "hardening" task, and will contribute to U.S. counterterrorism strategy by reducing terrorism- related constraints on U.S. freedom of action.

These efforts will be part of a larger global equation with regard to vulnerability and terrorists' choice of targets. Past terrorist behaviour suggests a considerable degree of adaptability in tactics, with a natural preference for soft targets. If U.S. military forces deployed in the Gulf become harder, less-attractive targets, terrorists might shift their focus to U.S. diplomats and businessmen or the oil industry. This displacement effect of hardening on other targets in no sense reduces the rationale for better force protection—it simply suggests that counterterrorism must be viewed in a comprehensive manner, with full recognition of all consequences.

- *Target terrorist funding and networks*. As traditional patterns of state sponsorship wane and are overtaken by a much more diffuse type of sponsorship, with cut-outs and a greater role for nonstate sponsors, our counterterrorism policies must adapt accordingly.

"Following the money" will help to identify sponsors and the terrorists themselves in this murkier environment. Understanding and severing the funding links between international crime and drug organizations and politically motivated terrorists will interrupt a major source of support for some of the most violent terrorist movements and make the most expensive and lethal technologies more difficult to acquire (e.g., agents of mass destruction, Stinger-class missiles). More diverse funding sources, including sympathetic individuals in the United States, also imply a larger group of potentially violent operatives.

To some extent, this linkage has already been borne out with the progression from fund-raising to international terrorist incidents on U.S. soil. The propensity for terrorist groups to seek "private-sector" funding, often in parallel with apparently nonviolent social and political activities (Hamas provides an example), may encourage victims of terrorist acts to seek financial compensation from terrorist movements, their fund-raisers, and donors. The recent compensation paid by the PLO to the Klinghoffer family, relatives of the victim of the 1985 Achille Lauro hijacking, sets a useful precedent.

If donors to causes linked with terrorism become aware that their assets can be placed in jeopardy, their enthusiasm may well be dimmed. Similarly, the propensity of modern terrorist movements to adopt network forms of organization in preference to more traditional, hierarchical patterns is to a great extent a consequence of the information revolution and the growing use of modern communications by terrorists. Inadequate scrutiny and control of students from countries implicated in terrorism resident in the United States raises issues related to terrorist infrastructure as well as the leakage of technical expertise on weapons of mass destruction.

Indeed, concepts of "leaderless resistance" as espoused

by anti-government militia groups in the United States or the highly compartmented cells seen in Hamas and other potent terrorist groups in the Middle East are greatly facilitated by encrypted phone communications and the Internet. This suggests that much of our counterterrorism effort in the future will be in the information warfare realm. Although networks will be more difficult to penetrate and disrupt than traditional groups, they too will have vulnerable nodes that can be targeted. Networks are likely to be required to fight networks, which argue for greater networking and coordination among counterterrorism services and agencies.

Hedging Strategy

The third dimension of counterterrorism strategy accepts that however effective other aspects of our strategy may be, terrorists will continue to operate and act against our interests. The terrorist threat can never be reduced to zero, and the growing tendency toward action by small, ad hoc groups—freelance terror—holds the potential for significant numbers of incidents with only a loose motivational link. Under these conditions, U.S. and allied policy will need to hedge against continued terrorism, limiting its scale and destructiveness, as outlined below.

- *Harden key policies and strategies against terrorist interruption.* Beyond hardening key civilian and military facilities, the United States must consider ways of hardening policies to limit terrorist risks to our national interests. Key negotiations, such as the Middle East peace process, might be put on a faster track to reduce the opportunity for extremists to disrupt the process through terrorism. Various operations other than war, especially peacekeeping deployments, might be timed and configured to reduce the potential for terrorist attacks on U.S. forces (e.g., without a prolonged and uncertain exit phase that makes terrorism an attractive option for elements aiming to end a deployment).

- *Emphasize stand-off and space-based capabilities for presence and intervention in the most chaotic and unstable regions.* In addition to moving toward an expeditionary approach to power projection as a means of shaping the strategic environment, U.S. and USAF strategy can hedge against terrorist risks stemming from anarchy and regime instability by emphasizing long-range strike and space-based surveillance as a contribution to regional security. Soldiers and aircraft on the ground, in-country and vulnerable to terrorist attacks, should not be the only measure of our security interests and commitments, although in some cases an in-theater presence will remain essential for deterrence and reassurance.
- *Prepare to mitigate the effects of conventional and unconventional terrorism.* The difficulty of eliminating the terrorist risk—regardless of national strategy—and the growing lethality of international terrorism point to a need for measures and capabilities aimed at limiting the consequences of terrorist incidents. The trend toward fewer but more spectacular attacks means that special operations forces for intervention and hostage rescue will be a vital "force in being," if infrequently employed. In fact, hostage rescue, a traditional raison d'être for antiterrorist forces, may be a declining mission as politically motivated terrorist groups with explicit agendas give way to religious, millenarian, and "asymmetric" terrorists with less finely calibrated and more destructive agendas.

Special operations forces are likely to be employed in the future for forcible apprehension, or for preemptive action, especially where agents of mass destruction are involved. The potential for highly destructive and disruptive terrorist attacks in urban areas, possibly with weapons of mass destruction, has encouraged more active efforts to prepare municipalities in the United States and elsewhere to recognize and respond to such attacks. In the wake of the Aum cult's chemical attack in the Tokyo subway and revelations about planned attacks by Islamic extremists on targets in New York, and many other minor incidents involving agents of mass destruction, this emphasis is likely to continue and deepen.

Policy makers and publics may eventually come to regard this as the leading post–Cold War civil defense issue. Civilian agencies are not yet well prepared to detect and manage the consequences of a disastrous chemical, biological, or radiological attack, not to mention the detonation of a nuclear device—although they are improving. Addressing these issues will be a fertile area for cooperation between civilian and defense agencies, as well as the military services, and a growing source of demands for operations other than war. In the realm of information operations, the United States and the USAF must weigh carefully the implications of modernization and the growing connections between military and civilian infrastructures. In some cases, we may wish to pay a price in terms of efficiency to harden and insulate critical communications links. Most contemporary analyses of terrorism focus on terrorist political violence as a stand-alone phenomenon, without reference to its geopolitical and strategic context.

Similarly, counterterrorism policy is rarely discussed in terms of its place in broader national security planning. Prior to the specter of "superterrorism" using weapons of mass destruction, terrorism, however horrible, never posed an existential threat to U.S. security. With the important exception of WMD, terrorism still does not pose a grave threat to America's future as it does to many other societies around the world. But many types of terrorism do pose a threat to U.S. interests, from homeland defense to regional security and the stability of the international system. As a global power, the U.S. perspective on terrorism is bound to differ in substantial ways from that of others, including allies such as Britain, France, and Israel, whose experiences provide lessons, but not necessarily direction, for U.S. counterterrorism policy. In light of the preceding analysis, and other RAND research, certain overall conclusions stand out:

- *Terrorism is becoming a more diverse and more lethal problem.* Contemporary terrorism occupies an expanded place on the conflict spectrum, from connections to drug trafficking and crime to its use as an "asymmetric strategy" by state and nonstate adversaries in a war paradigm. For a variety of reasons, primarily the rise of religious and millenarian groups with transcendent agendas but also the hardening of established political groups, terrorism has become more lethal. With the potential for catastrophic terrorism using weapons of mass destruction, lethality could increase dramatically.
- *The geopolitics of terrorism are changing.* Over the next decades, the prevailing image of terrorism affecting U.S. interests as a problem emanating largely from the Middle East is likely to be overtaken by a more diverse set of risks. The Balkans, the former Soviet Union, and Latin America are set to emerge as significant sources of terrorism aimed at or affecting U.S. civilian and military activities. Moreover, the vast bulk of global terrorism will continue to be confined within the borders of affected states. More anarchic futures in the Third World could fuel this type of terrorism, threatening America's systemic interests as a global power and placing constraints on our international engagement.
- *Much counterterrorism experience is losing its relevance in light of the "new" terrorism.* Many established images of counterterrorism policy, above all the use of force against state sponsors, are losing their relevance as

traditional forms of terrorist behaviour and organization—largely a product of the ideological and national liberation movements of the 1960s–1980s—give way to new patterns. The new terrorism often lacks a detailed political agenda against which the use of violence can be calibrated, and is therefore more lethal. It is less hierarchical in organisation, more highly networked, more diffuse in membership and sponsorship, and may aim at disruption as well as destruction. The absence of clear-cut sponsorship, above all, will complicate the task of deterrence and response. It will also compel a reorientation of policy to target nonstate sponsors and individual suspects.

- *Foreign experts see U.S. exposure increasing but view the problem in narrower terms.* A survey of expert British, French, and Israeli perspectives yields a gloomy outlook with regard to U.S. exposure to terrorist risks, which are widely seen as deepening, particularly with regard to U.S. forces in the Gulf. Policymakers and observers in these allied countries are not surprisingly focused on specific national risks, few of which are analogous to risks facing the United States at home and abroad. With the limited exception of France, which shares a global and expeditionary outlook in strategic terms, terrorist challenges are generally viewed in narrower, but starker, terms. Notably, experts in all three countries share a degree of skepticism about technology as a "solution" in counterterrorism.
- *A comprehensive counterterrorism strategy should have core, environment shaping, and hedging components.* Treating terrorism as one of many national security challenges suggests a multidimensional approach. Core, longer-term strategy must address the political, economic, and social roots of international terrorism, make deterrence relevant to nonstate actors as well as state sponsors, and reduce the risk of truly catastrophic

terrorism using weapons of mass destruction. The environment shaping aspect aims to create conditions for successfully managing terrorist risks: making terrorism more transparent, shrinking "zones of chaos," harnessing key alliances to the counterterrorism effort, reducing U.S. exposure, and cutting off terrorism's resources. Finally, the United States can hedge against inevitable terrorism by hardening policies as well as targets, and preparing to mitigate the effects of increasingly lethal terrorist acts.

Implications for Military Strategy and the U.S. Air Force

In many instances, air and space power will not be the best instruments in the U.S.-counterterrorism arsenal, and air power will rarely be used independently against terrorism. However, air and space power can play a role in intelligence and covert action. There will also be instances, as in the past, where air and space power will be instruments of choice in the fight against terrorism. Moreover, terrorism and counterterrorism policy are changing in ways that will significantly affect the future contribution of air- and space-based instruments.

- *Events in Sigonella and Afghanistan as well as Operation El Dorado Canyon may be key models for the future.* Air power in the service of counterterrorism will include, but will also go beyond, the surveillance and punishment of state sponsors. Deterrence and response will likely evolve in the direction of a more "personalized" approach, emphasizing the monitoring and attack of key nodes in terrorist networks and the forcible apprehension of terrorist suspects—with or without the cooperation of local states. Future demands on air power may be driven as Implications for Strategy much by requirements for intercepting and extracting suspects as by the need to attack terrorist training camps and strike regimes supporting the export of terrorism.

- *Air and space power will help make terrorism—an inherently amorphous phenomenon—more transparent.* The ability to identify and to target terrorist-related activity and to help expose terrorism and its sponsors for policymakers and international opinion will be key contributions of air- and space-based assets. As terrorism becomes more diffuse and its sponsorship increasingly hazy, finding the "smoking gun" will become more difficult but essential to determine strategies and build a consensus for action. Space-based sensors, surveillance by UAVs, and signals intelligence (SIGINT) will facilitate the application of air power and other instruments in the service of counterterrorism.
- *Gaining leverage in addressing the new terrorism will be a key strategic and technical challenge.* Future requirements for counterterrorism will be part of a broader need to tailor air and space power to challenges posed by nonstate actors, including networks of individuals. At the same time, policy instruments, including air and space power, will need to concentrate on detecting and preventing the use of weapons of mass destruction by terrorists—whether as a stand-alone apocalyptic act or as a low-tech delivery system in the hands of adversaries.
- *Much terrorism—and counterterrorism action—will focus on urban areas, with strong political and operational constraints.* Terrorism is increasingly an urban phenomenon, worldwide. One explanation for this is that the political fate of most modern societies is determined by what happens in cities. Terrorists seeking to influence political conditions have many incentives to attack urban targets. Terrorists with transcendental objectives will, similarly, find symbolic and vulnerable targets in urban settings.

The use of air power in a counterterrorist mode faces the more general problem of operating in an urban environment (the difficult Israeli experience in Beirut and south Lebanon is instructive). Terrorists and their facilities will be difficult to locate and target. Operations against them or to rescue hostages will pose severe challenges for the use of air power, not least the risk of placing uninvolved civilians in harm's way. The viability of air power as an instrument in such settings may depend on the capacity for discriminate targeting and the use of less-than lethal technologies.

- *Air power's pervasiveness and speed are advantages in the face of transnational and transregional terrorism.* In an era in which terrorist acts may take place across the globe and where sponsors cross national and regional lines, counterterrorism strategies will become "horizontal" in character. Where terrorists and their sponsors can be identified and attacked with purpose, the global sight and reach of air- and space-based assets will be valuable to national decision makers.
- *Air and space power will have a synergistic effect with other counterterrorism instruments.* Air and space power can be used in concert with covert action, diplomacy, economic instruments, and joint military operations. The notion of "parallel warfare," developed in relation to attacks on infrastructure in war, will also be relevant to counterterrorism operations. Operations using a range of instruments can be designed to act, in parallel, on terrorist supporters, terrorist infrastructure and networks, and the terrorists themselves.

Bibliography

Adams, James. *The Financing of Terror,* New York: Simon & Schuster, 1986.

Alexander, Yonah and Richard Latter, eds. *Terrorism and the Media: Dilemmas for Government, Journalists & the Public,* Washington, DC: Brassey's, 1990.

Andersan, Sean and Stephen Solan. *Historical Dictionary of Terrorism,* 2nd ed. Lanham, MD: Scarecrow, 2002.

Atkins, Stephen E. *Terrorism: A Reference Handbook,* Santa Barbara, CA: 1992.

Bell, J. Bower. *Transnational Terror, Washington,* DC: American Enterprise Institute, 1975.

Burton, Anthony. *Urban Terrorism: Theory, Practice, Response,* London: Cooper, 1975.

Chaliand, Gerald. *Terrorism: From Popular Struggle to Media Spectacle,* Atlantic Highlands, NJ: Saqi, 1987.

Comb, Cindy C. *Terrorism in Twenty-First Century,* 2nd ed. Upper Saddle River, NJ: Prentice Hall, 2002.

Crelinsten, Ronald D. and Denis Szabo. *Hostage- Taking,* Lexington, MA: Lexington Book, 1979.

Crenshaw, Martha. *Terrorism, Legitimacy, and Power,* Middletown, CT: Wesleyan University Press, 1983.

Gay, Kathleen. *Encyclopedia of Political Anarchy,* Santa Barbara, CA: ABC-CLIO, 1999.

George, Alexander, ed. *Western State Terrorism,* New York: Routledge, 1991.

Gurr, Ted Robert. *Handbook of Political Conflict: Theory and Research,* New York: Free Press, 1980.

Harmon, Christopher C. *Terrorism Today,* London: Frank Cass, 2002.

Hoffman, Bruce. *Inside Terrorism,* New York: Columbia University Press, 1998.

Jenkins, Brian. *International Terrorism: The Other World War,* Santa Monica, CA: RAND, 1985.

Kushner, Harvey W. ed. *The Future of Terrorism: Violence in the New Millennium,* Thousand Oaks, CA: Sage, 1998.

Laqueur, Walter. *History of Terrorism,* New York: Transaction Publishers, 2001.

Lesser, Ian O. et al. *Countering the New Terrorism,* Santa Monica, CA: RAND, 1999.

Lewis Bernand. *The Political Language of Islam,* Chicago: University of Chicago Press, 1988.

Miller, Abraham H. *Terrorism and Hostage Negotiations,* Boulder, CO: Westview, 1980.

Moss, Robert. *Urban Guerrilla Warfare,* London: International Institute for Strategic Studies, 1971.

Netanyahu, Benzamin. *The Terrorism Reader,* New York: Meridian, 1986.

O'Neill, Bard E. *Insurgency and Terrorism: Inside Modern Revolutionary Warfare,* Washington, DC: Brassey's, 1990.

Peters, Rudolph. *Jihad in Classical and Modern Islam,* Princeton, NJ: Markus Wiener, 1996.

Picard, Robert G. *Media Portrayals of Terrorism: Functions and Meaning of News Coverage,* Ames: Iowa State University Press, 1993.

Pillar, Paul R. and Michael H. Armacost. *Terrorism and U.S. Foreign Policy, Washington,* DC: Brookings Institution, 2001.

Rashid, Ahmed. Jihad: *The Rise of Militant Islam I Central Asia,* New Haven, CT: Yale University Press, 2002.

Rosie, George. *The Dictionary of International Terrorism,* New York: Paragon House, 1987.

Schamis, Geraldo Jorge. *War and Terrorism in International Affairs,* New Brunswick, NJ: Transaction Publishers, 1980.

Segaller, Stephen. *Invisible Armies: Terrorism in the 1990s,* San Diego, CA: Harcourt Brace Jovanovich, 1987.

Sofaer, Abraham D. and Seymour E. Goodman. *The Transnational Dimension of Cyber Crime and Terrorism,* Stanford, CA: Hoover Institution, 2001.

Sonn, Richard D. *Anarchism,* New York: Twayne, 1992.

Stern, Jessia. *The Ultimate Terrorists,* Cambridge, MA: Harvard University Press, 1999.

Tanter, Raymond. *Rogue Regimes: Terrorism and Proliferation,* New York: St. Maytin's, 1998.

Tucker, Jonathan B. *Toxic Terror: Assessing Terrorist Use of Chemical and Biological Weapons,* Cambridge, MA: MIT Press, 2000.

U.S. Department of State, *Patterns of Global Terrorism,* Washington, DC [Annual].

Venzke, Ben N. *First Responder Chem- Bio Handbook,* Alexandria, VA: Tempest, 1998.

Wardlaw, Grant. *Political Terrorism: Theory, Tactics, and Counter-Measures,* New York: Cambridge University Press, 1989.

White, Jonathan R. *Terrorism: An Introduction,* 3rd ed. Belmont, CA: Wadsworth, 2001.

Whittaker, David J. *The Terrorism Reader*, London and New York: Routledge, 2001.

Zinn, Howard. *Terrorism and War*, New York: Seven Stories, 2002.

Index

I

J

K

L

M

N